Economics of the Anthropocene Age

To the working class of the world

PREFACE

The economic growth process of the world economy in the post–World War II era has shown important empirical regularities. These include increasing per capita income over time, the persistence of a high and rising degree of inequality, and continuous degradation of the biophysical environment. In this period, per capita income has grown very rapidly, as never before, and so has income inequality. Environmental degradation, as measured by pollution of the atmosphere and climate changes, has also made a big jump in this relatively short period of human history. This is what empirical studies show.

Why and How Has Human Society Come to This Situation?

The pioneering work of Nicholas Georgescu-Roegen on bio-economics introduced the laws of thermodynamics into the economic process and was then able to explain why economic growth leads irrevocably to increased degradation of the biophysical environment. Thus, the correlation noted above between environmental degradation and economic growth in the world economy has been given a scientific explanation. Environmental degradation is the outcome of human actions; it is anthropogenic.

Earth science studies have gone even further. They have shown that the degradation of the biophysical environment in the last few decades has been very significant. Changes have occurred not only in the atmosphere, but in geological processes, which are also the result of human actions. The geological markers of change include waste accumulation of radioactive elements, plastic and concrete particles, and nitrogen and phosphorous in soils, which have become significant since the 1950s; in addition, wildlife is being pushed into an ever-smaller area of the Earth. According to these studies, human activity is the major force changing the Earth's behavior, of which climate change is just one. Furthermore, they argue that the Holocene Epoch ("the new whole") has ended, after 12,000 years of duration, and that we have already started (around the 1950s) a new epoch, which has been called *Anthropocene* ("the age of humans").

In the geological timescale, "epochs" correspond to the very long term, thousands and millions of years. In the social sciences, the relevant timescale runs for shorter periods, such as generations. Therefore, instead of the Anthropocene Epoch, we may use the *Anthropocene Age* to refer to the period initiated in the 1950s in which the Earth's behavior has changed in terms of pollution and climate. However, we should keep in mind that human actions not only are altering the Earth's climate behavior but are changing geological processes as well. We humans are destroying our planet, our only known ecological niche, and are thus endangering our survival as a biological species.

The question of the persistent inequality accompanying economic growth in the world economy is much harder to explain. The economic principles governing income distribution are society specific. The same can be said about economic growth itself. Therefore, the interrelations between economic growth, income distribution, and biophysical degradation can only be studied with reference to a particular social context. The object of this book is to explain those interrelations in the social context of the capitalist system.

The empirical regularities of the economic growth process under the capitalist system show the same traits as were found for the world economy, namely, an increase in per capita income accompanied by increasing inequality and increasing degradation of the biophysical environment. While rising per capita income over time is considered the main objective of the economic growth process, the other two can be seen as its side effects. However, the side effects have social consequences, leading to social maladies. As will be shown in this book, a degree of income inequality that is high and persistent leads to more acute social conflicts and social disorder, such as terrorism, illegal migration, illegal economic activities, urban violence, criminality, and insecurity. Increasing degradation of the environment—pollution and climate change—is in turn conducive to human health problems and hazardous human life and then to social conflicts and social disorder as well.

According to the World Bank data set, the countries that constitute the capitalist system represent nearly 70% of the world population and produced nearly 85% of the world output by 2005. The same source indicates that these percentages were 21% and 11% in the case of China (a non-capitalist country). China's output has grown very fast in the last decades, but its level is still relatively small in the world output. Therefore, the environment problem is highly dependent on the growth behavior of the capitalist system and we may safely link changes in the former to changes in the latter.

To be sure, clean skies and social order are two important public goods in human life, for they imply healthier, more peaceful, and less hazardous human society. However, both public goods have been degraded in the economic growth process. Therefore, the continuous rise in per capita income—the definition of *economic growth*—has been accompanied by rising income inequality and continuous environmental degradation, which have bad social consequences, namely, social maladies. The economic growth process has meant quantitative and qualitative changes: economic growth with social maladies. Considering the 200 years of capitalist development, economic growth with social maladies is a recent phenomenon. According to historian Eric Hobsbawm, we have lived in the age of violence since the 1960s. Therefore, in the age of economic growth, we live in an increasingly richer but increasingly inhospitable world.

The facts discussed above indicate that economic growth, income inequality, and environmental degradation are highly correlated. Beginning in the 1950s, and *as never before*, capitalism has experienced rapid economic growth accompanied by high levels of inequality and significant environmental degradation, so significant that the Earth has entered into another age: the Anthropocene. The question is to disentangle these correlations and identify the underlying causality relations. However, this question has not been a significant part of economic research.

By introducing the laws of thermodynamics into the economic process, Georgescu-Roegen created the field of bio-economics. However, bio-economics refers to the physical not to the social relations of the economic process. Hence, bio-economics needs to be integrated into a social context, into an economic theory. Indeed, in a letter of 1974, Marxian economist Paul Sweezy criticized Georgescu-Roegen for abstracting environmental problems from their social context.

Recently, this author has published a book with the title *Growth, Employment, inequality and the Environment. Unity of Knowledge in Economics*, which has indeed placed bio-economics in the social context of a capitalist system. This book has integrated Georgescu-Roegen's bio-economics analysis into a particular social context and developed the *unified theory of capitalism*. The unified theory is able to explain why the increases in per capita income, environmental degradation, higher income inequality, and a higher degree of social maladies have all come together. In the economic growth process, they constitute the endogenous variables, whereas the power structure—the initial inequality in the individual endowments in economic and political assets—is the exogenous variable, the ultimate factor determining that outcome. A concentrated power structure is the ultimate factor that explains why capitalism operates in this way.

What Does Remain to Be Explained?

The aim of scientific knowledge is to attain error-free knowledge. The findings of the unified theory imply that, regarding social maladies, capitalism is not a self-regulated system. Capitalism is unable to reduce or eliminate social maladies endogenously. This is too important a conclusion to be left right there. Therefore, one should insist on the question, why is capitalism unable to self-correct social maladies? The unified theory explains why the economic elites do not have the correct incentives to pursue the common good. What about the role of democracy? Economic growth with social maladies is indeed the outcome of *democratic* capitalism. This is certainly a scientific paradox. What about the role of the altruistic drive of human behavior? Under collective risk, such as unbearable social disorder and the survival of the human species, why have people not changed their behavior toward altruism to eliminate social maladies and seek to save the species?

The role of these factors—democracy and human drives—on the outcome of economic growth with social maladies needs a scientific explanation and this book takes up this challenge. If the results led us to reject the hypothesis that capitalism is not a self-regulated system, then we could conclude that capitalism has mechanisms to solve endogenously the social maladies, which eventually and somehow will appear. However, the book will show that this is not the case. Regarding social problems, democratic capitalism is not a self-regulated system. The initial conclusion of the unified theory is thus corroborated.

Then, what should human society do? The Anthropocene Age is already with us, an age in which the economic growth process takes place under stress of both the biophysical and the social environments. To answer this question, the second part of the book proposes a set of new economic principles, logically derived from the unified theory, that the new context of the Anthropocene Age needs. The new economic principles suggest introducing a set of institutional innovations, a new social order, which in turn implies a re-foundation of democratic capitalism. By construction, these are science-based policies.

BOOK CONTENT

As the human society has entered into the Anthropocene Age, what are the new principles that should govern the economic process in this age? This is the *fundamental economic problem of our time*. The answer depends upon the answer to another question: *Does the current capitalist organization of human society constitute a self-regulated system regarding social maladies?*

The fact that, so far, we have observed economic growth with social maladies implies that capitalism is not self-regulated. However, the question is whether there is scientific justification to expect that in the Anthropocene Age capitalism would endogenously change its current functioning and adopt new forms. If this were the case, then the fundamental problem would be solved endogenously; thus, capitalism is a self-regulated system. If this were not the case, then the solution of the fundamental problem would depend upon an accident or an event exogenously determined, that is, it would depend upon luck! Therefore, the question boils down to whether capitalism—democratic capitalism—is self-regulated. The question of self-regulation of the capitalist system constitutes one of the objectives of this book.

Self-regulation is an important characteristic of the functioning of society. It will be appropriate to give an example so that the concept is clearly understood from the very beginning.

Is the market system self-regulated? Consider the neoclassical theory in which all markets are Walrasian. In a single competitive market, such as the potato market, buyers and sellers exchange goods at the market price. Who is responsible for determining the market price? No one in particular, as all participants interact to determine the market price of equilibrium. At the equilibrium price, buyers and sellers are able to realize the quantities they are willing to exchange. Supply and demand interact.

If for any reason, the market price were different from that of equilibrium, there would be excess demand or excess supply, but then the market mechanism would be able to restore the equilibrium price *spontaneously*. If the price is below equilibrium, then there will be excess demand, then the price will tend to increase until the equilibrium value is attained, and thus the market is cleared. If the price is above equilibrium, then there will be excess supply, then the price will tend to fall until the equilibrium value is reached, and thus the market is cleared. Therefore, in the single market, the market price of equilibrium is self-regulated.

Oligopolistic, monopolistic, and other forms of imperfect competition market structures will have the same property. As long as markets are Walrasian, they will be self-regulated. The Walrasian market operates *as if* it were a big computer, which is able to solve the system of equations to determine the prices and quantities of equilibrium. This is the assumption of the Walrasian market theory.

Taking all markets together, the Walrasian market system will be able to determine the set of prices of equilibrium of all markets at the same time. The computer now solves the system of equations for all markets simultaneously. Thus, the market system is self-regulated. No interventions from outside are needed for the functioning of the market system. This is a beautiful property of the market system; however, we should remember that the theory assumes Walrasian markets, in which nominal prices are free to move up and down.

However, not all markets are Walrasian. The most important case is the labor market. Suppose that for any reason the nominal wage rate is above its Walrasian equilibrium price, then there will be excess supply of labor. Will the nominal wage rate fall spontaneously to clear the market? If that were the case, we would never observe unemployment. The fact is that unemployment is a permanent feature of the labor market in the First World. In the Third World, we also observe unemployment, but the large part of excess labor supply takes the form of underemployment or self-employment. Therefore, the theory that labor markets are Walrasian must be rejected because facts refute its predictions. Labor market equilibrium is with excess labor supply. The labor market is not self-regulated. It is different from the potato market.

The book contains eight chapters. The themes and the main findings are summarized here. Chapter 1 presents the unified theory of capitalism in its most elementary form. It shows how the theory explains the outcomes of the economic growth process under capitalism: economic growth with social maladies. The explanation of the phenomena is attained by assuming that the economic growth process is an evolutionary process—quantitative changes over time are followed by qualitative changes in society—and thus constructing an evolutionary model of the unified theory. This chapter is necessary to understand the logic of the themes discussed in the rest of the book and seeks to make the book self-contained.

Markets and democracy are the fundamental institutions of capitalism. The market system is the mechanism to solve prices and quantities in market exchange, which, at the same time, solves the problem of production and distribution of private goods in society. Democracy is the mechanism to produce public goods. The outcome of the economic process under capitalism, which includes per capita income growth with social maladies, is the result of both markets and democracy. What is the role of democracy in this outcome? Is it *in spite* of democracy or *due* to democracy?

Chapter 2 seeks to explain the paradox that social maladies prevail in a democratic capitalism. The chapter shows that in a capitalist society, electoral democracy—the particular form of democracy adopted in capitalist countries—is conducive to a perverse incentive system. Therefore, the outcome of economic growth accompanied by social maladies is not a paradox at all; it is the natural outcome of democratic capitalism. Electoral democracy does not lead to a self-regulated capitalism regarding social maladies.

Chapter 3 analyzes the role of the human drives in the economic growth process. A second evolutionary model (II) of the unified theory is constructed for this purpose. The model predicts that human egotism is increasing while altruism is decreasing in the process of economic growth, that is, the chapter shows that human behavior changes are also part of the economic growth process. As the chapter shows, the empirical predictions of this model are consistent with facts. Thus, we may accept the model. The implication of the model is that self-regulation of social maladies could hardly come spontaneously from a system—democratic capitalism—in which the incentives favor selfish, greedy, voracious human behavior.

Chapter 4 seeks to explain another characteristic of modern times: consumerism. Another evolutionary model (III) of the unified theory is constructed for that purpose. According to this model, the modernization process that comes with growth induces consumerism; thus, consumers' preferences are endogenous. As economic growth proceeds, new consumption goods are created, and people are induced through the different strategies of firms to consume these modern goods. Consumers are free to choose, subject not only to their budget constraints, but also to the social imposition of imitating the consumption of modern gadgets, of competing even in the consumption process. Consumerism leads workers to high demand for income and undersaving, which implies a vulnerable and stressful human life. The empirical predictions of the model are consistent with facts.

In addition, consumerism has negative effects upon the biophysical environment. The continuous modernization of consumption implies an increasing human dependency upon *exosomatic* instruments, physical goods that substitute *endosomatic* or biological organs (hands, feet, eyes, ears). It is part of the economic growth process that exosomatic instruments replace endosomatic organs. This occurs not only in the production process (where labor is replaced by machines), but also in the consumption process, in households, where exosomatic instruments include washing machines, air conditioning machines, automobiles, TV sets, computers, smart communication machines, and, more recently, robots. The production of exosomatic instruments is intensive in the use of mineral resource, and leads to pollution.

The process of economic growth is thus accompanied by endogenous changes in human behavior: increasing egotism and consumerism. Actually, consumerism can be seen as a form of increasing egotism. Therefore, given the power structure, self-regulation of social maladies could hardly come alongside the growth process: human behavior is induced to change but in the opposite direction!

Therefore, the initial conclusion of the unified theory is corroborated: regarding social maladies, democratic capitalism is not a self-regulated system. This trait of capitalism just reflects the power of the economic and political elites. As long as this power structure remains unchanged, economic growth with social maladies will persist. Leaving the system to continue operating as before—"doing business as usual"—and ignoring the fact that we are living in a different social and environmental context will just worsen the social maladies.

We live in the age of liberalism, also called neoliberalism. The liberal discourse promotes economic growth policies, of which the elites are the main beneficiaries, not only in terms of income concentration, but also in maintaining a privileged position in society. This discourse is against public policies— other than pro-growth policies, of course—for they are intrusions on individual freedom. Individual freedom and the freedom to choose are the most important human rights, according to this discourse. The pending question, before deriving public policies from the evolutionary models, is to analyze—theoretically and empirically—the question of whether individual freedom is indeed a feature of the current democratic capitalism and whether it can be so even in the Anthropocene Age.

Individual freedom under current democratic capitalism appears to be true, but it is not. It is a fallacy. Chapter 5 analyzes this fallacy in light of the evolutionary model III of the unified theory. According to biology, human behavior is changeable and is changed by the influence of society. Human behavior is the outcome of nature and nurture factors. Indeed, the economic and political elites have incentives to influence individual behavior under democratic capitalism. Capitalism does not operate under exogenously determined preferences and values of individuals, for they are endogenously determined in the economic growth process. Individuals have no autonomy to exercise their freedom. The liberal discourse condemns the intrusion of the state on individual freedom, but it does not condemn the power of economic elites through the market mechanism. The power structure includes both economic and political elites. Facts are consistent with the predictions of the theory.

The elites' discourse seeks to promote the idea that the democratic capitalist system guarantees freedom. Any social cost under capitalism can be justified because individuals enjoy freedom. In fact, however, democratic capitalism operates with power relations. The elites can control and change human behavior with the use of techniques of behavioral engineering—sometimes called techniques of manipulation and deception—and use them to induce people to behave according to their own interests. Those techniques are in the wrong hands, for these techniques could be utilized to seek the common good, such as the correction of social maladies.

In sum, the answer to the book's first question is that democratic capitalism operates with social maladies. The capitalist system is not self-regulated. Moreover, it can hardly become self-regulated, for the tendencies of the relevant factors move in the opposite direction. Surely, it will not be able to solve the new challenges that come with the Anthropocene Age.

The book's second major question is about the solutions to the fundamental economic problem of our time: *What are the new principles that should govern the economic process in the Anthropocene Age?* Thus, the policy implications of the unified theory are derived in Chap. 6. Five decades of economic growth have implied qualitative changes not only in the biophysical environment, but also in the social environment. The economic process in the Anthropocene Age operates under the stress of *both* environments. Therefore, we need new economic principles for the new context. A final evolutionary model (IV) is constructed for that purpose, the predictions of which are consistent with facts.

The chapter presents the social objectives, the public policies, and the institutional innovations that the new context requires. The new context implies that the objective of public policies cannot be economic growth—as it is today. In a no-growth society, the only social objective left is the *direct* improvement in the quality of society.

Institutional changes would then be required to impose upon social actors the appropriate incentive system. The most important institutional innovation derived from the unified theory is change in the form of democracy: to dethrone the current electoral democracy and substitute it with another superior form of democracy. Eliminating the political power originating from electoral democracy would imply a reduction in the current power structure. The new form of democracy should make viable the shift of public policies from pro-growth toward pro-quality of society.

Chapter 7 deals with the question of how a no-growth capitalist society would function. What would the new principles of production and distribution be? The chapter presents and discusses a set of new principles. The Anthropocene Age implies a new set of economic problems to be solved, which in turn implies a new social organization of capitalism, with new institutions that generate the correct incentives for solving the new set of problems that the current democratic capitalism has created. To solve the fundamental economic problem of our time will not be easy. This age is new and historical experiences cannot help. The only guide we have is the causality relations derived from the unified theory. It certainly helps to know that this scientific theory has been corroborated by facts.

Chapter 8 presents the epilogue.

According to the unified theory, the economic growth process under democratic capitalism is not a mechanical process, but rather an evolutionary process. As an evolutionary process, quantitative changes along a trajectory over time are accompanied by qualitative changes; thus, the outcome is economic growth with social maladies. In addition, the qualitative changes imply that economic growth cannot go on forever; moreover, this evolutionary process is leading to the collapse of human society, as we know it, in a shorter period. The current democratic capitalism has no mechanisms for the self-correction of these trajectories. The exogenous variable causing this result is the power structure, for the persistent trajectory of the endogenous variables just reflects those power relations. The observed trajectories will continue period after period as long as the current power structure remains unchanged.

However, there is nothing deterministic about the observed trajectories. Economics is not physics. A valid economic theory can suggest changes in society—new policies and new institutions—to move society to different trajectories, even in the presence of the continuous and irrevocable laws of thermodynamics. The current power structure is removable through institutional innovations. The new institutions that the Anthropocene Age requires are thus derived from the unified theory and are thus science-based. They imply a re-foundation of democratic capitalism. Therefore, an understanding of the fundamental economic problem of our time together with its solutions is the expected contribution of the book to the debate about the fate of human society.

BOOK READERSHIP

The book is primarily addressed to students of economics at advanced undergraduate and graduate levels. Students of the other social sciences may also find it useful, as the book deals with democracy and power structure in the functioning of capitalism. Students of the natural sciences may benefit from the book findings and learn about the interrelations between the social world and the biophysical world. The main findings of the book should be accessible to the general reader interested in the fate of human society. The most relevant findings are presented in simple English.

ACKNOWLEDGMENTS

I would like to thank my current institution, CENTRUM Graduate Business School, Pontifical Catholic University of Peru, and its Director Fernando D'Alessio, for providing me with support to the research that was conducive to this book. I also thank Franco Calle and Carla Glave for their work as research assistants. Two anonymous reviewers provided critical comments and suggestions that were valuable for the preparation of the final draft of the book. My thanks also go to them.

CONTENTS

LIST OF FIGURES

LIST OF TABLES

CHAPTER 1

Economic Growth with Social Maladies

This chapter presents the basic empirical regularities of capitalist economic growth process of the last decades. Then, the chapter summarizes the explanation given for the interrelations between income growth, income inequality, and biophysical degradation by unified theory. This is done by presenting an evolutionary model of unified theory. The reader will thus learn not only about the structure of the unified theory, but also about how it explains reality, which will facilitate understanding of the next chapters. This chapter intends to make the whole book self-contained.

EMPIRICAL REGULARITIES OF CAPITALISM: GROWTH, INEQUALITY, AND THE ENVIRONMENT

The aim of this chapter is to analyze the economic growth process under capitalism. The outcomes of this process will include changes over time in per capita income, income inequality, and the biophysical environment.

© The Author(s) 2017
A. Figueroa, *Economics of the Anthropocene Age*,
DOI 10.1007/978-3-319-62584-3_1

According to the estimates of economic historian Angus Maddison (2003, pp. 256–257), the world economy of the last two centuries was almost stagnant until the beginning of the 1950s (total output grew at nearly 1% per year between 1820 and 1950), when total output began growing very rapidly (at 4%). In a historical perspective, the post–World War II period has been the age of economic growth. Income inequality between countries also increased significantly in the period of rapid growth, as measured by the inequality between the richest and the poorest countries: the gap went from 3:1 in 1820 to 18:1 in year 2000 (cited in Galor 2011, p. 2).

Table 1.1 shows the basic facts about growth and distribution for the last decades. The first part of the table presents the degree of income inequality *within* countries, as measured by the Gini index. Due to the scarcity of data on the index by countries, the relevant information is averages by periods of several years and by group of countries. Since the 1950s, in the economic growth age of capitalism, the Gini index level is higher in the Third World than in the First World in the three periods of observations. Within the Third World, those countries having strong European colonial legacy, which constitute the large majority in the group, show higher degree of inequality than those few having a weak colonial legacy. The major fact is that Third World countries are *persistently* more unequal societies than First World countries. On the other hand, inequality within each group of countries shows no significant changes over time.

The second part of the table depicts inequality *between* countries. The income level of the First World is higher than that of the Third World, which conforms to the definition, but the gap has increased. The income level in the Third

Table 1.1 Income level and inequality in capitalist countries

Income inequality average Gini index			Per capita income (PPP)		
1950–1970	1971–2008	1992–2012	1980	2008	2014
First World/*epsilon*					
0.36	0.33	0.32	9508	41,642	46,019
(0.04)	(0.04)	(0.04)	(1977)	(12,115)	(14,496)
15	22	23	23	23	23
Third World with weak colonial legacy/*omega*					
0.39	0.36	0.43	3779	20,689	26,279
(0.09)	(0.07)	(0.06)	(2052)	(16,925)	(22,181)
5	7	11	9	10	10
Third World with strong colonial legacy/*sigma*					
0.47	0.49	0.45	2360	6163	7363
(0.09)	(0.07)	(0.09)	(3662)	(5179)	(5749)
30	32	92	65	88	88

Notes: On the entries of the table: (1) Gini index refers to average value of the period and countries. Per capita income is measured in PPP prices for each year. (2) Figures in parenthesis indicate standard deviation. (3) The third row under each side heading refers to the number of countries in the sample. The universe of countries in each category is 23, 13, and 138. Third World countries with weak colonial legacy include Argentina, Chile, Ethiopia, Costa Rica, Iran, Israel, South Korea, Singapore, Thailand, Turkey, and Uruguay

Sources: On Gini index: For 1950–1970 and 1971–2008 from Figueroa (2015, vol. 1, Table 2.2, p. 32), based on Milanovic database from national household surveys, using the definition "net income per capita." For 1992–2012: updated by the author, from the database of Branko Milanovic (2010). Web Page at World Bank, "All the Ginis Dataset": http://go.worldbank.org/9VCQW66LA0. Last date accessed 08/12/2016

On per capita income: For 1980, from Figueroa (2015, vol. 1, Table 2.2, p. 32), based on World Bank Development Indicators. For 2008 and 2014: updated by the author. The sample of 88 for sigma countries was taken from 114 countries with complete data. Countries that are small islands (15) and those with outlier data (11) were left out. Web Page at World Bank: http://data.worldbank.org/indicator/NY.GDP.PCAP.PP.CD?end=2015&start=2014

World with strong colonial legacy as percentage of that of the First World has declined over time: from 25% in 1980 to 15% in 2008 and to 16% in 2014. For the small group of Third World countries with weak colonial legacy, the gap is closing, from 40% to 57%. The major fact is that the gap between the few rich countries and the large group of poor countries under capitalism has widened in the economic growth age of capitalism.

Table 1.1 implies that overall income inequality in the capitalist system has increased since the 1950s, in the age of rapid economic growth. The inequality between groups (First World and Third World) has increased and the weight (population share) of the group with the highest inequality (the Third World) has also increased.

On the degree of degradation of the biophysical environment, the concentration of pollution in the atmosphere—measured by carbon dioxide, CO_2—was almost constant in the preindustrial period, increased a bit in the industrial period, but went up drastically also beginning in the 1950s. Today's CO_2 concentration level is almost 50% higher than that of the preindustrial period; three-quarters of this increase took place since the 1950s, when economic growth accelerated. Global warming is another feature that is highly correlated with pollution (Stavins 2011, p. 170). According to climate scientists, this correlation implies causality, for the observed climate change comes from the greenhouse effect of pollution (IPCC 2014).

The scientific question is the following: What is underlying the observed relations between output growth, inequality, and environment degradation? The explanation requires a scientific theory, which in turn requires a criterion to accept or reject scientific theories.

SCIENCE IS EPISTEMOLOGY

The needed criterion to accept or reject scientific theories comes from epistemology. Thus, scientific knowledge will have an epistemological justification. This book will adopt a composite epistemology that is the combination of the epistemologies of Karl Popper (1968) and Nicholas Georgescu-Roegen (1971), as proposed in Figueroa (2016). This section just summarizes the foundations of the composite epistemology.

According to Popperian epistemology, a scientific theory is required to explain the real world. No theory, no explanation. In addition, the theory must be empirically falsifiable. A falsifiable theory is one that is *in principle* empirically false. Under the falsification principle, the presumption is that the theory is false so that its testing becomes a necessity; that is, the theory is presumed false until proved otherwise. If the theory were presumed true until proved otherwise, then its testing would become discretionary. Through the falsification principle, science is protected from including untested propositions within its domain.

Therefore, the Popperian criterion to accept a proposition as scientific knowledge is not based on theory alone or on empirical data alone; it is rather based on the empirical refutation of theories, on the elimination of false theories. Falsification leads us to an evolutionary (in the Darwinian sense) scientific knowledge. "The evolution of scientific knowledge is, in the main, the evolution of better and better [scientific] theories. This is a Darwinian process. The theories become better adapted through natural selection: they give us better and better information about reality. (They get nearer and nearer to the truth)" (Popper 1993, p. 338). Popperian epistemology leads us to the construction of a critical science.

Social sciences seek to explain the functioning of human societies. We may say that human societies constitute highly complex realities. As some scientists of the natural sciences have recognized, the social world is a more complex reality than the physical world and thus the social sciences should be called the hard sciences, not the natural sciences (cf. Wilson 1998, p. 183). The notion of complexity refers to the large number and the heterogeneity of the elements that constitute the particular reality under study, and to the multiple factors that shape the relations between those elements. Human diversity and the multiplicity of human interactions make human societies intricate realities; moreover, the individuals that make up human society are not identical, as opposed to atoms in the physical world. Human society is a highly complex system because many individuals interact and individuals themselves are complex systems.

The problem is to find the proper epistemology for the social sciences. According to Popper, falsificationism is applicable to both the natural and the social sciences, for these types of sciences differ in scope, not much in method (Popper 1976). However, falsificationism does not say how to construct a scientific theory that is falsifiable, much less for complex realities. This question is resolved by using the *abstract process epistemology* of Georgescu-Roegen.

The complex real world can be reduced to a simpler world by transforming it into an abstract world with the use of the *abstract process.* Conceptually, a process refers to a series of activities carried out in the real world, having a boundary, a purpose, a mechanism, and a given duration; furthermore, those activities can be repeated period after period. The farming process of production, for example, includes many activities having a given duration (say, seasonality of six months), the purpose of which is, say, to produce potatoes, which can be repeated year after year. The factory process of production also includes many activities, but with a shorter duration, say, the hour; the purpose of which is, say, to produce shirts, which can be repeated day after day.

The abstract process epistemology rests upon the following principles:

> *First*, the complex real world can be represented in the form of an abstract process, with given boundaries through which input–output elements cross, and given duration, which can be repeated period after period. This representation is taxonomical. *Second*, the complex real world thus represented can be transformed into a simpler, abstract world by constructing a scientific theory, which assumes what the essential elements of the process are. This is the *principle of abstraction*. By transforming the complex real world into an abstract world, by means of a scientific theory, we can reach a scientific explanation of that complex real world.

The first principle indicates that to present the complete list of the elements of a process would be equivalent to constructing a map to the scale 1:1. As in the case of the map, a complex reality cannot be understood at this scale of representation. By using the abstraction method, the complex reality is represented at a higher scale, as in a map. This is the second principle.

The structure of an abstract process includes the boundaries. There are elements that cross the frontier from outside, called the *exogenous variables*, and those crossing the frontier from the inside, called the *endogenous variables*. The structure also includes the underlying mechanisms (unobservable) by which the endogenous and exogenous variables (observable) are connected. Finally, the structure includes the duration period of the process, which is going to be repeated period after period. The use of abstraction implies that some elements of the real-world process will be ignored.

How do we decide which elements are essential in a process and which are not? How do we construct an abstract process? By the introduction of a scientific theory, which is a set of assumptions. Hence, the assumptions of the scientific theory will determine the endogenous variables, the exogenous variables, the duration period, and the underlying mechanisms that are important. A scientific theory is, therefore, a logical artifice by which a complex real world is transformed into a simpler and more understandable abstract world.

Figure 1.1 depicts the diagrammatic representation of an abstract process. The segment $t_o - t_1$ represents the duration of the process, which is going to be repeated period after period; X is the set of exogenous variables and Y is the set of endogenous variables. The shaded area indicates the underlying mechanism by which X and Y are connected. What happens inside the process is not observable, as indicated by the shaded area in the figure. If it were, the interior of the process would be another process in itself, with other endogenous and exogenous variables and another mechanism; the latter mechanism would also be observable and then constitute another process, and so on. Thus, we would arrive at the logical problem of infinite regress. We may avoid this logical trap by making assumptions about the mechanism and maintaining it fixed. Ultimately,

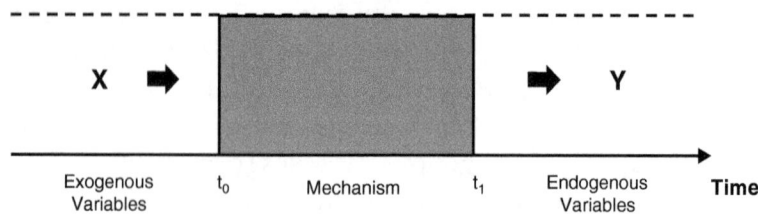

Fig. 1.1   Diagrammatic representation of an abstract process

there must be something hidden beneath the things we observe. Science seeks to unveil those underlying elements.

The scientific theory must also include assumptions about how the abstract process operates. The set of relations taking place within the mechanism constitute the *structural relations*. These refer to relevant physical and social interactions represented in equations, which include relations among endogenous variables, between endogenous and exogenous variables, and among exogenous variables as well. These structural equations must have a solution, represented by the *reduced form equations*, in which the values of the endogenous variables ultimately depend upon the values of the exogenous variables, that is, $Y = F(X)$. The solution, called *economic equilibrium*, implies that no social actor has both the power and the incentive to change it, and thus it is repeated period after period, as long as the exogenous variables remain unchanged.

This is the case of the static process. Given that the equilibrium is stable, the signs of the reduced form equation—showing the effect of changes in exogenous variables upon endogenous variables—are determined by the comparative statics method. Therefore, in the reduced form equations, the exogenous variables X constitute the *ultimate factors* in the abstract process that determine the values of the endogenous variable Y, after all internal relations or structural relations have been taken into account. The structural equations show only the *proximate factors* that affect the endogenous variables Y. Moreover, according to the reduced form equations, changes in the exogenous variables will cause changes of definite directions (positive or negative) upon the endogenous variables. Therefore, the reduced form equations also constitute the *causality relations* of the scientific theory. The reduced form equations, being observable, constitute the empirical predictions of the scientific theory. They are falsifiable or testable.

The abstract process may also take the form of a dynamic process. In this case, the solution of the structural equations varies for each period. Thus, the solution of period 1 implies new structural equations and new solutions for period 2, and so on. Therefore, the values of the endogenous variables show a trajectory over time (t), which represents the *dynamic equilibrium* curve, for given values of the exogenous variables. Both the reduced form equation and the causality equation can then be represented as $Y = G(t; X)$.

Given that the equilibrium in each period is stable, the effect of changes in the exogenous variables upon the endogenous variables will be determined by the comparative dynamics method. A change in an exogenous variable will shift the trajectory of the endogenous variables in a definite direction. Therefore, the value of the endogenous variable will move from its current position to the new dynamic equilibrium curve. This transition takes time and is called *transition dynamics*. Hence, in a dynamic process, there are two *dynamic trajectories*—showing changes due just to the passage of time—one showing the dynamic equilibrium curve and the other the transition dynamic curve. The dynamic process assumes mechanical time (t), in which only quantitative changes take place over time and thus the process can be repeated forever.

Finally, the abstract process can take the form of evolutionary process, in which the dynamic trajectory exists, but it is only temporal, for this trajectory is accompanied by qualitative changes as well, which in turn set limits to the repetition of the trajectory. The evolutionary process cannot be repeated forever. Here time is historical (T), not mechanical. Thus, both the reduced form equations and the causality equations are represented as $Y = H(T; X)$, such that $T < T^*$, and $T^* = f(X)$. Period T^* marks the collapse of the process and the regime switching to another process, the reduced form of which can be represented as follows: $\Upsilon = J(T; X)$, such that $T > T^*$ and X is another set of exogenous variables.

Comparing the set of principles of Popper's epistemology and Georgescu-Roegen's epistemology, we can see that they do not contradict each other; thus, they are complementary and can be combined into a single epistemology. Call this combination the *composite epistemology*. We can then integrate the principles of falsification and abstract process into one. Therefore, the composite epistemology rests upon the following principle:

> We can explain and understand a complex real world if, and only if, it is reducible to a simpler and abstract world in the form of an abstract process, by means of a scientific theory, which generates falsifiable empirical predictions; such scientific theory exists and can be discovered.

The principles of the composite epistemology are still too general. In order to make them operational, a set of more specific research rules is needed. This calls for a scientific research method, containing rules that are logically derived from the composite epistemology. This research method has been derived and it is called the *alpha–beta method* (Figueroa 2016). The method can be summarized as follows:

> The set of assumptions of the scientific theory is called the *alpha propositions*. These are non-observable and non-tautological propositions. A set of falsifiable empirical predictions, called *beta propositions*, is logically derived from alpha. The theory is falsifiable, not directly, but indirectly, through the beta propositions. Because the construction of the theory involves abstraction, the testing of the beta propositions must be statistical. If the beta proposition is statistically rejected, then the alpha proposition (the theory) is also rejected; if the beta proposition is statistically accepted, then the theory is also accepted, for the abstract world is a good approximation of the real world.

The particular trait of economics is that an economic theory is a family of models. The reason is that the economic process can take several forms, depending on the concept of time utilized: mechanical versus historical, chronological versus logical. Under mechanical time (t), the economic process is reversible, for endogenous variables can return to their initial position if the exogenous variables do. This is the case of static and dynamic processes. Under historical time (T), the economic process is irreversible, for historical time flows in one direction only, with past, present, and future. This is the case of evolutionary processes. Logical time refers to the degree of adjustments that people can make in the economic process. Compared to the short run, in the long run people can make more adjustments, which implies that some exogenous variables will become endogenous. The relation with chronological time is clear: people can make more adjustments in a year than in a week.

Therefore, the particular assumptions on the nature of the economic process—mechanical (static, dynamic) or evolutionary, and short run or long run—will lead to particular models of the economic theory. Beta propositions can only be derived from these models. Hence, economic theories are falsified through models.

The Unified Theory of Capitalism: Primary Assumptions

The foundations of a scientific theory are called primary assumptions or alpha propositions. The unified theory consists of the following set of alpha propositions, where the symbol (C) stands for capitalism:

α (C) (1). *Institutional Context*: (a) Rules. Markets and democracy constitute the basic institutions. People participating in the economic process are endowed with economic and political assets; economic assets are subject to private property rights; people exchange goods subject to the norms of market exchange, which include the norm that nominal wages cannot fall; the market system operates with Walrasian and non-Walrasian markets, in which the labor market is of the latter type. The political regime is democracy. (b) Organizations. Include firms, households, and the government.

α (C) (2). *Initial Conditions*: There are different types of capitalist societies, which differ by two initial conditions: factor endowments and the initial inequality in the individual distribution of economic and political assets. Factor endowments make capitalist societies underpopulated or overpopulated. Initial inequality in the individual distribution of economic assets makes capitalist societies class societies (constituted by capitalists and workers), whereas unequal political entitlements make them socially homogeneous or heterogeneous (first-class and second-class citizens). The economic process works differently in each type of society. The legacy of the European colonial systems is the essential factor that underlies the existence of types of capitalist societies.

α (C) (3). *Economic Rationality of Agents*: Consistent with the institutional context of capitalism, individuals act guided by the motivation of self-interest. Capitalists seek two particular objectives, hierarchically ordered: firstly, maintenance of class position and, secondly, maximization of profits. Politicians seek to capture the state to obtain incomes. In the labor market, workers seek to maximize wages and minimize effort, while capitalists seek to minimize wages and maximize labor effort. Due to this conflict in labor relations, capitalists use devices to extract effort from workers. Individuals have a limited tolerance for inequality.

Two groups of countries, the rich and poor, usually called the First World and the Third World, constitute the capitalist system. Unified theory seeks to explain this system. As shown in Table 1.1, First World countries are richer and less unequal compared to Third World countries. Why is this so?

Assumption (2) says that there exists an underlying qualitative difference between the First World and the Third World, which originates in their European colonial history. The Third World started as capitalist with the legacy of European colonialism. This is not the case for the First World; on the contrary, some countries were colonial powers. Therefore, these two groups started capitalist development under different initial conditions. Relative to the First World, the Third World began as overpopulated implying that capital per worker was relatively lower and as heterogeneous implying that individual political endowments were unequally distributed, giving rise to first-class and second-class citizens, the latter being the descendants of the dominated population in the colonial times.

As with any scientific theory, as an abstract representation of the real world, unified theory consists of a set of assumptions. The economic process operates differently in each type of capitalism. Therefore, there must be partial theories to explain each type of society taken separately and then a unified theory that can explain the system taken as a whole. Unity of knowledge is an epistemological requirement for a good scientific theory: One theory for one world. Thus, economic theory that seeks to explain capitalism as a whole could only take the form of a unified theory.

The two abstract capitalist societies that constitute the capitalist system are called *epsilon* and *sigma*, and are thus abstract representations of the First World and Third World countries. Therefore, epsilon society is underpopulated and socially homogeneous, whereas sigma society is overpopulated and socially heterogeneous, with first-class and second-class citizens. Epsilon and sigma constitute partial theories of the unified theory of capitalism. Thus, the unified theory seeks to explain the functioning of each type of capitalist country (First World and Third World) taken separately and then the capitalist system taken as a whole.

AN EVOLUTIONARY MODEL (I) OF UNIFIED THEORY

In order to give a precise answer to the scientific question posed above—how to explain the outcome of economic growth with its side effects, inequality, and environment degradation—a model of the unified theory is needed. For the problem at hand, the appropriate model is the evolutionary process, in which quantitative changes in the economic growth process are accompanied by qualitative changes in society. Just to make the book self-contained, this model is presented here in its most elementary form.

Two auxiliary assumptions for the construction of the evolutionary model include the following. First, the production process is entropic, that is, it is subject to the laws of thermodynamics, which deals with matter and energy relations. Second, only three social actors are considered: capitalists, workers, and politicians, where each social group is homogeneous. Power structure is highly concentrated in the economic and political elites.

The implication of the entropic assumption is that waste is an irrevocable side effect of the economic process. According to the *first law of thermodynamics*, matter and energy cannot be created or destroyed, only rearranged. Thus, part of the matter and energy that enter as inputs into the production process of goods will become waste. According to the *second law (entropy law)*, as rearrangement takes place, there will be qualitative changes in the biophysical environment, which implies its continuous and irrevocable degradation. Thus, the waste part of the energy burned from mineral resources utilized in production (carbon dioxide, CO_2) will be dumped into the atmosphere, which will have the consequence of polluting it. These are physical laws imposed by nature, not by man or technology.

Therefore, an entropic economic process assumes that production of goods and its waste are both endogenous in the economic process. Quantitative and qualitative changes in the biophysical environment take place in the economic process; thus, an entropic economic process implies an evolutionary economic process. This is to say that an entropic economic process cannot be mechanical; it cannot be repeated period after period *forever*.

Table 1.2 presents the entropic economic process in the form of an input–output table. This is a form of representing the abstract economic process, as evolutionary in this particular case. The economic process produces only one good. There is only one type of labor. There are fund factors, which enter into the process *and* come out; then, there are also flow factors, which *either* enter *or* come out. The assumptions about the fund factors are as follows:

- Capital per worker (k) enters into the production process and comes out, but as a trajectory that is increasing over time, as there is capital accumulation in the process and population increase as well.
- Stock of renewable natural resources (R), from which matter and energy enter into the process. The stock comes out unchanged, for the quantity used in production (m) is regenerated in the same period.

Table 1.2   Input–output table of an entropic economic process

	Inputs	*Mechanism*	*Outputs*
		Markets	
		Democracy	
		Technology	
		Thermodynamics	
Funds			
Capital per worker	k_0		$k(T)$
Natural resources			
Renewable	R_0		
Non-renewable	N_0		$N_0 - n = N(T)$
Pollution concentration	Π_0		$\Pi_0 + \pi = \Pi(T)$
Power structure	δ		δ
Flows			
Inputs from renewable	m		
Inputs from non-renewable	n		
Total income			$\Upsilon(T)$
Income per person			$y(T)$
Income distribution			$D(T)$
Waste/pollution			π

Source: Author's elaboration

- Stock of non-renewable resources or mineral resources (N), from which material inputs go into the process in quantity (n), in the form of matter and energy. The initial stock falls by that amount (n); thus, the outcome will be a trajectory of continuously declining stocks until its total depletion.
- Stock of pollution in the atmosphere (Π), which is increased over time due to the waste flow that production of goods generate irrevocably, which is dumped into the atmosphere in a given amount (π), which depends upon the quantities (m,n). The model assumes that pollution (not depletion) sets the limit to the reproduction of the process.

- Finally, there is an initial inequality in the distribution of economic and political assets (δ), which enters into the production process as power structure and comes out intact.

The flows of the economic process include the flow of natural resources utilized in production as inputs (m, n); then, total income (Υ), per capita income (y), and income distribution (D), all as trajectories. Finally, we must include the flow of waste (π), which is not the purpose of the economic process, but of the irrevocable effect of the laws of thermodynamics.

From the input–output table, it is clear that the economic process is under expanded reproduction and thus represents the economic growth process. However, as the economic process is repeated period after period, the growth of per capita income is accompanied by qualitative changes in society: pollution and depletion of non-renewable natural resources in the biophysical environment and income inequality in the social environment. Depletion of each period cannot continue forever, for the stock of mineral resources in the crust of the Earth is given. Pollution cannot continue forever either, for human life is aerobic and thus viable only in a particular ecological niche. Income inequality cannot continue forever either, for social tolerance for inequality is limited, and then social disorder will increase. Therefore, this process cannot be repeated forever. At some finite period, these changes, whichever comes first, will set limits to the economic growth process, and then the process will collapse and will be switched endogenously to another process. This is an evolutionary process.

The input–output table can be transformed into categories of the abstract process, which was shown in Fig. 1.1. The endogenous variables include all variables that appear under "output." The exogenous variable is the initial distribution of assets or power structure, which enters into the process and can change only independently during the process. This is the only exogenous variable. The mechanism by which the exogenous variable generates the outcomes of the endogenous variables is also given, which includes institutions (the market system and democracy), technology, and the laws of thermodynamics. The economic rationality of people in society is shaped by the institutions of capitalism, which leads them to act guided by self-interest.

In the abstract process, static and dynamic processes are defined as mechanical. They can be repeated period after period forever. In contrast, an evolutionary process sets limits to its mechanical repetition, so that the process will eventually collapse and switch to another process. Therefore, the study of economic growth as an evolutionary process starts with a dynamic process, the duration of which is temporary. Therefore, the dynamic trajectory—either as dynamic equilibrium curve or as transition dynamic curve—is just a mirage.

The quantitative outcome of economic growth refers to the continuous increase in per capita income or output per worker, which are equivalent terms under the assumption that the labor participation rate remains fixed. The dynamic trajectory assumes that output per worker is the result of a production process in which total output depends upon the quantity of labor and how labor is equipped with capital and technology. In the growth process, all these factors will change. Assuming that technological change is labor productivity augmenting— that is, labor saving—we can combine labor and technology into a single factor of production, measured in efficiency units or effective labor, the other factor being physical capital.

The dynamic equilibrium trajectory will occur when the economy reaches its steady state, which means that the ratios output per effective labor and capital per effective labor remain constant over time. This equilibrium condition implies that capital stock and effective labor will grow at the same rate (say 5% per year), which implies that total output will grow at 5% as well (assuming that returns to scale are constant). Therefore, the two ratios will remain constant. On the components of the effective labor factor, assume that labor supply increases at 2% per year and technology at 3% per year. Thus, under dynamic equilibrium, in the long run, output per worker will grow at the rate of 3% (the difference between total output and labor supply rates), which is equal to the rate of technological change.

The dynamic equilibrium trajectory of output per worker can be represented by a rising curve over time. We may call this dynamic trajectory the *growth frontier curve* of society. The slope of this curve is determined by the growth rate of technological change and its intercept depends upon the parameters that determined the steady-state situation. These parameters are the investment rate, years of education, and labor supply (or population) growth rate. The first two parameters have positive level effects upon the frontier—shifting upward the level of the frontier curve—whereas the latter has a negative effect.

From its current initial position of output per worker, society will move toward the frontier curve spontaneously through transition dynamics. The growth rate of output per worker along the transition dynamics will be higher than that of the frontier, for it is the only way to reach the frontier. Once the frontier is reached, economic growth proceeds along the frontier. Certainly, changes in the frontier will change the trajectory of the transition dynamics. What is observable is the transition dynamics.

Epsilon society and sigma society have different growth frontiers due to differences in the parameters determining the frontier, which depend upon differences in the initial inequality. Compared to sigma society, epsilon society has lower initial inequality. A lower initial inequality is a more favorable context for growth, for it leads to social order in society, and makes it a stable and low-risk society. Therefore, the investment rate and the average years of education are higher and the population growth rate is lower in epsilon compared to sigma; consequently, the level of the frontier is higher in the former. Epsilon and sigma move along parallel paths. A necessary condition for sigma society to catch up with epsilon society is to have a common growth frontier, which is not the case. The difference in the growth frontier between epsilon and sigma will persist as long as the difference in the initial inequality (δ) also persists. Therefore, the evolutionary model predicts that the gap of output per worker will be persistent in the economic growth process.

Differences in the observed growth rates of output per worker between epsilon and sigma societies will mostly refer to changes along their transition dynamics trajectories. Therefore, they will depend upon how close countries are from their frontiers, which are unobservable. Therefore, the evolutionary model has no predictions about growth rate differences. However, even if sigma were growing faster than epsilon is, the model predicts that there will be no catching up, for they would be approaching different frontiers.

As to differences in the degree of income inequality, the model predicts that the *level* of inequality will be higher in sigma compared to epsilon. The reason is that, in the long run, the degree of income inequality (D) is determined essentially by the initial inequality in economic and political assets (δ), which is higher in sigma society. Therefore, according to the evolutionary model, in the process of economic growth there is path dependence; that is, history matters. Neither the income level nor the level of inequality will tend to equalize between epsilon and sigma.

As to *changes* in income inequality along the transition dynamics, income inequality will tend to remain constant in epsilon society, but will tend to increase in sigma society. The reason is that in epsilon, market competition leads to increases in the average real wage rate at the same pace of the growth of labor productivity or output per worker, which originates in technological change. In sigma, an overpopulated society, in addition to the capitalist sector, there exists the subsistence sectors in which excess labor supply is able to generate their incomes. Output per worker grows faster in the capitalist sector than in the subsistence sectors. Real wage rate growth also follows labor productivity in the capitalist sector and then the gap with the average income of the subsistence sectors tends to increase.

The evolutionary model predicts that the overall income inequality in the capitalist system will increase in the growth process. In transition dynamics, as shown above, income inequality tends to remain unchanged in epsilon society, but tends to rise in sigma. Moreover, the higher growth rate of population in sigma will have the effect of increasing the weight of the more unequal region and, thus, will lead to a rise in the overall average degree of inequality.

The evolutionary model also predicts economic growth with degradation of the biophysical environment. Taking the capitalist system as dominant in the world economy (justified earlier, see preface), total output increase implies higher levels of pollution emissions and higher levels of pollution concentration in the world atmosphere. This effect is irrevocable, as it comes from the physical laws of thermodynamics, which refer to the relations between matter and energy.

According to the evolutionary model, the side effects of economic growth are rising income inequality and environment degradation, which have social consequences. The overall income inequality increase leads to increasing social disorder. The unified theory assumes that individuals have a limited tolerance for inequality; therefore, as income inequality increases, a higher proportion of the population will have their threshold values of tolerance surpassed and will react by challenging the institutional rules of society, such as private property and law obedience. The social conflict about inequality will be increasingly intense in the capitalist system.

The degradation of the environment also leads to more intense social conflicts, due to its effect on human health, as people have limited physical tolerance for polluted atmosphere, and due to the increasing shocks coming from consequent climate change. The exploitation of mineral resources usually generates negative externalities over other sectors (agriculture, forestry) and upon water resources, adding to social conflicts. Social order and clean skies are public goods, which degrade with economic growth. As a result, people live a more hazardous human life.

In sum, the evolutionary model predicts that economic growth is accompanied by qualitative changes in society: income inequality and environment degradation, which together imply social maladies. Given the limited social tolerance for those maladies, economic growth cannot continue forever. The limit to economic growth will be determined by any of the following threshold values: the limited social tolerance for inequality, the limited tolerance of human health for pollution, or the total depletion of non-renewable natural resources, whichever comes first. The model predicts that, due to the incentives system under capitalism, pollution will more likely come first, and will thus be the *effective* limiting factor. Human health has limited tolerance for pollution and eventually this threshold will be reached, which will imply the collapse of human society, as we know it.

Figure 1.2 depicts the predictions of evolutionary model I. The vertical axis measures output per worker and the horizontal historical time. The upward slopping curve R shows the trajectory of economic growth (output per worker). Along this curve, qualitative changes occur in society, such that both income inequality and environment degradation are higher at point B than at point A, and higher at point C than at B, and so on. Human tolerance for pollution reaches its limit at output per worker y^*, which occurs at period T^*. Then regime switching takes place at this period endogenously and the new

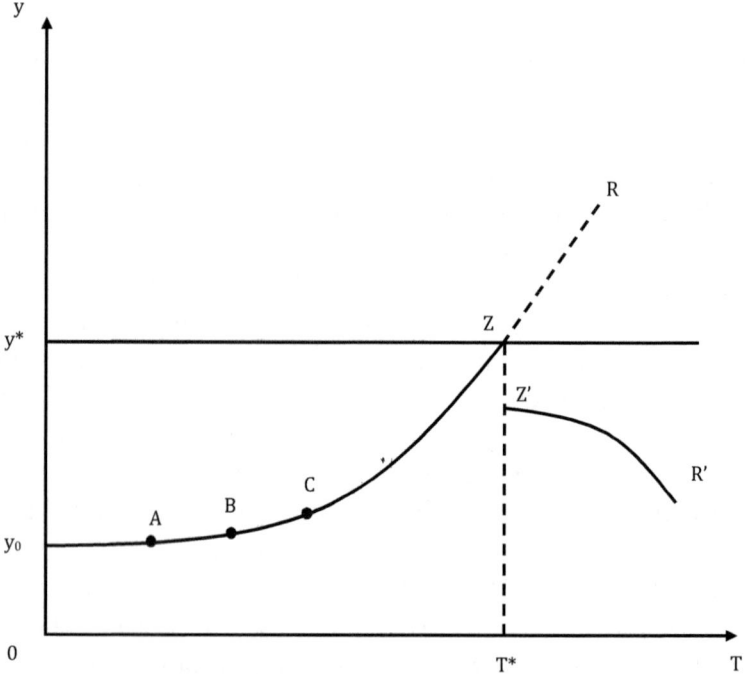

Fig. 1.2   Evolutionary economic process

trajectory is given by the curve Z'R', which will end in a col-lapse of human society, if the exogenous variable—the power structure—remains unchanged.

The economic growth process is evolutionary, in which any dynamic trajectory (as represented by curve R) is only temporal, a mirage, for eventually the process will collapse and regime switching will take place. The entropic economic process is the source of the evolutionary process—rising income inequality is not the factor that leads to the break-down of the growth process; it is pollution. In sum, the empirical prediction of the evolutionary model, on the dynamic trajectory—economic growth with rising income inequality, environment degradation, and social maladies—is falsifiable.

EMPIRICAL CONSISTENCY

The predictions of the evolutionary model tend to be consis-tent with facts. In particular, they are consistent with the facts given in Table 1.1. In the age of rapid economic growth, in the last five to six decades, the degree of income inequality is persistently higher in the Third World than in the First World and the overall inequality in the capitalist system taken as a whole has become more unequal. The income gap between the First World and the Third World has widened.

The income gap is closing only for the Third World coun-tries with weak or no colonial legacy, a group of few countries, which are called *omega societies*. The abstract omega society is overpopulated and socially homogeneous—one class of citi-zens only. Omega and epsilon have similar growth frontier curves, with differences only in the current income level. Through economic growth, omega will then be able to move toward the epsilon frontier.

Economic historian Angus Maddison (1995) has shown that in the very long run there has not been catching up between poor and rich countries. The only case of success is Japan. This country belonged to the group of poor countries in 1820 and today is a member of the exclusive club of the First World. Japan started its capitalist growth process as an omega society. This is consistent with the prediction of the evolutionary model.

Maddison also has estimated the gaps between rich and poor countries in the very long run, which indicate significant increases in today's gap compared to those in 1820, as shown above. The conclusion is that today's degree of income inequality in the capitalist system has never been observed before. The age of rapid economic growth is also the age of higher degree of inequality. According to the evolutionary model, growth and distribution are the outcomes of the same economic process.

The observed correlation between total output and pollution is also consistent with the predictions of the evolutionary model. Measures of pollution—carbon dioxide, CO_2, in the atmosphere—indeed show a great jump in pollution around the beginning of the 1950s (Stavins 2011, p. 170); moreover, the observed correlation between pollution and climate change implies causality, according to climate scientists (IPCC 2014). To recall, Maddison's calculations place the 1950s as the beginning of the rapid growth process. The beginning of the new Anthropocene age is also located around those years. Therefore, according to the evolutionary model, income growth, inequality, and pollution are all endogenous variables of economic growth process; hence, Anthropocene is also endogenous.

Finally, the prediction of the evolutionary model that the side effects of growth, rising inequality, and environment degradation have social consequences that lead to social maladies also tends to be consistent with facts. Data for these facts are scarce, revealing that they are outside of mainstream thinking. However, the scatter available data tend to support the predictions of the model, as shown in Figueroa (2015). Some relevant updating follows now.

Environment degradation is making human life much more hazardous. Pollution is becoming one of the top killers in the world; actually, according to a recent study, it is already the fourth leading risk factor of premature deaths worldwide (World Bank and IHME 2016). Pollution is also a significant factor in the higher rates of morbidity, which is due to the increase in non-communicable diseases, such as skin cancer and respiratory diseases. Higher temperatures are causing more frequent and intense floods and droughts; more extreme temperatures imply both higher average temperature and higher variance as well.

A recent paper by Environmental Health scientist Michael Brauer (2016), based on the Global Burden Disease study of 2013, reported that 85% of the world's population lives in areas where the WHO Air Quality Guideline is exceeded. In New Delhi, the number of fine particles (known as PM2.5) can be higher than 300 micrograms per cubic meter. The WHO's limit is in the range of 25–35 micrograms.

A prediction of the evolutionary model is that pollution and climate change will set the limit to economic growth rather than the total depletion of mineral resources. A scientific study, using an integrated assessment model to explore the implications of the 2°C limit in climate change, found that this limit would be reached in 2100; moreover, the current fossil reserves would remain unused before that year, the proportions being 30% of oil reserves, 50% of gas reserves, and 80% of coal reserves (McGlade and Ekins 2015). Thus, these findings render unnecessary continued investment in fossil fuel exploration because any new discoveries could just increase the unused rates. There would be more minerals in the ground than we can afford to burn.

Another implication of this scenario is that the long run supply of fossil fuel is higher than the long run demand, which in turn implies that long run relative prices will not tend to rise sharply. Fossil energy may even become relatively cheaper and thus there would not be incentives for substituting them through innovations in technology or consumption.

The problem of pollution and climate change is global. The Earth is a closed thermodynamic system, as it exchanges energy (solar) but not matter with its environment. Thus, globalization of environment degradation must be higher than other forms of globalization, such as finance and trade. Who are the big polluters? The higher the total output, the higher the pollution. This relation implies that large countries (the USA, China, India) are bigger polluters than small countries. At the level of households, some estimates indicate that wealthy families are bigger polluters than poor families: the top 10% of the world generates 50% of total pollution, whereas the bottom 50% does only 10% (Oxfam 2015). These figures roughly follow the world income distribution by individuals (Milanovic 2005, p. 109).

Furthermore, pollution is increasing social conflict between big corporations and rural communities of the Third World, in whose territories mineral exploitation projects are mostly located, with governments taking side with corporations. The Third World peasantry seek their livelihood in agricultural marginal lands, so marginal that these lands contain mineral deposits. Had the peasantry left those territories to become city workers, the empty land could have been exploited without much conflict; however, the economic growth process could not generate that transformation and the peasantry remain in the marginal lands.

As predicted by the evolutionary model, increasing income inequality has social consequences. It has led to higher degree of global social disorder. Illegal activities, illegal migration, terrorism, insecurity in the cities characterizes today's social environment. The need of "law and order" is often demanded everywhere, and increasingly so.

Life expectancy is usually taken as the measure of social progress. The empirical evidence is that life expectancy has been rising in the economic growth process. Therefore, one may conclude that social maladies, after all, are not that important for the human well-being. This fact would refute the prediction of the evolutionary model. However, there are reasons to doubt that the correlation between life expectancy and growth in per capita income implies causality.

It is a fact that life expectancy is higher in the First World than in the Third World. However, it is also a fact that among First World countries (controlling for income level), it is higher in those countries that have higher degree of *equality* (Bergh et al. 2016). In addition, some empirical studies suggest the following relationship: High inequality in society leads to high stress and decreased health quality not only for those at the bottom of the distribution, but for all the population (cited in Bergh et al. 2016). Therefore, countries with lower income inequality tend to be qualitatively better societies, as the evolutionary model predicts.

Consequently, life expectancy depends not only on income levels, but also on the degree of inequality. The effect of the former is positive, while that of the latter is negative. The relative higher life expectancy of the First World (compared to the Third World) is due to the sum of both effects, for they move in the positive direction: higher relative income and lower relative inequality. Furthermore, some empirical studies have shown that the income elasticity of life expectancy by countries is positive but less than 1 (Deaton 2013, p. 30). The fact that the income effect of life expectancy is positive but it is subject to diminishing returns implies that the inequality effect becomes increasingly more relevant for the improvement in life expectancy.

Another doubt is whether life expectancy is a good measure of social progress. Although this concept is considered a qualitative measure of social progress, life expectancy is quantitative (number of years). Some studies have shown that *people live longer, but are sicker.* Table 1.3 depicts some calculations made for the First World and Third World, between 1990 and 2013. The table shows that life expectancy falls significantly when measured as *healthy* life expectancy, taking into account days lost due to sickness. The loss is around 10 years, from 81 years to 69 in the First World countries, and from 68 years to 59 in the Third World countries. Hence, if the criterion is healthy life expectancy, then social progress is less bright in the economic growth process. This criterion seems more appropriate to have a summary measure of social maladies. The health effects of social disorder and pollution would be included under this criterion.

The same limitation applies to infant mortality rates as a measure of social progress. Infant mortality rates fall in the economic growth process. However, low mortality rates can coexist with a high incidence of undernourished children. This fact is reported in the literature. "A much larger proportion of South Asia children are undernourished (nearly half) than Sub-Sahara African children (nearly one-third). The interesting (apparent) paradox is that infant mortality rates are much lower in South Asia. In South Asia, the physician network is much larger and widespread, so the life-saving

Table 1.3 Life expectancy and healthy life expectancy by group of countries, 1990–2013

Life expectancy			Healthy life expectancy		
1990	2005	2013	1990	2005	2013
First World/*epsilon*					
76.33	79.77	81.07	65.93	68.53	69.62
(1.23)	(1.12)	(1.06)	(1.27)	(1.18)	(1.11)
23	23	23	23	23	23
Third World with weak colonial legacy/*omega*					
70.46	75.21	77.30	61.83	65.69	67.46
(7.95)	(6.27)	(5.17)	(7.22)	(5.57)	(4.52)
12	12	12	12	12	12
Third World with strong colonial legacy/*sigma*					
63.62	65.61	68.30	54.98	56.83	59.35
(8.56)	(9.50)	(8.04)	(7.61)	(8.30)	(6.95)
112	112	112	112	112	112

Notes: (1) Third World countries with weak colonial legacy include Argentina, Chile, Ethiopia, Costa Rica, Iran, Israel, South Korea, Singapore, Taiwan, Thailand, Turkey, and Uruguay. (2) Figures in parenthesis indicate standard deviation. (3) The third row under each side heading refers to the number of countries in the sample. The universe of countries in each category is 23, 13, and 138. (3) Each country HLE (healthy life expectancy) and LE (life expectancy) is based on the simple average between women and men indices reported by IHME (Institute for Health Metrics and Evaluation)

Source: Elaborated by the author using data from IHME (2016) Web Table 3. Last visit: 29-08-2016. Web page at: http://ghdx.healthdata.org/global-burden-disease-study-2013-gbd-2013-data-downloads

medical facilities [supervised births and vaccinations] are better than in Africa" (Mehrotra 2006, p. 56). The children who survive are not healthy but undernourished and having an impaired life. The survival life as destitute (children and adults) is not human life at all, as analyzed by some researchers (Dasgupta 1998).

The evolutionary model explains why we have come to this outcome of economic growth with social maladies. The exogenous variable is the power structure under capitalism. The economic and political elites have incentives to promote pro-growth public policies everywhere: They are the main beneficiaries of the economic growth process. It is not only that they benefit in the income distribution of the productivity gains brought about by growth, but it is also the means to maintain their privileged position in society. The persistence of social maladies just reflects the exercise of the power of the elites. Capitalism operates under power relations.

CONCLUSIONS

The evolutionary model (I) of the unified theory predicts that the economic growth process under capitalism produces a continuous increase in per capita income with two side effects. These include higher degree of inequality and higher degree of biophysical degradation, which have social consequences, leading to social maladies. This outcome is just the reflection of the power of economic and political elites in the economic process. Facts tend to be consistent with these predictions. Available facts tend to corroborate the economic growth process depicted in Fig. 1.2. Therefore, there is no reason to reject the evolutionary model (I) at this stage of our research and we can accept the model as a good approximation of real-world capitalism. The model explains this reality.

The exogenous variable in the evolutionary model is the power structure of society. The endogenous variables will move along particular time paths as long as the power structure remains unchanged. The concentrated power structure is the ultimate factor that explains the observed economic growth with social maladies. The persistence of social maladies reflects the power of the economic and political elites, who have no incentives to solve social maladies. The current concentrated power structure can change, but only exogenously; it could change toward an even more concentrated power. According to the model, no mechanism exists in the economic growth process that can lead endogenously to less concentrated power structures. Therefore, regarding social problems, the implication of the evolutionary model is that the capitalist system is not self-regulated.

Another implication of the evolutionary model is that the economic growth process cannot go on forever because it is an entropic process, which implies an evolutionary process; that is, there is no such thing as sustainable economic growth or steady-state economy. Under the evolutionary process, dynamic (mechanical) equilibrium is a mirage, as is steady state. Even static equilibrium is a mirage. In a static process, the same level of output (the no-growth society) is repeated period after period, as long as the values of the exogenous variables remain unchanged. The stock of mineral resources will decline by a given amount in each period until it becomes depleted! The stock of pollution will reach intolerable levels for human health by adding the same amount of pollution period after period!

An additional implication is that future generations will live under a more polluted atmosphere than does the current generation. Therefore, along the economic growth trajectory there exists implicitly another qualitative change: intergenerational negative externalities increases.

A final implication is the following. The international inequality in asset endowments or the international power structure refers not only to the concentration of economic assets (physical and human capital), but it includes the concentration of political assets as well (first- and second-class citizens), which, according to the unified theory, is part of the European colonial legacy of capitalism. The consequence of the persistent inequality in world capitalism is that international relations are also power relations. Rich nations have the power to intervene in the life of poorer nations. The superpower nations that emerged from the World War II (the USA, UK, France) have frequently intervened in Third World countries. Historian Eric Hobsbawm (2007) has argued that this is the age of the American imperialism; the collapse of the Soviet Union left the USA as the only superpower.

Furthermore, these interventions and invasions have surely exacerbated the social intolerance for international inequality, which is an important underlying factor in the international social disorder that we observe. As long as the power structure in the capitalist system taken as a whole prevails, international social disorder will remain. Therefore, overall inequality is also one of the fundamental problems of our time.

The current period is one in which economic growth is taking place under environment stress—the economic growth process has changed the Earth from the Holocene age to the Anthropocene age. In other words, and for practical purposes, we have already reached the end of the economic growth age. This is unfortunate, for social maladies remain unresolved. The question of how to change the economic process in the Anthropocene age and still reduce or eliminate social maladies will be analyzed in the rest of the book.

To be sure, the conclusions of unified theory differ from those of neoclassical economics, the standard economics. The growth models of neoclassical economics assume a mechanical economic growth process. These models assume that current economic growth process is taking place within the same biophysical environment we had around year 1800 and that nothing of significance has changed since. These models also ignore the social consequences of increasing income inequality. Therefore, the current economic growth is sustainable and can go on forever. There are no physical or social limits to economic growth. Furthermore, neoclassical theory assumes a capitalist system where power relations are not among the essential factors. Neoclassical theory predicts that economic growth is conducive to social progress. However, the fact that economic growth is accompanied by social maladies refutes this prediction and thus the neoclassical theory of economic growth.

Market and democracy are the fundamental institutions of capitalism. Therefore, economic growth with social maladies is an outcome of *democratic* capitalism. The outcome of social maladies under democracy is certainly a paradox. What role does democracy play in this outcome? Is it in spite of democracy or due to democracy? This is the topic of the next chapter.

REFERENCES

Bergh, A., Nilsson, T., & Waldenström, D. (2016). *Sick of inequality? An introduction to the relationship between inequality and health*. Cheltenham, UK: Edward Elgar.

Brauer, M. (2016). *The global burden of disease from air pollution*. Paper presented at the American Association for the Advancement of Science, 2016 Annual Meeting, February 13, 2016.

Dasgupta, P. (1998). *An inquire into well-being and destitution*. Oxford, UK: Oxford University Press.

Deaton, A. (2013). *The great escape*. Princeton, NJ: Princeton University Press.

Figueroa, A. (2015). *Growth, employment, inequality, and the environment: Unity of knowledge in economics* (Vol. I & II). New York: Palgrave Macmillan.

Figueroa, A. (2016). *Rules for scientific research in economics*. New York: Springer.

Galor, O. (2011). *Unified growth theory*. Princeton: Princeton University Press.

Georgescu-Roegen, N. (1971). *The entropy law and the economic process.* Cambridge, MA: Harvard University Press.

Hobsbawm, E. (2007). *Globalization, democracy, and terrorism.* London, UK: Abacus.

IHME. (2016). Institute for Health Metrics and Evaluation: Global burden of disease study 2013 data downloads. Retrieved from http://ghdx.healthdata.org/global-burden-disease-study-2013-gbd-2013-data-downloads

IPCC (Intergovernmental Panel on Climate Change). (2014). Climate change 2014: Synthesis report. In Core Writing Team, R. K. Pachauri, & L. A. Meyer (Eds.), *Contribution of working groups I, II and III to the fifth assessment report of the intergovernmental panel on climate change* (151 pp.). Geneva, Switzerland: IPCC.

Maddison, A. (1995). *Monitoring the world economy, 1820–1992.* Paris: OECD.

Maddison, A. (2003). *The world economy: Historical statistics.* Paris: OECD.

McGlade, C., & Ekins, P. (2015). The geographical distribution of fossil fuels unused when limiting global warming to 2.6 °C. *Nature, 517,* 187–190. doi:10.1038/nature14016.

Mehrotra, S. (2006). Child poverty. In D. Clark (Ed.), *The Elgar companion to development studies.* Cheltenham, UK: Edward Elgar.

Milanovic, B. (2005). *Worlds apart: Measuring international and global inequality.* Princeton, NJ: Princeton University Press.

Milanovic, B. (2010). All the Ginis dataset. *World Bank.* Web page. Retrieved October 18, 2010, from http://go.worldbank.org/9VCQW66LA0

Oxfam. (2015). *Extreme carbon inequality.* Retrieved from https://www.oxfam.org/en/pressroom/pressreleases/2015-12-02/worlds-richest-10-produce-half-carbon-emissions-while-poorest-35

Popper, K. (1968). *The logic of scientific discovery.* London: Routledge.

Popper, K. (1976). The logic of the social sciences. In T. W. Adorno et al. (Eds.), *The positive dispute in German sociology* (pp. 87–104). New York: Haper & Row.

Popper, K. (1993). Evolutionary epistemology. In M. Goodman & R. Snyder (Eds.), *Contemporary readings in epistemology* (pp. 338–350). Englewood Cliffs: Prentice Hall.

Stavins, R. (2011). The problem of the commons: Still unsettled after 100 years. *The American Economic Review, 101*(1), 141–188.

Wilson, E. (1998). *Consilience: The unity of knowledge.* New York: Alfred Knopf.

World Bank & IHME. (2016). *The cost of air pollution: Strengthening the economic case for action.* Washington, DC: The World Bank.

CHAPTER 2

Power Structure and Democracy

Market and democracy constitute the fundamental institutions of capitalism. Therefore, economic growth with social maladies found earlier as the outcomes of the economic process corresponds to *democratic* capitalism. This is certainly a paradox, which needs a scientific explanation. This chapter intends to supply such an explanation. To be sure, this chapter is not a philosophical or doctrinaire discussion of democracy (which is abundant), but a scientific one (which is scarce). It is not about what democracy *ought to be*; it is rather about what democracy *is*.

THE STANDARD ECONOMIC THEORY OF ELECTORAL DEMOCRACY

The classic book by Anthony Downs (1957) presented an economic theory of democracy, which actually referred to *electoral democracy*. It was an extension of neoclassical economic theory to the electoral democracy behavior. The theory assumes that people act guided by self-interest not only in the economic process, but also in the democratic process. Politicians seek power,

© The Author(s) 2017
A. Figueroa, *Economics of the Anthropocene Age*,
DOI 10.1007/978-3-319-62584-3_2

prestige, and income, which leads them to seek winning elections, which in turn implies seeking maximization of votes. Politicians are interested in gaining office to obtain personal benefits, not in promoting a better society. Political ideologies are just instruments in the struggle for office. On the other hand, the individual citizen seeks self-interest and votes for the political party he or she expects will provide them with more benefits than any other.

Downs' theory thus assumes that democratic government behavior is endogenously determined. Like in the case of any other social actor, such as consumers, business people, or investors, governments respond to incentives. The assumption is that individuals in the capitalist society have a private motive and a social function; however, people primarily seek to further their own interests and only secondarily to provide benefits for society. Thus, according to Downs' theory, democratic governments do not seek social well-being, but private interests; that is, social objectives are subordinated to private interests.

The literature that followed Downs' work has made many elaborations on the theory, but it seems that the theory has not been submitted to the empirical falsification requirement. Downs himself was able to derive a set of empirical predictions from his theory—25 to be exact! However, not all these empirical propositions are falsifiable (as they are unobservable), but several are. One prediction is particularly relevant: "Democratic governments tend to redistribute income from the rich to the poor" (proposition 6). However, the fact that the degree of income inequality is one of the structural features of capitalism (Chap. 1) refutes this prediction. One could argue that inequality would be much higher without government policies, or that tax policies reduce market inequality.

A survey article of the international literature about the relationship between democracy and the magnitude of income redistribution has found that there is no consensus on empirical results (Acemoglu et al. 2015). Thus, the fact remains that income inequality is persistent under electoral democracy, a paradox that needs an explanation.

We could consider Downs' work just a particular model of the neoclassical theory. This would open the option of constructing another neoclassical model by introducing other auxiliary assumptions. However, the empirical predictions will be the same because the assumption of neoclassical theory that power relations can be ignored will prevail for any other model. Ignoring the power structure in the functioning of electoral democracy seems to be the reason for the theory failure. Thus, a new theory of democracy is needed.

ELECTORAL DEMOCRACY IN A SMALL SOCIETY OF EQUALS

Electoral democracy is usually seen as one of the greatest human inventions. Instead of reviewing the history of electoral democracy (which is abundant), it would be interesting to review its logical foundations. Therefore, consider the following introductory question: What are the implicit assumptions about the type of society in which electoral democracy would lead to the common good? It can be proved that these assumptions include a society of equals and a small society.

Consider an abstract society that is small and equal. Individual endowments of economic and political assets are equally distributed. No capitalist class exists. Equal political entitlements imply that all people are first-class citizens.

Suppose electoral democracy is the rule in this society. The government is elected through voting. This democratic rule implies that the political power of the people is transferred to the group elected for the government, but the transfer is *temporary* only and not to a political class. There are no incentives for the existence of political parties and a political class. The problems of the community and the policy alternatives—the means and the ends—can be discussed openly in a small society and competition between political parties is unnecessary. Citizens know what they want and are aware of the constraints, and consensus can be reached on the common good. What is needed as government is a group of good managers, selected by voting. Citizens will have the incentives to participate in public affairs and in elections, as the chance to influence in the issues through elections will be high. The individual motivation of free-riding behavior on public affairs would be limited by the social control mechanism. The government is thus subject to social control. In such a society, therefore, seeking to buy votes would be unviable.

In such a small and equal abstract society, the functioning of electoral democracy would have several traits. First, the best ideas for improving the common good in society would be chosen. Information about policy alternatives would be uniform. There would exist a kind of Darwinian competition among proposals: the bad political ideas would be eliminated and the good ones would be selected. Second, a political class from which government officials are elected would be unnecessary. Third, social control would play a significant role in the functioning of democracy. Fourth, if preferences over public policies were heterogeneous, and if consensus were difficult, then majority rule would prevail. In any case, the policy choice would be directed toward the common good; if it did not work, another policy will be sought and implemented. Democratic public choices would thus be self-regulated.

The elected government would tend to seek the common good, not because people in government are altruists rather than egotists, but because of incentives. Social control would be very strong, not only on government behavior, but also on citizens. Thus, the government would be accountable to the people and to the people alone. The government would have the proper social incentives to perform well: social prestige for good performance and social stigma and ostracism for bad performance. Social incentives, rather than economic incentives, would prevail in the democratic process.

In sum, in this small and equal society, electoral democracy would lead to a *government of the people, by the people, and for the people*. Democracy (from the Greek *demos*, people, and *kratos*, power) is usually so defined. The institution of electoral democracy would thus generate incentives for attaining the common good. It would indeed represent one of the greatest human inventions. It would be more efficient than the alternative forms of government, such as dictatorship, dynasty, or gerontocracy.

Therefore, the essential factor explaining the failure of electoral democracy under capitalism would have to do with the fact that capitalist societies do not conform to the implicit society that electoral democracy assumes. Real-world capitalism is indeed very different from that abstract small society of equals that electoral democracy assumes. Once this is recognized, the fact that electoral democracy fails under capitalism should not come to us as a surprise.

In what ways does the existence of inequality in individual endowments distort electoral democracy under capitalism? How about the effect of large size societies? These questions need a scientific explanation, namely, the construction of a theory that is falsifiable.

A THEORETICAL MODEL OF ELECTORAL DEMOCRACY

The unified theory assumes that market and democracy constitute the fundamental institutions of capitalism. This theory also assumes that the significant trait of democratic capitalism is the initial concentration of economic assets in the hands of the capitalist class. How about political endowments?

The unified theory assumes two types of capitalist societies that constitute the capitalist system, namely, the epsilon society (intended to resemble the First World) and the sigma society (the Third World). Sigma societies have the legacy of the European colonial systems; moreover, as part of this colonial legacy, there are two classes of citizens, not formally but de facto, in the workings of electoral democracy. First-class citizens comprise the descendants of the dominant groups during colonial times, whereas second-class citizens comprise the descendants of the dominated groups (natives and workers who were brought into the colonies as slaves, mostly of African origin).

As a result, the initial inequality in assets is more concentrated in sigma than in epsilon. In the former, there exists inequality in political entitlements, as there are first-class and second-class citizens, whereas in the latter there is only one class of citizens. Taking the capitalist system as a whole, the initial inequality in political endowments is such that individuals of sigma societies are second-class citizens in the capitalist world taken as a whole. This is also rooted in European colonial history.

The unified theory also assumes that individuals' acts are guided by the motivation of self-interest. Under capitalism, it is rational for individuals to be selfish. Altruism, the other human motivation, is thus subordinated to egotism. Therefore, consider the following auxiliary assumption on the individual motivations that guide the behavior of the political class:

Alpha proposition: *In an electoral democracy, politicians act guided by the motivation of self-interest. They seek to capture the state to have political power and income. This objective implies seeking to maximize votes, subject to budget constraints.*

The institution of electoral democracy implies that people transfer their political power to their representatives by the mechanism of voting. Politicians seek to be elected for office because they expect to gain political power, and with it high personal incomes. Politicians anticipate that if elected they can capture the state for their personal benefits. Entrepreneurs seek to create firms in order to have profits: no firms, no profits; similarly, politicians seek to capture the state to have political power and income: no state control, no political power and no income. Firms and the state are the means to obtain personal objectives. Any concern for social progress is a secondary objective.

Markets and electoral democracy constitute the fundamental institutions of capitalism. The production and distribution of private goods operates through markets, whereas the provision of public goods does through electoral democracy.

In order to explain the workings of electoral democracy in its most elementary form, a static model of political behavior is constructed now. The model includes the following assumptions: (a) the assumption on the behavior of politicians, as stated above; (b) three social actors will be taken into account in the social interactions: capitalists, politicians, and workers; (c) the democratic process is static, which consists of two sequential stages: first, the elections stage and then functioning of the elected government. Furthermore, in this model, capitalist and political classes will constitute the elites, a very small fraction of the population, even including their organic professionals; hence, workers being the large majority of the population will constitute "the people" and "the voters."

Political Behavior in the Election Process

Consider firstly the stage of the election process. Politicians form political parties and compete with each other for the votes of citizens. Votes are the necessary and sufficient condition to be elected and to gain political power. Politicians know that electoral democracy is a mechanism to transfer the political power of voters to the government.

What do politicians do in order to win elections? The model assumes that politicians seek to maximize the number of votes, which come from different social groups with different interests. Attracting voters depends upon the investment made in reaching them in the campaign and the promises made to them, given the investment and proposals of the competitors. Politicians must allocate their given budget or investment fund in reaching out to groups to maximize the number of total votes. Therefore, politicians seek to buy votes by means of political campaigns and by spending money to persuade voters.

Therefore, the politician or political party will seek to allocate their given investment fund according to their vote returns. Assuming that returns are subject to diminishing marginal gains in attracting voters, investment will be allocated in such a way that marginal gains are equalized in attracting each group.

Each political party will act in a context in which few competitors offer different products. This resembles the market structure of oligopoly with some product differentiation. In this context, competition implies interactions among the players. Political parties know what the others are offering and know that strategies followed by one political party will lead to responses from the others. Due to these interactions, the initial proposals of the individual politician will be adjusted and will tend to move to the center of the spectrum, seeking to attract voters siding with the opposite view without losing voters from his or her own side. Thus, the well-known Hotelling theorem on oligopoly markets—initial product differentiation among firms tends to move to the center of the spectrum—is applicable to political competition as well. Investment funds are needed to propagandize and manipulate the preferences of voters, just like in the oligopoly market structure.

Workers—"the people," under capitalism—also act guided by self-interest. They may be committed to vote for a particular political party on ideological grounds. However, the model assumes that this is not the essential factor in the electoral process, and that a large majority of voters in the electoral democracy will vote guided by self-interest. The individual worker votes for the political party he or she expects will provide the highest benefits. Workers are *in principle* free to choose among the political candidates depending on their proposals. However, the use of propaganda and manipulation techniques, the extent of which depends upon the budget of the competing parties, will change workers' preferences in the election process.

We know from biology that human behavior is the result of both nature and nurture; given nature factors (genes), the social environment shapes human behavior. Therefore, social influences can control and change human behavior. The mechanism is the so-called techniques of *behavioral engineering* (more on this in Chap. 3). These techniques are widely utilized in society, as in education, in religion, in commercial advertising, and so on. In the electoral case, the social influence and the techniques of behavioral engineering come via electoral propaganda.

The electoral process operates, according to this theoretical model, as a monopolistic market of ideas. Competition is among the few, where the investment capacity of candidates to manipulate and change the preferences of voters through advertisement—the capacity to buy votes—is fundamental for competition. Therefore, the model predicts that political parties with the largest investment funds will be able to buy more votes, and thus have a larger share of the total votes. The model predicts that money plays a fundamental role in the voting process.

Economic elites have promoted the idea that the free market is socially desirable because market competition transforms individual self-interests into the common good. This idea is socially imposed as true knowledge and thus becomes the economic discourse in society. In large societies, the discourse is disseminated via mechanisms that the elites control, such as the media. Therefore, the discourse becomes common knowledge, the "commonsense knowledge," for it is believed to be true, and may even take the form of sacred or magical.

To be sure, the elites' discourse has nothing to do with scientific knowledge about the real world; it is rather a particular form of knowledge that is socially imposed as true, which is in the interests of the elite. This is the concept of *discourse* utilized in this book.

According to the discourse, firms are price takers in the market, that is, they have no market power. Therefore, firms compete to produce goods at the lowest cost, whereas consumers freely choose the cheapest goods, according to their preferences. This is the natural economic efficiency of capitalism. Market competition is Darwinian, in which high-cost firms are eliminated from the market and low-cost firms prevail to the benefit of consumers.

Actually, the discourse is against facts. In the real-world market, indeed, there exists competition, but it is not perfect competition (powerless); it is mostly imperfect competition, oligopolistic competition, and competition among the few, which originates in the fact that physical capital ownership is highly concentrated in a few hands. In the real-world market competition, firms operate as big business, corporations, and conglomerates, and have market power, that is, they are price makers, not price takers. These firms use sophisticated devices to control and change consumers' behavior in the direction of maximizing their profits, such as publicity and sales promotion techniques (see more in Chap. 4). The discourse serves the purpose of legitimizing both their social position of privilege and their profits; so, they have the incentives to sell this belief. Moreover, in large societies, they have the mechanisms to do this (the media, which they also control).

Similarly, political elites have created a discourse that promotes the public belief that electoral democracy is the best system, for voters are free to elect the best alternative for them. Competition among politicians is also Darwinian: those proposing bad public policies will lose the elections and those proposing the best policies for the people will be elected. This belief serves the purpose of legitimizing the politician's political power, prestige, and incomes; that is, politicians have the incentives to sell this discourse—moreover, they have the mechanisms to do it in large societies, through the electoral machinery, which includes the media.

Therefore, the market of political ideas is an imperfect market, an oligopolistic type of market. Political parties seek maximization of votes by using different strategies. The social conflicts in a capitalist society appear in labor relations, between firms and workers; in market relations, between buyers and sellers of goods and services; in the provision of public goods, between those who pay the taxes and receive the benefits; in the distribution of income between capitalists and workers, and among workers as well. However, politicians seek to manipulate and distort all these social conflicts, according to their objective to maximize votes. Thus, they offer pro-growth policies, for everyone gains with economic growth, as the discourse says. Economic growth is thus sold as the panacea.

Furthermore, in the election campaign, the market of ideas is a *market of promises*. The political market is not like the potato market. Therefore, there is room for different strategies to sell promises; moreover, these strategies easily include the manipulation of the preferences of voters through publicity and other devices. Electoral democracy leads to the existence of the industries of strategists, advisors, and publicity.

In this context, citizens can hardly choose according to their *given* preferences. The use of behavioral engineering in the electoral democracy process implies that the preferences of voters are not exogenously given, but are changeable, and ultimately endogenous. Controlling people's behavior in large societies implies using mass communication publicity, which in turn implies millionaire electoral campaigns. Political competition is about the capacity of financing the electoral campaign. Thus, politicians need financing to control and change people's behavior; therefore, electoral competition implies the operation of manipulating voter's preferences, which is equivalent to the operation of *buying votes*.

Political competition is about buying votes with *promises* of politicians to follow some policies. It is not the case that political parties have a given set of policies and seek to win voters in order to apply it; instead, political parties construct an appropriate set of policies they promise to apply with which they expect to win the elections. Thus, the market of political ideas is a market of promises only, as discussed above.

Democracy is the method to decide collectively over the production of public goods. Once we have assumed that individuals act guided by self-interest, it follows that individuals will follow free-riding behavior on collective action. Hence, the voter's motivation to participate in the elections is not strong. Once public goods have been produced, all would benefit from their services, even those who did not participate in its production.

The political market of promises contributes to free-riding behavior. Voters know that political competition is about promises and that they are seeking to buy votes using advertisement to manipulate voters. Voters also have expectations about the likelihood of implementation of promises. Once in government, the promises need not come true, as politicians, once elected, will concentrate the political power and will be able to elaborate "sound" excuses. Thus, as this process is repeated, voters have low incentives to participate in the elections. However, the strategy followed by political parties induces high participation of citizens in the electoral process to gain political power that is legitimate.

Would scientific knowledge be present in the political debates about public policies? Society needs to decide on means and ends that are of public interest. Science is the natural source to obtain the knowledge needed about the means (the causality relations) and thus make the ends to be consistent with the means. Although the ends are not necessarily derived from science, the use of science-based public policies would give consistency to ends and means. However, scientific knowledge is absent in the political competition. There are no incentives for that.

On the contrary, politicians have the incentive to distort reality in the direction of their own interests. Political discourse is utilized not to help voters to understand reality, but to obscure and distort it. The end-means alternatives are not left to the experts or scientists but to politicians themselves. On the other hand, the voters—workers—do not have enough education or information to have access to scientific discussion; moreover, they know that the political debate is mostly about promises and thus seek to free-ride. Hence, even if politicians are willing to introduce scientific knowledge into the political debate, they would find that it is not useful to buy votes. Therefore, the political discourse of candidates is based not on scientific knowledge (from the natural and social sciences), but rather on arguments that are intuitive and based on rhetoric, manipulation, and fallacies, but attracting the interest of voters. Compared to the professional strategies of politicians, workers appear as amateur participants in the election process.

The electoral democratic system is thus conducive to a kind of *Galton's law of mediocrity* in society. The political debate about means and ends takes place not at the level of current scientific knowledge, but at levels closer to popular beliefs, which in turn are based on the discourse of the elites. The norm in scientific work says that it is better to be wrong than vague; the incentive in the political process goes in the opposite direction: It is better to be vague than wrong. Electoral democracy leads society to mediocrity.

On the behavior of capitalists, the model assumes that private investors who contribute to the financing of political parties seek economic returns, as they do in any investment; they can even follow the portfolio diversification strategy by supporting several political candidates at the same time. Capitalists know that politicians once elected will capture the state and that business opportunities travel through the state and markets. Thus, private investors have incentives to finance political campaigns. Therefore, money plays a major role in the election process, as politicians need money to buy votes and capitalists have incentives to finance and have a legitimate government to do business with later on.

In sum, the election process is business! Workers have no mechanisms to resist the manipulations (as discussed above) and are dominated by the power of money. The "free choice" of voters is just another myth created by the political discourse.

Political Behavior of the Elected Government

Consider now the second stage of the political process, namely, the behavior of politicians when in government. Once elected, politicians become the representatives of the people in the state. *Electoral democracy implies the transfer of people's political power to their representatives.* Thus, elected politicians are endowed with political power and are able to capture the state in the name of workers. Thus, there is a qualitative change in the behavior of politicians before and after being elected: from begging people for their votes to becoming their masters. Once elected, politicians need not execute what they promised in the election competition; no mechanism exists that can ensure that, much less when the politicians in government now hold political power. For the next elections, conditions and main issues of society will be different, or politicians will make them appear different, as they are the experts in distorting reality.

In the production of public goods, workers will tend to adopt free-riding behavior, as they have no incentives to go into collective action to ensure the application of policies that benefit society. In a large society, selfish individuals seek to behave in this way regarding public goods (Olson 1965). As the saying goes, "Everybody's business is nobody's business." Workers will be willing to exercise pressure on some policies that affect them directly; however, even in this case of producing a local public good, free-riding behavior will tend to prevail, and will weaken the collective action. On the other hand, politicians will find easy ways to circumvent those pressures, given the weakness of collective action and asymmetric information. Governments operate with secrecy, not with complete transparency, for it is needed to exercise political power.

Once in power, politicians will still seek to maximize votes in the form of popularity. They have incentives for that. Popularity gives them legitimacy to act seeking their own interests and keeps them politically viable for the next election process. Thus, governments will have incentives for supplying those public goods that have a high public impact, and have it now, before the next election, rather than in the long run. Long-term problems of society, policies leading to qualitative progress of society, but having low short-run public impact, will have no priority in public policies. Thus, the incentives are for new buildings of public schools or public hospitals, which can be inaugurated and can become big news in the media, rather than institutional innovations to improve, say, the quality of schools and hospitals, which cannot be inaugurated or propagandized, although it will have significant effects upon the common good in the long run.

Government policies of great public impact will thus have priority. This is usually called "populist policies" and is very often criticized. However, according to the theoretical model, the incentive system in the electoral democracy is such that it inevitably leads to populist policies, that is, populist policies are embedded in the system. It is just like the case of oligopolistic markets, where firms are price makers (not price takers), and it would be pointless to criticize that. Once they have captured the state, politicians seek to buy popularity. The myopic rationality of politicians in government is inconsistent with the state role, which is supposed to be the concern about the common good and the fate of society.

On accountability, politicians will have incentives to be accountable to capitalists rather than to workers. The reason is that the capitalist class controls capital, the basic economic resource of society. The popularity of the government depends upon the well-being of workers, which in turn depends upon the labor market conditions, which in turn depend upon the decisions of capitalists; thus, the popularity of government depends upon the behavior of the capitalist class. Therefore, the incentive to be accountable to workers is relatively low, not that governments will ignore social protests, but governments know how to use devices to control human behavior, and even to buy popular support, given the weakness of collective action and asymmetric information, as discussed above.

On the other hand, governments face serious threats from capitalists, who are free to invest abroad rather than domestically if government policies are not capital-friendly. We may call it the Kaleckian threat, for economist Michal Kalecki (1971 [1943]) was one of the first to understand it. Therefore, politicians will tend to side with the capitalist class, not with workers. Moreover, politicians may also govern without much popularity as long as they have the support of the capitalist class. The opposite situation would be unviable. For the case of re-election, political parties will then have the financial support from capitalists and thus will have greater financial capacity to buy votes.

Up to now, the model has referred mostly to the epsilon society. Some particular traits of electoral democracy in the sigma society are in order. Compared to epsilon society, sigma society is unequal in political entitlements among citizens. There are first-class and second-class citizens, which implies first-class and second-class workers. To recall, second-class workers are the descendants of the population that were dominated during the European colonial systems. The political behavior of workers who are first-class citizens will be very similar to those of the epsilon society. Compared to these, second-class workers, who also have the formal right to vote, have no political voice or lower political voice, and lower education level; thus, their capacity to pressure government for policies on their particular interest is even weaker. Thus, they will have less incentives to participate in the political process, unless voting is mandatory. Given their low level of education, they are excluded from the political process and political debate. Voting is just a formality.

In the sigma society, the mechanism of political competition will be similar to the one in epsilon society. The difference is that second-class citizens will be much easier to manipulate and deceive in the objective of buying votes. Once in government, politicians will have even lower incentives to be accountable to those workers who are second-class citizens. These workers can be manipulated more easily not only in the electoral campaign, but also from the government, given the fact that information asymmetry will be even more marked in this case. Thus, workers in general will be in a weaker position to be a main social actor in the political process. Capitalists will have the power over governments as in the epsilon society, but this power in the sigma society will be even greater, given the relatively lower voice of workers.

According to the theoretical model, in short, workers transfer their political power to the government; thus, workers elect their masters, not their servants. Workers' entitlements of political power are thus reduced and those of politicians in government increased. The government so elected becomes part of the power structure of the capitalist society. Electoral democracy constitutes an underlying mechanism to generate and support the power structure in which the power of the capitalist class is dominant. This is the nature of electoral democracy. Schutz (2011) analyzes comprehensibly the ways in which money rules in electoral democracy. Thus, electoral democracy is plutocracy. Electoral democracy is business.

Taking the capitalist system as a whole, as composed of epsilon and sigma societies, if such global government existed and were elected under the rules of electoral democracy, the same conclusions would follow. Electoral democracy would be a mechanism by which the political power of the people is transferred to the elected politicians. Money would rule in electoral democracy.

The theoretical model of electoral democracy under capitalism can be represented as a static abstract process. Consider Fig. 1.1 again. The exogenous variables (X) are, in this model, the initial inequality in the individual distribution of economic and political assets (δ), competing political parties, and money. The endogenous variables include the new distribution of economic and political assets, the new power structure (δ'), which implies a more concentrated power structure than that related to the initial inequality; and then the composition of political parties in government (Υ), which determines the public policies. The mechanisms (underlying factors) include institutions—the formal rules of electoral democracy, rights, and duties—and electoral technology, which refers to the behavioral engineering techniques.

To be sure, there are two effects to consider. Electoral democracy implies a transfer of workers' political power to politicians. This has a *level effect* in the power structure (from

δ to δ'). This is a long-run effect, as the new level will remain unchanged as long as the initial inequality also remains fixed. *The power structure, with which capitalism operates, is more concentrated than the initial inequality.* In the short run, as the process is repeated election after election, electoral democracy leads to a redistribution of political power among the political class (short-run variations of δ'). Thus, in the short run, money is the essential variable that determines changes in who captures the state. The new governments will choose different public policies. However, these changes in governments and policies are of second order of importance, while the level effect is the fundamental change in society brought about by the electoral democracy institution.

From the assumptions of the theoretical model, the following equilibrium conditions under which electoral democracy will tend to operate (beta proposition) can be derived:

> Beta proposition: *Under electoral democracy, workers transfer their political power to politicians elected for government posts, who then capture the state apparatus and use it to seek their own interests, subject to the constraints given by the capitalist class' interests. Thus, electoral democracy is the mechanism to increase the initial concentration of the power structure of a capitalist society to a higher level, which now includes political power over workers.*

These equilibrium conditions are observable; therefore, they constitute the empirical predictions of the static model. It says that electoral democracy is the mechanism to increase the initial concentration of power under capitalism to another level. It is falsifiable. The model would be refuted if electoral democracy had given workers the political power—the government—in society, which is not the case. Not to be confused with political parties that carry the name "workers party," "labor party," or similar names, for they are playing the electoral democracy game. The reason is that both economic and political power is based on the power of money. Electoral democracy is also business. Money rules in the current democratic capitalism.

In the small and equal society that we referred to above, electoral democracy did not lead to the concentration of political power because the power of money was not involved, because in this case electoral democracy was not business; that is, electoral democracy was based on social incentives, not on economic incentives. In the capitalist society, in contrast, the electoral democracy is based on economic incentives. According to this theoretical model, it is not ideology that underlies the workings of the electoral democracy; it is money.

GENERAL EQUILIBRIUM UNDER CAPITALISM WITH ELECTORAL DEMOCRACY

How does capitalism operate under electoral democracy? The theoretical static model of electoral democracy is now introduced into the static economic process under capitalism, as constructed by the unified theory. Consider Fig. 1.1 again. In a very elementary static or short-run model of capitalism, the exogenous variables (X) will be the capital per worker, the international terms of trade, and the initial inequality. The mechanisms are the institutions, which include the market system and the electoral democracy. The exogenous variables (Y) will be output per worker and the degree of inequality in income distribution. The reduced form equation of the model shows the endogenous variables as a function of the exogenous variables, that is, $Y = F(X)$.

Where does the electoral democracy model appear in the economic process? It will be part of the structural equations.

The first structural equation says that the endogenous variables (average income and income inequality) depend upon the initial capital per worker ratio, the international terms of trade, and the public policies. We already know that the public policies chosen by the government are an outcome (endogenous variables) of the electoral democratic process, which depend upon the new exogenous variables of the electoral process (political parties and money). This is the second structural equation. Hence, the reduced form equation will show average income and income inequality as a function of the initial capital labor ratio, international terms of trade, and public policies.

How is the general equilibrium attained? The market system operates *as if* it were a big computer, which is able to solve a system of equations for the prices and quantities of equilibrium of market exchange. The system of equations now includes, say, the government fiscal policies. The simplest way is to assume the tax rates and the government budget structure as given; then, there will be general equilibrium values of prices and quantities in the market system. Total government tax revenues and expenditures will thus be endogenous. If this outcome is not what the government expects, then by changing the initial givens, the government can determine the acceptable outcome. This is to say that the tax rates and expenditure structure are ultimately endogenously determined, together with the average income and income inequality results. Therefore, the outcome of the general equilibrium will include the production of private and public goods. The distribution of private and public goods among the three social classes is also determined endogenously. Thus, general equilibrium in the short run will be attained.

Democratic capitalism as epsilon or sigma society has the same market mechanisms to solve production and distribution spontaneously. This holds true even on considering the coexistence of Walrasian and non-Walrasian markets. In a non-Walrasian market, the nominal prices are exogenous; thus, the market system has one less unknown to solve for, but, at the same time, one equation is lost in the entire system of equations. Moreover, if for some reason nominal market prices were out of equilibrium in Walrasian markets, the entire market system would be able to restore equilibrium, also spontaneously. The market solution is thus stable.

In the short run, the outcome of general equilibrium implies excess labor supply and excess income inequality. In order to distinguish the effect of government policies on the general equilibrium outcome, we could analytically separate the general equilibrium of the market system alone from general equilibrium including government intervention. In the first case, the outcome would imply excess labor supply and excess income inequality. Capitalism needs excess labor supply to operate, for this is the mechanism to extract effort from workers and thus maximize profits. This would be unviable under full employment. Labor markets are by necessity non-Walrasian. Given the concentration in the initial inequality in the distribution of economic assets, income inequality would also be very unequal.

Government policies cannot solve these problems. Excess labor supply can hardly be eliminated by public policies; it is a necessity for the functioning of capitalism, as discussed above. To eliminate excess income inequality would imply, in the short run, significant income redistribution, which would affect the elites. Elites do not have the incentive to accept that. Therefore, the general equilibrium with government intervention could modify the pure market solution, but it would not constitute a significant change. Hence, the observed outcome of the economic process in the short run is with excess labor supply and excess income inequality, that is, with social maladies.

Therefore, in what sense are we calling this outcome "equilibrium"? Conceptually, an economic equilibrium situation means that no social actor has both the power and the incentives to change the situation and thus the situation will be repeated period after period as long as the exogenous variables remain unchanged.

In the dynamic or long-run model, dynamic general equilibrium implies a dynamic trajectory showing economic growth—the continuous increase in output per person. Physical and human capital accumulation and technological progress are the proximate factors that determine economic growth. The ultimate factor is the initial inequality. However, excess labor supply and excess income inequality—and thus social maladies—will persist in the process of economic growth, for the dynamic trajectory can be seen just as a sequence of static equilibrium situations. The same principles apply to the dynamic trajectory showing the transition dynamics.

In the evolutionary or very long-run model, the economic process of production and distribution is an entropic process, in which the dynamic trajectory of output per worker is accompanied by excess labor supply, excess income inequality, and degradation of the biophysical environment. Because the quantitative increase of output per worker over time is accompanied by qualitative changes in society (income inequality and degradation of the biophysical environment), the dynamic process becomes an evolutionary process ending in a switching regime, as shown in Fig. 1.2. In the evolutionary process, we also have economic growth with social maladies.

Therefore, in all its analytical models, the unified theory predicts that the economic process under the current democratic capitalism is conducive to social maladies. How could social maladies be the outcome of a system that operates with democracy? Certainly, this is a paradox. Unified theory explains this paradox as follows: democracy takes the form of electoral democracy, which, given the initial inequality, generates a perverse incentive system.

Considering again the evolutionary model (I), the essential mechanisms of electoral democracy in the economic growth process can be summarized as follows.

Excess labor supply is a necessity for the functioning of capitalism, for it is a device to attain higher labor productivity and thus higher profit levels. Because workers and capitalists are not full partners, capitalists must apply devices to discipline workers and extract effort from them. A situation of full employment would be against this objective, for workers would face no cost of shirking in the job. There are two separate devices, one for each type of capitalism. In an epsilon society, which is under-populated, the device to discipline workers is unemployment; therefore, the cost of shirking is unemployment. Labor market equilibrium is thus with unemployment. In a sigma society, which is overpopulated, the device to discipline workers is a gap between the market wage rate and the income workers can make if self-employed. This gap is the cost that workers will face if shirking. Therefore, the self-employed become the excess labor supply, which is called underemployment.

In the economic growth process, technological change takes place. The unified theory assumes that technological change is endogenously determined, for capitalists have incentives to generate labor-saving new technologies, which leads to higher profits and also constitutes another mechanism to maintain the needed excess labor supply situation.

Therefore, no matter how hard workers seek wage employment, not all will succeed. No matter what democratic governments do to apply policies that promote employment, full employment will not be attained. A full employment situation is against the interests of capitalists. General equilibrium with excess labor supply is the main feature of capitalism. Therefore, the social malady of excess labor supply cannot be self-regulated under democratic capitalism. This outcome reflects the power of the capitalist class over government and workers, as predicted by the electoral democracy model.

Furthermore, the use of labor discipline devices is conducive to inequality among workers of similar skills. One could say that the general labor discipline device is to maintain inequality among homogenous workers. Hence, the problem of excess labor supply can be seen as part of the problem of income inequality. Because excess labor supply implies inequality among workers, we could consider it included in income inequality; thus, the endogenous variable may be reduced to excess income inequality.

In the long run, the level of income inequality tends to reflect the initial inequality in the distribution of economic and political assets; that is, the higher the latter, the higher the former will be. (In the short-run model of the unified theory, due to changes in the terms of international trade, income inequality will show temporal variations around its long-run value.) This relation holds true in both epsilon and sigma societies. The difference is quantitative: the observed degree of income inequality is higher in sigma than in epsilon because the initial inequality is higher in the former.

If income inequality is excessive, one would expect that workers should protest and press the democratic government—their representatives—for redistribution policies, until a socially tolerable inequality is attained. Moreover, in an asymmetric distribution of income, the median voter belongs to the poor group of society, which should lead to public policies in favor of the poor. Given the size of the working class, the government should have incentives to apply those policies. Why does democracy not regulate excess income inequality?

Redistribution of income from the rich to the poor groups is unviable under electoral democracy. The economic elites—as owners of capital—would resist this policy. The *Kaleckian threat* also applies in this case. Free capital movement limits the tax rates that can be imposed upon the wealthy. In a world of free capital movement, capitalists can invest somewhere else, and thus the after-tax rate of profits in the country must be in line with the international rate, corrected by risk factors. Hence, the government's redistribution policies are subject to this constraint.

Some redistribution would be viable in the context of economic growth. Profits and high incomes are increasing in absolute amounts, which also increase total tax revenues. Then, through income transfer policies, real income of the poor could be increased. Thus, as the current discourse goes, everybody can win in the economic growth process. However, this outcome shows reduction in poverty, but it does not imply reduction in income inequality.

Furthermore, economic and political elites will manage to propagandize the social benefits of pro-growth policies, which can be demonstrated in the rise in the absolute incomes of the poor and the consequent fall in the poverty rate. However, they will hide the fact that the real income of the wealthy has also increased and that the degree of income inequality has increased or has remained unchanged. The incentives of the economic and political elites are for reducing absolute poverty, not relative poverty (inequality). As social disorder will not disappear, the discourse will then put the blame on ideological or political motivations underlying the social disorder.

The economic and political elites will then seek to sell the pro-growth discourse. As with any discourse, it is very effective upon public information or disinformation. The content of this discourse includes ideas (mostly fallacies) such as "with growth, we all win," "growth is the only way to reduce poverty," "redistribution is unethical: it is against individual freedom," and more notably the following: "in poor countries, where the average income is low, redistribution of income is a bad policy, for it is just redistribution of poverty." The latter proposition is a fallacy because the degree of inequality in the capitalist system is so pronounced that redistribution from the very wealthy to the poor can raise the income of the poor significantly *now*, instead of waiting for the same increase via economic growth for decades. (Numbers involved are provided in Chap. 7.)

Therefore, under electoral democracy, reducing the excessive degree of income inequality to a socially tolerable level through income redistribution is unviable. There are no incentives for that. Capitalists will favor pro-growth economic policies. Governments also prefer economic growth, for they can collect more taxes and have a higher budget to spend on buying public popularity. If growth proceeds with higher income concentration in the marketplace, the better, for tax revenues will be higher and the government can use those funds to buy popularity by applying anti-poverty policies. If there were no poverty—if incomes were equally distributed—governments would have problems to buy votes. Poverty is thus good business for the government! Both capitalists and governments have incentives to promote economic growth, not to redistribute income.

Finally, pro-growth policies imply an acceleration in the rate of degradation of the biophysical environment. This effect is independent of who the main beneficiaries of economic growth are.

The problem of the environment is a problem of a public good, known as *the commons problem*. The process of production and consumption implies depletion of mineral resources and pollution of the atmosphere. According to the laws of thermodynamics, depletion and pollution are irrevocable. Firms produce goods and pay all the costs involved, which are transferred to market prices, except the costs of depletion and pollution. There are no markets for these public goods. Mother Nature has no cashier.

Because the environment is a problem of public goods, capitalists and workers adopt free-riding behavior. Democracy has a clear role here. However, governments do not have incentives to reduce pollution or depletion, for it would imply no-growth policies and then income redistribution policies, as the only way to raise the income of workers. Their incentives just go in the opposite direction: promote economic growth and apply anti-poverty transfers, as shown above. In any event, the environment problem is a long-run problem that goes beyond the government period and the calendar of next elections. No incentives to tackle this problem exist under electoral democracy.

Economic growth with social maladies is a structural trait of the current democratic capitalism. This particular outcome just reflects the power of the economic and political elites. This is what the unified theory predicts.

Empirical Consistency

The predictions of the evolutionary model (I) remain when the workings of the electoral democracy are explicitly included in the model. Therefore, they also tend to be consistent with facts. Indeed, we have observed increases in both income inequality and environment degradation in the growth age of capitalism, as shown above. Further evidence follows.

A survey of the international literature on the relationship between democracy and the magnitude of income redistribution has found that there is no consensus on the empirical results (Acemoglu et al. 2015), as discussed earlier. Furthermore, empirical evidence for the long run suggests that the tax rates on top incomes in the First World countries do not show progressive taxation. The tax rates were very low at the beginning of the twentieth century, then increased significantly until the 1950s, and thereafter have shown a tendency to fall, with greater force since the 1980s. In the United States, for example, the tax rate on top incomes was 70% in 1980 and fell to nearly 30% in 2010 (Piketty 2014). Free capital movement has increased with globalization in the last decades and it is possible that governments have felt the Kaleckian threat with increasing force and have had to reduce the tax rates on profits and top incomes.

The number of capitalist countries that have adopted electoral democracy has expanded continuously in the last decades. Calculations made by this author from the database built by IDEA (2016) indicate that the number of Third World countries that has held presidential elections has increased tremendously over time: 18 in 1945–59 to 66 in 1990–1999 and to 75 in 2010–2015. If electoral democracy is good for equality, then overall income inequality should tend to diminish as electoral democracy expands. However, and as predicted by the dynamic model of the unified theory, the degree of income inequality has not declined in the Third World countries over time, as shown in Table 1.1 (Chap. 1).

Excess income inequality has social consequences: it leads to social disorder. The income redistribution failure through public policies will generate illegal forms of redistribution. Redistribution will take the form of private and forced redistribution, which leads to the weakening of institutions, such as private property rights and law and order, and the expansion of crime and insecurity and illegal economic activities. This is how excess income inequality leads to social disorder.

However, this social disorder will be absorbed by the system easily, for it does not challenge the system itself. Furthermore, the economic and political elites will seek to present the social disorder not as a social problem, but as individual problems of bad behavior, of criminals, which should be treated by the police and justice departments. Thus, the control of social disorder usually falls in the realm of the ministry of repression, not of the ministry of economy and finance. According to the theoretical model presented here, people's criminal behavior is not exogenous, but rather endogenously determined.

Environment degradation is also an outcome of democratic capitalism. Facts are also consistent with this prediction of the unified theory. The conference of governments—called Conference of the Parties (COP)—has failed to control greenhouse gas emissions. Since COP 3 (Kyoto, 1997) up to COP 21 (Paris, 2015) no agreement that is mandatory to reduce emissions has been reached, only the accord about what has been termed "pledge and review." Politicians will not be willing to exchange policies that are unpopular in the short run for those that seek a better social situation in the future.

We also observe social conflicts associated to environment degradation in the short run. These conflicts mostly involve the big multinational corporations extracting minerals, petroleum, and gas, on the one hand, and the poor rural communities in the Third World, who are defending their lands and water resources, and their livelihood, on the other. In this conflict, as the unified theory predicts, we observe that democratic governments side with big corporations, to which they are subordinated, and against rural populations who are mostly second-class citizens.

In sum, the unified theory predicts that the outcomes of the economic process under democratic capitalism include economic growth accompanied by excessive inequality and environment degradation. The unified theory explains why. Democratic capitalism has no mechanisms of self-regulation that can eliminate those social maladies. This lack of self-regulation just reflects the power concentrated in the economic and political elites. These elites will tolerate equilibrium with social disorder as long as it does not challenge their privileged position in society. Therefore, this is an equilibrium situation, for there are no internal social forces in the economic process that can modify the outcome.

The paradox that social maladies are an outcome of democratic capitalism has an explanation. Electoral democracy is a particular form of democracy under the current capitalism. Electoral democracy generates political power and thus increases the level of concentration of power structure with which the capitalist system operates. It also generates a perverse incentive system to solve social problems.

Other traits of democratic capitalism are worth mentioning. Under electoral democracy, the people's representatives in government, the politicians, will act following their own interests, not that of the people. Therefore, electoral democracy does not lead to the *government of the people, by the people, and for the people*. For one thing, the members of the government do not constitute a random sample of the people—the workers in this case.

The important qualitative outcome of the electoral process is the concentration of political power, which increases the initial power structure based on the initial inequality in the distribution of economic and political assets. In the case of epsilon society, this proposition is clear. Regarding political entitlements, people are equal. The outcome of the electoral process is that a significant part of that entitlement is transferred to the elected government. Thus, electoral democracy is the mechanism to concentrate political power and with it to concentrate even more the overall power structure of society. In sigma society, where political endowments are unequally distributed, and thus the initial political power is already concentrated, electoral democracy is a device to concentrate it even more.

Electoral democracy empowers the politicians in the government and not the voters. The political discourse says that electoral democracy implies popular control of government, but it is empirically false. We observe that social protests are blocked and crashed. Because general equilibrium is with social disorder, electoral democracy operates with social and political repression over workers. Nowhere has electoral democracy implied the workers' capture of the state, even if some political parties in power carry the name of "workers party" or "labor party," as mentioned earlier. Electoral democracy is, according to the unified theory, plutocracy. It also shows elements of despotism through the power of the democratic state over workers.

Economic growth with social maladies implies a capitalist society with intense social conflicts. Conflicts include a duality, between workers and capitalists and between workers and the state. The conflict between the capitalist class and the state is of second order of importance because electoral democracy is also in the interest of capitalists. Capitalists can control politicians through the discipline of capital, that is, private investment may be reallocated to other countries, and through financial support for the electoral campaign may go to rival political parties. It follows that electoral democracy increases, not reduces, the degree of social conflicts in society. Electoral democracy leads to additional social conflicts and tensions and to further divisions in a class society, now along political party lines. Social cohesion is much harder under electoral democracy.

According to the unified theory, under the current democratic capitalism, the working class has two masters. As labor, they are subordinated to the capitalists' will, and, as citizens, to the power of the state, which has been captured by politicians. The initial inequality implies a certain degree of power relations under capitalism, which are increased through the institution of electoral democracy. The stronger asymmetry in the new power relations can be seen as follows: In the market social relations, capitalists act as professionals, while workers as amateurs; in the political social relations, politicians act as professionals, while workers as amateurs.

It is not that workers cannot learn as the electoral democratic process is repeated period after period. The fundamental problem lies in the power of money. Money can buy almost everything in both the marketplace and the electoral democratic process; that is, electoral democracy is business too! Capitalism is a hierarchical society because of electoral democracy too, not in spite of it.

THE CORRUPTION QUESTION

Another undisputed fact is that the current democratic capitalism operates with corruption, which is another component of social disorder. This fact also needs a scientific explanation.

Analytically, corruption can be seen as an illegal exchange of goods between government officials and private individuals. Government officials are willing to sell a state contract or license for a price (bribe), whereas individuals or private firms are willing to obtain those privileges paying the price (the bribe).

The exchange may be voluntary or may have some elements of coercion. Therefore, corruption is different from *open market exchange*, which is voluntary and subject to legal constraints. It has elements of *black market exchange*, which is voluntary but illegal, where the risk of losses is related to the penalties established by the law and the degree of enforcement. Corruption also has elements of non-market exchange because coercion from one of the parties may be involved. ("Make him an offer that he cannot refuse" is the law of mafia, as popularized in the novel *Godfather.*) Finally, corruption could also be part of an exchange of favors, as in the case of politicians returning favors to investors for their financing of the electoral campaign. Corruption is thus a complex form of exchange.

The production of public goods creates opportunities for corruption. First, property rights are not well-defined and thus open market competition is unviable. The opportunities are for illegal exchange. Second, state purchases of goods and services are in large amounts—state investment projects are usually of great economic size; hence, the decision as to who are going to be selected as the few suppliers or contractors also creates opportunities for corruption. As long as public goods are needed in society, these opportunities will exist. Electoral democracy transforms these opportunities into incentives for corruption, for individuals who have captured the state seek their own interests and private individuals seek their own interests as well. Under electoral democracy, the interests of the people—the common good—is thus subordinated to private interests, as the theoretical model says.

Corruption is subject to the risk of paying the penalties established by law. The participants in the illegal exchange take this risk into account when calculating the expected income gains. Selfish individuals will choose to obey or not to obey the law, depending on which alternative is more profitable. There is nothing sacred about what the law says.

The behavior to comply with the law is subject to economic incentives only. Income gains are all that matters, as in any other economic decision. If the expected economic gains of not obeying the law, net of bribe costs and the risk of penalties, are higher than the economic gains of not obeying the law, the individual will choose to go illegal. Ethical considerations are not taken into account and social incentives do not matter under selfish behavior.

To be sure, given the institutional context of markets and electoral democracy, corruption is a rational behavior. Under democratic capitalism, people tend to act guided by self-interest. This is the rational thing to do. According to this economic theory, people see fines, penalties, lawyer expenditures, and the risk of years in jail as the price to pay for buying goods or services illegally, in the same way that bread or other consumer goods are bought for a price; hence, the decision to comply with the law is endogenous: it depends on the price. Thus, a market for illegal exchange is endogenously generated, given the constraints established by the law. This is the "market revenge" to legal constraints.

Politicians who have captured the state to make money will seek to buy votes through the supply of public goods, even if corruption is involved in its production. Private individuals who find it profitable will participate. Big projects will buy more votes; but big projects imply big money, which is an incentive for corruption behavior. Paying and receiving bribes is rational behavior under the context of markets and electoral democracy institutions, as discussed above.

In sum, the theoretical model of corruption proposed here assumes the following:

Alpha proposition: *The institution of electoral democracy creates incentives for corruption behavior of social actors in the production of public goods; that is, corruption is rooted in the electoral democracy system.*

Therefore, electoral democracy would not be a system that deters corruption, just the opposite. It is a mechanism that makes it rational to get into corruption behavior.

Introducing this assumption into the static model of the unified theory, we can determine the new traits of the general equilibrium in the short run. For the sake of simplicity, assume that the bribe rate (b) is included as a markup to the real total cost of the infrastructure project (G). Also, assume that the bribe rate of equilibrium is determined in the same way as the tax rate is, by trial and error. The general equilibrium outcome of the economic process now includes the total government expenditure as $G = G(1 + b)$. The value of G goes to pay for the cost of labor and material inputs and for normal profits of the contractor firm, whereas bG (the amount of corruption) is distributed to the government officials involved as extra income and to the contractor firm as extra profits. Assume that this behavior also applies to other illegal activities, such as trafficking of drugs, arms, commodities, and humans.

The effect of corruption is to reallocate the government budget structure (increasing the total expenditure in big projects), whereas the distribution of the total amount of the corruption will feed into the demand for goods in the economy. Then the market mechanism will solve the prices and quantities of equilibrium in all markets. Total income and its distribution will be endogenous; so will the extent of corruption. Hence, general equilibrium with corruption will be the outcome of the economic process in the short run. It can be shown that the same conclusion follows for general equilibrium in the long run.

Therefore, the prediction of the static model of the unified theory is as follows:

Beta proposition: *General equilibrium with corruption will be the outcome of the economic process under capitalism, with markets and electoral democracy as basic institutions.*

This prediction is consistent with the fact that capitalism operates with corruption. The model is able to explain why.

Therefore, any general equilibrium solution of capitalism will include the existence and persistence of corruption income. Moreover, as long as electoral democracy remains as the form of democracy, corruption behavior will persist. Corruption is thus endogenous. Illegal economic activities are also endogenous. The general equilibrium with corruption implies a kind of "impunity trap equilibrium," for illegal behavior is embedded in the system and is socially tolerated as inevitable. People internalize the risk involved in their behavior; hence, they have possible economic disaster situations under control, and corruption behavior can be repeated in the economic process.

General equilibrium with corruption implies the triumph of economic incentives over social incentives—social prestige, reputation, and the risk of ostracism matters less or does not matter any longer in society. Money is the only thing that matters in society. Money is the measure of individual and social success. It matters less how it is obtained.

The outcome of the economic growth process includes corruption. Corruption is part of the structural equations of the dynamic model of growth and thus contributes to more rapid growth outcome. The great scandals of corruption have taken place in the cycles of economic boom. The outcome also includes excess income inequality. The possible effect of corruption behavior on income inequality will not be to decrease it. Small amounts of corruption will be transacted between the poor and low-level bureaucrats, whereas large amounts will be transacted between political leaders and business leaders of big corporations, the "grand corruption," as it is called by economist Rose-Ackerman (2010). Hence, the size of gains will tend to be higher (maybe proportionally higher) for the rich than for the poor groups. Income inequality will tend to increase or remain unchanged.

Corruption cannot reduce the damage to the environment either; on the contrary, it will become a mechanism to circumvent the law intending to control environment degradation. Thus, corruption is a mechanism to increase the rate of economic growth.

Increasing the penalties, but maintaining the electoral political system, will not change the general corruption behavior in society much. As experience has shown, these measures increase the price of the "good" to be transacted, but that does not imply that corruption will decline. Even at the new prices, it could still be profitable to many people. On the other hand, there is path dependence in the corruption exchange: once you are in, you cannot get out. (The mafia rule is binding, "Make him an offer he cannot refuse.") Given the opportunities for corruption income that the electoral democracy generates, people will hardly change their corruption behavior. Citizens have no power to change the situation. Therefore, economic equilibrium is with corruption, which just reflects the power of the economic and political elites. Capitalism is not a self-regulated system.

The standard literature on corruption has proposed several hypotheses on the causes of corruption, but the role of electoral democracy is usually ignored. This can be seen in a recent book presenting the state of the art on empirical and theoretical works about corruption (Dutta and Aidt 2016). In addressing corruption, the typical proposal is that political reforms are a priority, including the democratization and modernization of political parties and the judiciary, including an open and meritocratic system in the selection of party leaders and judges (cf. Kaufmann 2015). This view retains electoral democracy, which is, according to the unified theory, the main root of corruption. Moreover, the discourse is not against democracy or against capitalism, but against the bad behavior of individuals. On the other hand, the empirical works presented in the literature tend to conclude that corruption increases inequality (cf. Gupta et al. 2002). This result is consistent with the hypothesis presented here. However, this conclusion must be taken into consideration with great care, for one can hardly expect to accurately assess the size of illegal incomes, such as those coming from corruption, which is, by definition, not registered.

INSTITUTIONAL INNOVATIONS IN THE DEMOCRATIC SYSTEM

In light of the results shown up to now, the fact that electoral democracy has prevailed for so long constitutes another paradox. Citizens' behavior often indicates complaints against electoral democracy (not only against governments). It seems that citizens take electoral democracy for granted and they do not see alternatives.

What are the alternative forms of democracy? Could another type of democracy replace electoral democracy? Any superior form of democracy would have to solve the basic problems of electoral democracy: (a) political power should be eliminated; (b) individual free-riding behavior toward public goods should be reduced; (c) governments should have the correct incentives to attain the common good. Does this new form of democracy exist or does it need to be invented?

Consider direct democracy. In this case, people themselves, not their representatives, are in control of the state. However, the implementation of direct democracy is known to be very difficult. Modern capitalism is too complex to be operated under direct democracy, especially in large population societies. It may be utilized as a mechanism in which citizens vote on major political decisions or laws in the form of referenda. This form of direct democracy is practiced in some countries, such as Switzerland, where new laws often need a referendum in order to be passed. Direct democracy could operate well in an equal and small society. In this type of society, even electoral democracy is expected to work well, as shown earlier.

Are there representative democracy alternatives other than electoral? Some analysts have proposed the use of the mechanism of sortition or random selection for appointing government authorities as the alternative to electoral democracy (Burnheim 2014; Carson and Martin 1999; Delannoi and Dowlen 2010; Dowlen 2008; van Reybrouck 2016).

Examples of using sortition democracy include the ancient Greek city-state of Athens, where democracy originated. In Athens, citizens were by right members of the Assembly and had the duty to participate and vote on legislation. The City Council (in charge of the administration) had 50 citizens elected by lot from the list of candidates who had passed the required examinations and were older than 30 years. Thus, citizens exercised direct democracy in the Assembly and had control over the City Council. Political parties did not exist(!). Political rights and citizenship were granted only to adult males, not to women or slaves. Dowlen (2008) describes the Athenian and other ancient cases of sortition democracy. Sortition democracy has not been applied in modern democracies.

Sortition democracy would certainly operate better in an equal society. The pool of citizens would then be composed of equally informed and educated people. In an unequal society, in contrast, the pool would have to include the qualified people only; hence, the poor, the uneducated, the second-class citizens would be excluded to participate in the democratic process; thus, this would become the modern version of the Athenian democracy.

Under capitalism, and just for the sake of illustration, consider sortition democracy operating under the following rules. Members for the government would be selected through a random sample mechanism drawn from the universe of all adult people. People will expect to be selected and to comply with this civic service duty. Because random selection is required, individuals may not volunteer for service. The appointment is for a limited period and covers all instances of the state. In order to have social control, small groups will constitute decision units in the different sections of the state. Decisions in all instances will be reached by consensus. Sampling selection may be weighted to ensure the presence of minority social groups, such as some ethnic groups and the rural population. Given the difficulty of involving everyone in the deliberative process of public policies (as in direct democracy), weighted random selection is a mechanism that allows a cross section of the people to be involved in the public decisions that affect them.

Given the fact that workers constitute the largest majority in society, the mechanism of random selection will lead to a government that is composed mostly of workers. A balance of power would then be reached in society: capitalists control capital and workers control the state. Another consequence of sortition democracy is that political entitlements are equalized among individuals in society. First-class and second-class citizenship would be ruled out by the random sample mechanism.

Does sortition democracy generate the correct incentives to seek the common good? The political class would be eliminated under sortition democracy. It may exist as political organizations and may participate in the public debates about public policies, in the market of ideas. These organizations may still seek to manipulate public opinion in the direction of their particular interests, and use money for that. However, whatever they do would not lead them to capture the state. The logic of truly ideology differences on social issues (the social objectives) would mobilize political groups. The market of ideas would now become real. The economic elites who used to finance the election of politicians in the electoral democracy would not play any role in government decisions. Therefore, those selected for government would have the incentive to be accountable to the people and to the people alone.

The mechanism of random sample selection implies social duties and social responsibilities on the population. Because citizens know they can be selected for serving in government, they would seek to be involved in public issues continuously, which would generate incentives for political participation, which in turn would imply social control upon government actions. The reward for performing social duties well while in government is not economic, but social. The reward is social respect. If government officials failed to serve the people, they would suffer a social sanction, including ostracism. Thus, there will be no incentives for free-riding behavior.

Under these rules, seeking selfish interests while in government would not be rational behavior. The incentives are not only economic, but also, and mostly, social. The "impunity trap equilibrium" could hardly happen. Thus, the government will act guided by the motivation of the common good. Government decisions by consensus would be necessary to ensure a public policy that leads to the common good, which a government of workers would facilitate.

Under the sortition rule, democracy would not be plutocracy because to be representative of the people in government is not business any longer. Money would be out of the workings of democracy. Long-run problems of society, and not just short-run problems, would be part of the public debate and of public policies.

Randomly selected government authorities would imply a government of low-educated people, not of the highly educated, who are a minority in society. Under this system, scientists and professionals could not control the government. However, they could be part of the bureaucracy and technocracy. They could be in charge of presenting the technical alternatives for public choice, the technocratic part of the solution; however, the choice between alternative ends will be in the hands of the government authorities. This is in accord with the principle that the role of scientific knowledge is to present the best means to attain given objectives, not necessarily to establish the objectives themselves. The latter is a normative problem, over which scientists have no clear advantage over non-scientists. Government could then select science-based public policies.

The power of the bureaucracy is always a risk. However, in this case, the bureaucracy is not at the service of politicians, as is the case under electoral democracy. They are state workers and the bosses are the randomly selected authorities, the bosses of whom are their fellow workers. Meritocracy in the public career could be established and organized through especial bodies. The group of government authorities alone is responsible for the decision, which must be by consensus. Sortition democracy could thus imply powerful rules against corruption and factionalism.

Sortition democracy would comply with the very concept of democracy: the government of the people, for the people, and by the people. The people would be in control of the state. Given that under capitalism, the people are the workers, sortition democracy would give workers political power. Therefore, workers would be able to control the power of the capitalist class. Second-class citizens and minority groups would participate in public decisions, that is, they would be empowered as well. Sortition democracy would be conducive to citizenship equalization. More importantly, the incentive system is such that individuals selected for government will have the right incentives to pursue the common good in society.

Under sortition democracy, forms of direct democracy, such as referendum, would operate better than under electoral democracy. The government would have incentives to decide the alternatives and the terms of the referendum, which would have no class bias or political bias (as in electoral democracy), and the people will decide the outcome by exercising direct democracy voting.

In sum, sortition democracy under these rules appears to be a superior alternative to electoral democracy. Furthermore, sortition or any other democratic system that complies with the three conditions indicated above will make capitalism a socially self-regulated system, which means that if market equilibrium outcome were with social maladies, the mechanisms of democracy would be able to introduce new policies to generate another equilibrium that corrects those social maladies. This type of democracy would be more efficient than electoral democracy, where the criterion of efficiency is not voting turnout and regular calendar of elections (as is today), but the quality of society. Society with low social maladies is clearly a high-quality society. Other forms of democracy that are equally efficient or superior to sortition democracy need to be discovered. More research in this theoretical area is thus needed. Before application, some creative forms of testing these new forms of democracy would also be needed.

CONCLUSIONS

The outcomes of the economic growth process under democratic capitalism include continuous increase in per capita income over time, which is accompanied by qualitative changes, such as rising income inequality and degradation of the biophysical environment, which have social consequences, leading to social maladies. The fact that social maladies result from a democratic capitalist system is a paradox.

Unified theory is able to explain the paradox: The particular form of democracy under capitalism is electoral democracy. Electoral democracy generates a perverse incentive system to attain social progress, as individuals seek their own interests not only in the marketplace, but also in the democratic process. Furthermore, electoral democracy implies a transfer of the workers' political power to politicians, thus increasing the concentration of the power structure in society.

Consequently, the democratic capitalist system is not self-regulated, that is, social maladies cannot be eliminated endogenously. The persistence of social maladies is not despite electoral democracy, but because of it too. The persistence of social maladies just reflects the influence of the power structure, which is concentrated in economic and political elites. This prediction of the unified theory is consistent with facts.

In spite of its shortcomings, electoral democracy has been taken for granted for almost 200 years of capitalist development. Economic and political elites have the incentives to defend electoral democracy and promote its expansion. Other forms of democracy have simply been neglected in the scientific literature. The scientific study of other forms of democracy is a pending task.

These conclusions are contrary to the political conjecture presented by Francis Fukuyama (2006), which has become today's paradigm: *Democratic capitalism has defeated all other forms of human organization and has marked the end of human history.* This may be true when democratic capitalism is compared to slavery and feudal systems; or compared to communist systems, which were the alternative for many years; or compared to capitalism under dictatorships. However, the current democratic capitalism—capitalism under electoral democracy— is a socially inefficient system, as shown in this chapter.

According to the scientific theory developed here, capitalism operates with a particular form of democracy—electoral democracy—which has become a device utilized by economic and political elites to construct a concentrated power structure. The fact that democratic capitalism has produced economic growth with social maladies is just a reflection of this power. The failures of electoral democracy are not just a matter of incomplete implementation of the principles of democracy either, as Fukuyama also argues. First, this is a tautological statement ("incomplete implementation" is unobservable), useless for science; second, the failure has to do with the concentrated power structure, which is a structural feature of capitalism, as shown in this chapter.

To be sure, according to the unified theory of capitalism, power structure is the ultimate factor, the essential exogenous variable, that explains the functioning of the current democratic capitalist system. This conclusion does not mean that the current power structure is fixed; it can change, but exogenously only. More precisely, what the theory says is that the concentrated power structure cannot be reduced endogenously, for the system is not self-regulated; however, it can be reduced exogenously, through interventions from outside the system. This is the major challenge in today's capitalism. Thus, one can hardly say that we have come to the end of history. Furthermore, we are just at the beginning of a new age, the Anthropocene, in which human species face the risk of its own extinction if we keep doing "business as usual," which includes maintaining electoral democracy as the form of democracy under capitalism.

In brief, the unified theory predicts that democratic capitalism operates with a concentrated power structure in the hands of the economic and political elites. Under capitalism, electoral democracy increases the concentration of power structure; it does not reduce it, much less eliminate it. This prediction may seem strange, but it is derived from a logical system (the theory), which is, in addition, consistent with facts. In light of the unified theory, electoral democracy can hardly be considered the "greatest" human invention, as it is presented in the current discourse. It is simply a human invention. Electoral democracy is not an institution that can help to solve social maladies, for it generates a perverse incentive system. One could even say that, for class societies, it is a regrettable human invention.

References

Acemoglu, D., Naidu, S., Restrepo, P., & Robinson, J. (2015). Chapter 21. Democracy, redistribution, and inequality. In A. B. Atkinson & F. Bourguignon (Eds.), *Handbook of income distribution* (Vol. 2, pp. 1885–1966). Oxford, UK: Elsevier.

Burnheim, J. (2014). *Is democracy possible? The alternative to electoral democracy* (Third ed.). Clovelly, Australia: Jump Up Publishers Sydney.

Carson, L., & Martin, B. (1999). *Random selection in politics.* Westport, CT: Prager.

Delannoi, G., & Dowlen, O. (Eds.). (2010). *Sortition. Theory and practice.* Exeter, UK: Imprint Academic.

Dowlen, O. (2008). *The political potential of sortition. A study of the random selection of citizens for public office.* Exeter, UK: Imprint Academic.

Downs, A. (1957). *An economic theory of democracy.* New York: Harper.

Dutta, J., & Aidt, T. (Eds.). (2016). *Corruption and economic development.* Cheltenham, UK: Edward Elgar.

Fukuyama, F. (2006). *The end of history and the last man.* Paperback edition with new afterword. New York: Free Press. Originally published in 1992.

Gupta, S., Davoodi, H., & Alonso-Terme, R. (2002). Does corruption affect income inequality and poverty? *Economics of Governance, 3,* 23–45.

IDEA (Institute for Democracy and Electoral Assistance). (2016). Voter turnout database. Retrieved from http://www.idea.int/vt/

Kalecki, M. (1971). *Selected essays in the dynamics of the capitalist economy 1933–1970.* Cambridge, UK: Cambridge University Press. Chapter 1 on effective demand was originally published in 1943.

Kaufmann, D. (2015). Corruption matters. *Finance and Development, 52*(3), 20–23.

Olson, M. (1965). *The logic of collective action: Public goods and theory of groups.* Cambridge, MA: Harvard University Press.

Piketty, T. (2014). *Capital in the twenty-first century.* Cambridge, MA: Harvard University Press.

van Reybrouck, D. (2016). *Against elections: The case for democracy.* London, UK: The Bodley Head.

Rose-Ackerman, S. (2010, November 9). Corruption: Greed, culture, and the state. *The Yale Law Journal, 120,* 125–140.

Schutz, E. (2011). *Inequality and power: The economics of class.* Abingdon, UK: Routledge.

CHAPTER 3

Evolutionary Human Behavior

According to unified theory, selfish human behavior has generated the Anthropocene age. Are people in the capitalist system becoming more concerned with the fate of human society;
that is, are they becoming more altruists and less egotists in
their behavior in the economic growth process? Is the risk of
collapse of human society a force for changes in human behavior? This chapter seeks to answer these questions.

A Biological Theory of Human Behavior

Changes in human behavior have been the concern of writers
and scientists. Among the former, writers of utopia novels,
such as George Orwell and Aldous Huxley, have expressed
this concern in the form of fictitious inhuman societies
intended to give us a warning: unless the course of history
changes, men will tend to lose their most human qualities,
will become soulless automatons, and will not even be aware
of that. This warning is in marked contrast with common
Western thinking: the faith in man's capacity to create a very
human society, characterized by peace, justice, and social
progress.

© The Author(s) 2017
A. Figueroa, *Economics of the Anthropocene Age*,
DOI 10.1007/978-3-319-62584-3_3

Among scientists, physicist Albert Einstein (1954) wrote an article comparing capitalism and socialism, in which he presented a conjecture on the evolution of human behavior under capitalism:

> Man is, at one and the same time, a solitary being and a social being. As a solitary being, he attempts to satisfy his personal desires. ... As a social being, he seeks to gain recognition and affection of his fellow beings. The relative strength of these two drives is, in the main, not fixed by inheritance. It is fixed by society. The individual can only be understood within the framework of society. (1954, p. 153)
>
> In the capitalist society, the individual's position in society is such that the egotistical drives of his make-up are constantly being accentuated, while his social drives, which are by nature weaker, progressively deteriorate. ... Capitalism leads to the crippling of the social consciousness of individuals. (1954, p. 155, 158)

Coming from a physicist, this conjecture is impressive and sound for the social sciences. On the other hand, Einstein added, the problem with socialism is that bureaucracy, not the people, controls the state.

Einstein's conjecture assumes that *human makeup exists, but it is changeable, and changeable by society.* According to this conjecture, we could say that people act guided by two motivations at the same time: egotism and altruism. Self-interest implies that individuals act seeking their own benefits alone, with complete disregard of the well-being of others, even if their actions cause damage to others. Altruism implies that individuals have unselfish regard for the well-being of others. Altruist people are thus willing to sacrifice their own welfare in order to increase the welfare of others. According to the conjecture, capitalism tends to exacerbate the selfish against the altruist makeup of humans.

Why and how does selfish human behavior tend to become dominant under a capitalist society? No answer is found in Einstein's conjecture. This is why it is a conjecture.

The old debate about whether human behavior is the result of heredity or environment, nature or nurture, has ended. Recent discoveries in biology support the theory that human behavior is the result of the interactions between *both* nature and nurture. Biologist and science writer Matt Ridley has explained these discoveries and has concluded with a more precise relation: it is not nature versus nurture, but nature via nurture (Ridley 2003).

To put it differently, human behavior is the result of the interactions between both genes and the social environment. Genes alone do not determine human behavior. There is no biological determinism in human behavior. There is no social environment determinism either. Humans are not a blank sheet of paper on which society writes its text. The interactions between genes and the social environment underlie human behavior.

Moreover, genes constitute the mechanism by which the social environment influences human behavior; that is, genes are designed for nurturing. For example, the human brain is built for nurturing. "It is genes that allow the human mind to learn, to remember, to imitate, to imprint, to absorb culture. Genes are not puppet masters or blueprints. Nor are they just the carriers of heredity. They are active during life ... they respond to the environment" (Ridley 2003, p. 6).

We can then state the *biological theory of human behavior* as the following set of assumptions:

Alpha proposition: *Individuals are endowed at birth with genes, which are determined by heredity and are immutable. Human behavior is the result of the influence of social environment through genes. The social environment does not change genes, but operates through the given genes.*

The epistemology of abstract process allows us to transform a complex social reality into an abstract process that resembles the real world by using a scientific theory. As shown in Fig. 1.1 (Chap. 1), the analytical structure of the abstract process includes the exogenous variables, which come from outside and go into the process, and the endogenous variables, which come from inside the process. The process also includes a mechanism by which the exogenous variables generate the endogenous variables.

The biological theory of human behavior just stated can be represented in the abstract process form. In particular, the theory assumes that the exogenous variables that enter into the process come from the social environment, the endogenous variables include the traits of the human behavior, and the mechanism is the following: The influence of the social environment operates through genes. Thus, genes belong to the mechanism. Genes are not exogenous variables, the changes of which can change behavior.

Therefore, given the genes endowments of an individual, his or her behavior will be determined by the influence of the social environment. The individual's predispositions and talents are contained in his or her genes endowment and whether they are developed or suppressed will depend upon the influence of the social environment; that is, different social environments will determine different behaviors of the same individual. The individual's genes are immutable, but they vary across people. Therefore, given the same social environment, individuals with different genes will behave differently.

Given the genes endowments of individuals in society, the behavior of people will be determined by the elements of the social environment. Genes constitute the makeup of humans at birth. Therefore, we could say that the adult is endowed with two types of genes: biological genes, which carry his parents' heredity, and "social genes," which carry his social heredity, which together determine behavior. The individual is son of John and Mary, but he is also "son" of New York City, where he grew up. Changes in New York City's social environment will change his behavior. This is what the biological theory of human behavior says.

The biological theory predicts the following:

Beta proposition: *Human behavior is changeable and can be changed by the influence of the social environment.*

Studies in biology have shown that this prediction tends to be consistent with facts. These include observed human behavior regarding mating, sexuality, criminality, athletic, and education (cf. Ridley 2003).

According to biological theory, the discussion regarding whether human behavior is due to nature or nurture is out of place. However, it is still widely utilized. This is the case of lawyers intending to defend their clients in court, sometimes on the ground of genetic fate underlying crime: "It was not his fault, your honor, it is in his genes," and sometimes using nurturing as the determinant: "The defendant was driven to crime because he was abused as child."

The individual is born with a particular endowment of genes, and thus with a particular set of talents, which will set his or her natural propensities for human behavior. Consider, for example, intellectual and manual work as the talents. If the individual with a relatively higher endowment of intellectual over manual talents is living in a peasant society, he will have the influence of this particular society and will tend to learn manual work; hence, manual work skills will be his relative strength at adult age. Suppose those talents at birth are normally distributed in the population. Now considering the aggregate, in a given period, there will be more people with a relative strength in manual over intellectual skills. This is fixed by society. Over time, therefore, the average mix will change toward manual work, departing from the initial average mix, which was given by the normal distribution of the biological genes in the population. The average mix will change in the opposite direction if individuals lived in a university town.

In light of the biological theory of human behavior, we may then restate Einstein's conjecture as follows. Given the individual's biological genes, he is endowed at birth with two drives—the solitary and the social. The initial drive mix will later be influenced by the social environment, which will change the initial drive mix and thus the behavior. Therefore, human drives or motivations are, in the long run, *endogenously* determined. Suppose these two drives at birth are evenly distributed in the population. Aggregating over all individuals, at a given period, there will be another distribution of human drives fixed by society. If living in a capitalist society, people will tend to develop the egotistic drive relatively more; hence, over time, there will be more people having a higher mix of egotistic over social drives.

In the rest of the chapter, the theory of human behavior proposed above will be introduced into the study of the evolutionary economic process. Hence, a new evolutionary model of the unified theory of capitalism is now constructed and then submitted to the falsification process.

A New Evolutionary Model (II) of Unified Theory

The previous evolutionary model (I) predicted that in the process of economic growth two qualitative changes take place: both income inequality and biophysical environment degradation increase (Chap. 1). We showed that facts are consistent with this prediction. Chapter 2 showed that the same outcomes were obtained under electoral democracy. Now we need an evolutionary model that should be able to predict another qualitative change in the process of economic growth under capitalism: changes in human behavior, namely, people become increasingly egotists.

In economics, when dealing with human behavior, we make an analytical distinction between the motivations—the drives—and the constraints. Observed economic behavior is the result of both. Therefore, given the motivations of individuals, changes in constraints will cause changes in behavior, in what people do and choose as producers, consumers, investors, laborers, and so on.

In the standard consumption theory, for instance, the individual acts guided by the motivation of egotism, which is reflected in his or her utility function, which he or she seeks to maximize. Thus, given the preferences of individuals for goods (the utility function), which are unobservable and exogenously determined, people will choose certain consumption baskets based on their constraints. Changes in the consumption baskets will come from changes in real incomes or relative market prices, which are the determinants of the budget constraint, and are the exogenous variables of the theory. Therefore, this theory assumes that human behavior is changeable; moreover, it is changeable by the influences of society that come through real incomes or relative market prices, but the egotist drive or motivation—individual utility maximization—is given.

Einstein's conjecture addresses a different question. Does the social environment change the drives or motivations of people? His answer is yes. The biological theory that human behavior is the result of nature and nurture predicts that human behavior can change and is changeable by society. We now need to use the biological theory of human behavior to construct the economic behavior of people. The assumption of the economic behavior theory is now the following:

> Alpha proposition: *In the short run, given people's motivations, social environment affects people's behavior through changes in their constraints; in the long run, social environment changes their motivations.*

This assumption may be called the *general economic theory of human behavior*. It deals with the influence of society upon economic behavior of individuals through both constraints and motivations. This assumption does not contradict any assumptions of unified theory; therefore, it can be included within the auxiliary assumptions needed to construct an evolutionary model of unified theory.

The short-run and the long-run effects of social influence need to be analytically distinguished. Again, take the theory of consumer as an example. In the short run, changes in the social environment imply changes in the people's budget constraints, which will modify economic behavior—the basket of goods purchased in the market will change. People seek to maximize their utility function and the basket that satisfies this objective will now be different to the previous one. In the long run, changes in the social environment, such as a higher degree of competition among individuals, a more aggressive environment, and modernization of the way of life, will induce people to change their motivations toward more egotistic economic behavior, which in turn implies a change in the basket of goods purchased, maintaining budget constraints fixed. The change in the basket of goods now reflects the influence of society upon motivations, not upon the budget constraints.

We also need to be more precise on the assumptions of human drives or motivations. The egotistic and social drives or motivations of individuals can be represented by the following taxonomy:

Typology A: Pure egotist individual, who has disregard for the well-being of others, including when damages are inflicted onto others by pursuing self-interest in the consumption of private goods, and free riding on the production of public goods.

Typology B: Quasi-egotist individual, who has some concerns for the well-being of others and for the supply of public goods.

Typology C: Pure altruist individual, who is concerned only with the well-being of others, including here the supply of public goods.

The first category refers to persons with full egotistic drive. This kind of person disregards, or even opposes, anything that implies cooperation, solidarity, and the attainment of the common good. Typology B combines both selfish and pro-social drives. The individual has some concern for the well-being of others. Thus, the individual's behavior combines activities leading to his or her own benefit and doing something for the rest, such as volunteering work out of leisure time, charitable giving, blood donations, and seeking to find ways for the partial compensation of the negative externalities inflicted upon others. In addition, the individual has solidarity with the needs of others, incurring sacrifices for that, as part of his or her budget is allocated to provide goods for others. Moreover, he or she pays his or her share (taxes) for the supply of public goods and is willing to participate in some collective actions.

Under typology C, the individual regards the well-being of others and the main objective of his or her life and economic activity aims at that objective; thus, he or she allocates all of his or her resources to that end, reserving for himself or herself only the necessary goods to serve others productively. Adam Smith is known for his liberal thinking published in the *Wealth of Nations*, but in his previous book *Moral Sentiments* (Smith 1976 [1759]), he presented a clear idea about altruistic behavior. The altruist person is interested in the fortune of others, and renders their happiness necessary to himself or herself, though he or she derives nothing from it except the pleasure of seeing it. Therefore, if the individual is concerned with the well-being of others seeking "to gain recognition and affection of his fellow beings" he or she will be classified under typology B.

The above typology refers to consumption behavior. However, it can easily be extended to producers' behavior as well. Individual A has disregard for the unintended damage inflicted upon others and about the supply of public goods. Individual B is concerned with the negative externalities that his or her production activity may create upon others; he or she is also concerned about some solidarity with others. However, a distinction must be made here. If the solidarity is anonymous, then it will be part of altruism; if it is propagandized, this is just part of the strategy to maximize profits with guile and thus the producer belongs to typology A. To recall, altruism means *unselfish* regard for the well-being of others. Typology C can also be found among producers, whenever all profits are channeled to serve the needs of others.

It should be noted that the individual's altruistic behavior is voluntary, who enjoys doing the transfer of the product of his or her effort to others. Altruist behavior that is costless to the individual is not altruism. Altruism is also different from doing transfers with business motives. Altruism does not seek rewards. Anonymous transfer is sufficient to recognize an altruistic behavior. If the transfer seeks rewards, it is investment, as economic returns are expected. Under this criterion, most of the observed firms' social responsibility programs are not altruism, but strategies to seek more profits with guile, as the transfers are highly propagandized, as discussed above. Altruistic behavior that benefits the "altruist" is not altruism.

Why does the economic growth process lead to changes on people's drives, increasing their egotist drive? The following evolutionary model will provide an answer.

The outcome of the economic growth process includes higher output per worker over time, a quantitative change, accompanied by qualitative changes in society, such as higher excess labor supply, higher income inequality, and higher degree of degradation of the environment, as shown in evolutionary model I (Chaps. 1 and 2). Other qualitative changes include new technologies, new types of human capital (skills embodied in workers), new capital goods, and new consumption goods. Modernization is also an outcome of the economic growth process.

The first assumption of the new evolutionary model (II) is that economic growth implies modernization, which in turn changes human behavior toward more competition and less cooperation in society. Competition for profits among producers will be stronger in the context of technological innovations, as compared to a static economic process. Competition for jobs among workers will be stronger in the context of increasing excess labor supply, to which labor-saving technological innovations and increasing population will have contributed. In the context of new consumer goods, the need for higher real incomes is increasingly pressing. Increasing scarcity of natural resources, due to depletion and pollution and to increasing population, will also lead to increased competition for real incomes. In brief, overall competition will become more intense in the economic growth process; thus, competition will tend to displace social relationships of friendship and cooperation. People will learn that it becomes increasingly costly to treat others with friendship and altruism.

The second assumption is that modernization leads to social disorder. Increasing excess labor supply, income inequality, and environment degradation all imply higher levels of social conflict, as shown in model I. Now as modernization implies an increase in competition and a decline in cooperation, society would require the law to play a stronger role to maintain social order; however, the law constitutes only a partial mechanism to maintain social order, as people's selfish drive implies behavior that could transgress the law. To disobey the law is rational behavior. Therefore, social disorder will tend to increase. Trust among people will decline under a higher degree of social disorder. Cooperation will then weaken, which in turn will lead to a higher degree of competition.

Both assumptions put together imply that economic growth is conducive to a higher degree of *relative scarcity*, which leads people to choose more competition than cooperation. This conclusion may seem strange when economic growth means expansion in the productive capacity of society and more abundance of goods. Economic growth, by definition, implies more goods per person over time, but that does not mean that scarcity tends to diminish in society. No amount of goods will be enough in *human* society. Furthermore, relative scarcity will increase for many due to unequal income distribution. Losers will compete more intensively with winners to have the same access to modern life that economic growth offers and advertises by means of market competition or private and forced redistribution mechanisms.

Employment level increases in the growth process; however, growth does not imply full employment. Relative scarcity of jobs is thus another factor leading workers to compete rather than cooperate. Finally, degradation of the environment implies relative—and absolute—scarcity of natural resources, which is also conducive to more competition than cooperation in society. This type of scarcity plays in human society the same role that scarcity of natural resources does in the Darwinian competition among other biological species.

The third assumption is that economic and political elites have incentives to promote selfish behavior or individualism. In labor relations, capitalists can exercise their power more strongly dealing with workers on an individual basis rather than collectively. Competition among workers is to the firm's benefit. Meritocracy as the rule of promotion also leads to individualism. In electoral democracy, governments can exercise their power more strongly by dealing with citizens on an individual basis rather than collectively. Economic and political elites seek to promote self-interest drives and individualism in society because it is in their own interest to do so. Therefore, the discourse will promote individualism rather than collective actions in society.

In sum, the outcome of the economic growth process includes qualitative changes in the social environment, which in turn leads to changes in human behavior. This is in accord with the economic theory stated above. Consequently, the influence of the new social environment will change the "social genes" of people, which, via their given biological genes, will change their human drives. Therefore, it will be rational for people that had altruistic drives or quasi-altruistic drives to behave more egotistically now; that is, the share of budgets or outputs or time allocated to the well-being of others, including the production of public goods, will tend to diminish. Then, typology C individuals will tend to become

B or A, and typology B individuals will tend to become A; therefore, typology A will endogenously become dominant in society, and increasingly so. Hence, in the long run, human drive is endogenously determined, by changes in society, not by changes in inheritance. Moreover, it poses personality problems upon individuals because humans are, by nature, social animals.

THE ROLE OF INSTITUTIONS: MARKET AND DEMOCRACY

What is the role of market and democracy—the two basic institutions of capitalism—in the evolutionary process of human drives? Do these institutions set limits to this evolution or promote it?

Social relations through the market system need to be understood theoretically. Unified theory assumes that market exchange is a particular form of exchange, the rules or norms of which include:

(a) It is voluntary.
(b) It is based on the motivation of self-interest.
(c) Economic incentives dominate social incentives. Money can buy everything. Market exchange is constrained only by the resource endowments of individuals; that is, any other constraint, such as social, cultural, or legal, is embedded in the economic cost–benefit calculations, where any transgression has a price and an economic return. Ethical and social values are included in the preferences, not in the constraints.

These rules imply a particular system of incentives to play the market game. People who participate in market exchange have the incentive to take advantage of every exchange opportunity to make economic gains for their own benefit. The aim of economic gains implies cold calculations of costs and benefits of exchange, including the costs of disobeying the law, destruction of competitors, opportunism, and so on. Ruthless competition is the name of the market game.

Market exchange has two additional implications. The first is that the *law of one price* will prevail in any particular market. Buying dearer or selling cheaper than what is the market price of a standardized good is not a way of taking advantage of exchange opportunities to make gains.

The second implication is that market exchange tends to be impersonal in the sense that the objective of market exchange is not personal ties, friendship, but rather economic gains. Some markets may seem to operate on a personal-ties basis. The usual examples include labor, credit, and insurance markets. Due to the problems of incomplete information on the goods or services exchanged, these particular markets imply personal interactions among participants, whose identification is necessary for the exchange. However, acquaintance needs for market exchange should not be confused with personal ties, which refer to membership of a social network, a group of close relatives, and close friends. For example, if the employer faces a slack in demand, he will dismiss workers to avoid economic losses, including among the dismissed even the worker with whom he has some personal ties: He is the godfather of the worker's child. The same will happen with a bank enforcing the collateral to "a friend" who is now unable to repay the credit.

By contrast, non-market exchange may take the form of command or reciprocity. Command exchange of goods retains rules (b) and (c), but excludes rule (a). This is the case of forced labor exchange, such as human labor trafficking.

Reciprocity refers to exchange of favors within social networks. A social network is an interconnected group of people, who are close relatives or close friends, not just acquaintances. This form of exchange includes rules (a) and (b), but not (c). The exchange of goods is part of a larger system of exchange of favors. People still act guided by self-interest, but personal ties are now essential for the exchange of goods. Thus, the law of one price need not apply under reciprocity, for its deviation will be consider a favor, which will be compensated later on when another exchange of goods will be carried out; the balance of exchange is thus attained in the long run, not in every transaction, as is the case in market exchange. We could define this type of exchange as *reciprocal altruism*: the individual accepts a short-term loss to benefit others in exchange of long-term gains.

As the market system expands with capitalist development, reciprocity forms of exchange will tend to diminish, and thus a progressive weakening of social ties would accompany this expansion. Therefore, the social drives of people's makeup will tend to decline. Individual behavior as members of a social network will weaken and selfish behavior will become dominant. The example of this type of change in behavior is found in the literature on peasant communities of the Third World. As the market system expands in rural areas, the egotistic drive substitutes the traditional social drive (e.g., Vincent 2012).

In sum, market exchange promotes the domination of egotistic behavior over altruistic. Although market exchange implies egotism, the efficiency of the market system requires some ethical values of individuals. Adam Smith (1976 [1759]) in his *Moral Sentiments* argued that trust and honesty are required for market exchange; otherwise, market exchange will be overwhelmed with transaction costs.

WHAT IS THE ROLE OF ELECTORAL DEMOCRACY?

Democracy in the capitalist system takes the particular form of electoral democracy. The incentive system here is such that politicians and voters act guided by self-interest (Chap. 2). Therefore, electoral democracy is a mechanism that promotes the selfish drive of individuals, even though democracy is, in principle, the mechanism intended to attain the common good. Therefore, free-riding behavior will dominate over collective action.

As the egotistic drive of people become dominant in society, institutional norms will be introduced in society to regulate this behavior. Laws will seek to penalize those creating negative externalities upon others and to those evading taxes or engaging in corruption behavior. However, people will make an economic calculation of the cost–benefit to obey or not to obey the law, considering the expected penalties just as a price, as in any other economic choice, just as considering the price to buy bread. Thus, egotism implies that people's own interests are, in principle, above the law. It will be a matter of economic choice whether people decide to obey or not to obey the law. This is what rule (c) above implies.

State regulation will have a limited effect on selfish behavior. It will change the constraints (the relative price of transgression of the law), but not the egotist motivations.

In sum, in the process of economic growth, quantitative and qualitative changes take place in society, which tend to change the social environment over time, which in turn leads to changes in human behavior. Therefore, economic growth leads to endogenous changes in human behavior. These changes include the increasing predominance of the selfish drive in the human makeup. Economic incentives play an increasing role and social incentives decline in human behavior.

EMPIRICAL REFUTATION OF THE EVOLUTIONARY MODEL II

We have incorporated the economic theory of human behavior into the unified theory to generate a new evolutionary model (II) of unified theory. The general equilibrium along any form of dynamic trajectory—the growth frontier curve or the transition dynamics—will be attained in a manner that is similar to that followed in model I. Given the objectives seeking social actors, which are represented in a system of equations, the market system operates *as if* it were a big computer and thus is able to solve for the endogenous variables—prices and quantities of private goods and the equilibrium quantities of public goods—in each period. The solution of this period generates new initial conditions for the next period, and again the market system is able to solve this system of equations, and so on. The outcome of the economic growth process is a trajectory of endogenous variables, which includes per capita income, income inequality, environment degradation, and (now) increasing selfish behavior of people.

In particular, the following prediction of this model can be stated as follows:

> Beta proposition: *In the economic growth process under electoral democratic capitalism, selfish behavior will tend to dominate over altruistic and free-riding behavior over collective action behavior over time; that is, economic incentives will tend to dominate over social incentives in the behavior of people.*

According to abstract process epistemology, the predictions of a theoretical model must be observable. To be sure, human behavior is observable, but human drives or motivations are not. Thus, in the evolutionary model, changes in the endogenous and exogenous variables are observable, but human drives—the forces underlying that behavior—are not. As we know, human drives belong to the mechanisms of an abstract process (Chap. 1). Therefore, changes in human drives can only be identified when the exogenous variables remain constant. In the evolutionary model, the only exogenous variable in the long run is the initial inequality. Although the initial inequality can change exogenously, it has not changed in a significant manner in the last decades in world capitalism (Figueroa 2015). Therefore, changes in human behavior will reflect mostly changes in human drives.

For example, if society is changing people's drives toward egotism and away from social drives, we should observe that the participation of citizens in the electoral process is declining over time; that is, the model predicts falling rates of voter turnout over time. Citizens are increasingly selfish and free riders on the common good issues. This prediction is testable.

The empirical data on political participation as measured by voter turnout rates are available from the database of IDEA (2016). Its data set covers 22 countries of the First World and 145 of the Third World, for the period 1996–2015, and includes elections for president and parliament. The data set separates mandatory and non-mandatory regimes for voting, but non-mandatory is predominant in both groups of countries. This is then the relevant category.

About levels, the voter turnout rates for non-mandatory regimes in the First World and the Third World are very similar, with average value for the period of around 60%. This figure does not show a great commitment with public affairs. On trends, the rates decline over time in both cases, and are statistically significant in both cases (at p-value of 5% in the Third World and 10% in the First World). Over time, voting participation is declining all over capitalist countries. This fact is consistent with the predictions of the evolutionary model: people are *increasingly* less concerned about public affairs and more concerned about their private life.

In the public sphere, the model predicts weakening in the workings of electoral democracy. It includes weakening of citizens' participation in political parties over time; increasing degree of corruption, not only petty corruption, but grand corruption; increasing tax evasion, not only by the poor, but also by the economic elites, through mechanisms such as *off-shore* companies for financial management; increasing privatization of the state through a more plutocratic electoral system. These traits are common observations, but empirical hard data are not available.

In the private sphere, the model also predicts weakening in the significance of collective actions in society. Thus, according to the model, we should observe less relative significance of labor organizations, such as labor unions, peasant organizations, and consumer organizations as well. This is indeed the case in labor union membership in the USA. According to the Bureau of Labor statistics, the proportion of workers who are members of a labor union showed a continuous decline: from 16 workers per thousand workers employed in 1994 to 11 in 2015 (BLS 2016). The other cases are hard to substantiate empirically due to the lack of information.

The conclusion is therefore that along the economic growth trajectory, showing quantitative increase in per capita income over time, there are also qualitative changes in society. Not only income inequality and biophysical environment degradation will increase along the trajectory, but also people's drives will become increasingly egotistic. The latter is a prediction of the new evolutionary model of unified theory. It can be represented in Fig. 1.2 (Chap. 1). Along the economic growth curve (R) various qualitative changes now take place in society, as indicated by points A, B, and C: increase in income inequality, increase in environment degradation, and increase in the egotistic drive of the population. In the economic growth process, the relative strength of these two drives—self-interest and altruism—are endogenously changed in favor of self-interest.

The predictions of this new evolutionary model of the economic growth process also tend to be consistent with the available facts. Data sets about the variables involved in the model are scarce, as these questions are not part of standard economics. However, the available data show consistency with the model's predictions.

CONCLUSIONS

The initial evolutionary model of the unified theory predicted that the economic growth process under capitalism also led to qualitative changes in society. Along the economic growth path, the degree of income inequality increased continuously, so did the degree of degradation of the biophysical environment (Chaps. 1 and 2). This chapter has presented a new evolutionary model, which predicts yet another qualitative change in society: changes in human drives, as the egotistic drive of the human makeup increases over the altruistic drive over time. The predictions are consistent with the available empirical data. Therefore, there is no reason to reject the evolutionary model II at this stage of research and we may accept it as a good approximation of the real world.

According to the initial evolutionary model, economic growth has two side effects—increase in income inequality and increasing degradation of the biophysical environment—which have social consequences, leading to economic growth with social maladies; hence, capitalism is not a self-regulated system to solve social maladies (Chap. 1). Then we showed that the institution of electoral democracy does not generate the correct incentives; hence, it does not make capitalism a self-regulated system (Chap. 2). In this chapter, we discovered another side effect of economic growth: the continuous increase in the egotistic human drive. Regarding self-regulation of social maladies, this change goes in the opposite direction. Selfish behavior can hardly seek to resolve collective problems, which requires cooperation. The risk of collapse of the capitalist system, and that of the human species, is thus reinforced with the change in the human drives toward egotism.

If people could live with private goods only, all exchanged in the marketplace, then the selfish behavior of people would be rational. However, people also need public goods. Actually, the existence of public goods makes a group of people a true human society, with common problems and a common fate. On the other hand, in the capitalist society, the individual's dependence upon society is high, that is, there is a low degree of individual self-sufficiency, and yet individuals are increasingly egotists and less concerned with collective problems. Thus, people tend to behave as isolated individuals rather than as members of society, and assuming social responsibilities. People increasingly seek individual solutions to their problems, whereas social solutions are increasingly pressing. This theoretical finding about human behavior is certainly a paradox.

The new evolutionary model presented in this chapter has provided an explanation of this paradox. Individuals have no *autonomy* to exercise their egotistic and altruistic drives. Our theoretical and empirical findings give support to Einstein's conjecture stated above: "The relative strength of these two drives is, in the main, not fixed by inheritance. It is fixed by society." The influence of society upon these drives and thus upon human behavior is significant. In the economic growth process, people increasingly tend to behave as isolated individuals rather than as members of society because they are *induced* to do so.

The current discourse of the economic and political elites promotes individualism and selfish behavior as the correct human behavior because it is in their own interest; moreover, the elites have the mechanisms for that—applying the techniques of behavioral engineering. The observed increased *individualism* is thus endogenous. Playing the market and democracy games, people arrive at this paradox situation.

The discourse is also embedded in the education system. The school contributes to this outcome by promoting the values of self-sufficiency and glorifying individual effort and success. At the university level, for instance, economics textbooks indoctrinate students on the value of individual selfish behavior. It is a fact that economics students compared to students of other fields become more inclined to self-sufficiency and self-interest than to cooperation (Frank et al. 1993). However, they study general equilibrium models where the individual dependence upon the rest of society is the main trait of capitalism. The paradox is solved if we remember that the general equilibrium models of the neoclassical theory—appearing in the popular textbooks—show that individual selfish behavior is conducive to the common good. This is just pure indoctrination, for the theory is proved empirically false (Chap. 1).

Crippling the individual's social drive, and his or her social consciousness, as Einstein's conjecture says, is one of the outcomes of the capitalist economic growth process. The culture of individualism glorifies individual success in any aspect of human life, even in collective sports performance, and thus undermines efforts for collective action and collective success. Thus, one can understand why celebrity culture has becomes the most significant trait of capitalism. This is a side effect of economic growth under capitalism, which leads people to perverse incentives regarding the common good.

Therefore, social maladies of capitalism could hardly be resolved endogenously by these evolutionary changes in human behavior. Human behavior is changeable and it is indeed being changed by society; however, the change is going in the opposite direction to what is needed to solve the social maladies created by the capitalist system itself. The conclusions we reached earlier (Chaps. 1 and 2) are thus corroborated: Regarding social maladies, capitalism is not a self-regulated system.

Increasing consumerism is another trait of the economic growth process under capitalism. It will be analyzed in the next chapter.

REFERENCES

BLS (Bureau of Labor Statistics, Current Population Survey—USA). (2016). Retrieved from www.bls.gov/cps/tables.htm

Einstein, A. (1954). *Ideas and opinions.* New York: Crown Publishers.

Figueroa, A. (2015). *Growth, employment, inequality, and the environment: Unity of knowledge in economics* (Vol. I & II). New York: Palgrave Macmillan.

Frank, R., Gilovic, T., & Regan, D. (1993). Does studying economics inhibits cooperation. *Journal of Economic Perspectives, 7*(2), 159–171.

IDEA (Institute for Democracy and Electoral Assistance). (2016). Voter turnout database. Retrieved from http://www.idea.int/vt/

Ridley, M. (2003). *The agile gene: How nature turns on nurture.* New York: Perennial.

Smith, A. (1976). *The theory of moral sentiments.* Oxford, UK: Oxford University Press. Originally published in 1759.

Vincent, S. (2012). *Dimensions of development: History, community, and change in Allpachico, Peru.* Toronto: University of Toronto Press.

CHAPTER 4

Consumerism in the Economic Growth Process

Is the selfish behavior of individuals leading them to attain their supreme objective of individual well-being? This question may seem useless. If people seek their own interests, there is no reason to expect that the final outcome could be damaging them. Even more precisely, the question is whether selfish behavior could lead the individual to bad results for his or her well-being. This chapter seeks to answer it by analyzing consumption behavior. Forget for a moment about the common good. It will come later on in the book.

THE STANDARD CONSUMER MODEL

The standard consumption model of neoclassical theory seeks to explain consumers' behavior in a capitalist society. The model assumes that the individual has a personal utility function, which he or she seeks to maximize subject to his or her personal budget constraints. The utility function is exogenously determined. The endogenous variables are the quantities of goods demanded and the exogenous variables are

© The Author(s) 2017
A. Figueroa, *Economics of the Anthropocene Age*,
DOI 10.1007/978-3-319-62584-3_4

relative market prices of goods and real income. Thus, people are free to choose, but within the feasible set of goods determined by their budget constraint.

What are the predictions of the model? If the relative price of a good rises, the quantity demanded of this good will take any direction. If the quantity falls, it is a *normal good*; if it increases, it is a *Giffen good*. How do we know what good is which? Well, it is a normal good when its quantity decreases as its relative price increases; it is a Giffen good when the quantity increases as its relative price increases. Thus, we reach the problem of tautology, as the model only provides definitions for each outcome. Therefore, the model does not generate empirically refutable propositions on relative price effects.

The same characteristic is found regarding real income effects. If the quantity demanded increases as real income rises, then it is a *normal good*; if the quantity demanded falls, it is an *inferior good*. Again, the predictions are tautological propositions. Therefore, these predictions cannot be utilized to falsify the model either.

The only prediction that could be utilized to falsify the model says that a Giffen good has to be an inferior good. The price effect has two components: the substitution effect (always negative) and the real income effect (positive or negative). For any given consumption good, an increase in its market price will, if the real income were held constant, lead to a fall in its quantity, as the good has become relatively expensive; but the increase in the price reduces real income, the effect of which on the quantity consumed is undetermined. Thus, the net price effect will depend on whether the good is normal or inferior.

If it is a normal good, the net price effect will lead to a fall in the quantity demanded, for the fall in real income will lead to a fall in its consumption, so the negative real income effect will reinforce the negative substitution effect. If it is an inferior good, the net price effect will be undetermined, for the fall in real income will lead to an increase in the quantity demanded, so the positive real income effect tends to offset the negative substitution effect. Therefore, the consumption of the good can decrease, remain unchanged, or increase; in the latter case, the good is Giffen. The Giffen good must necessarily be an inferior good.

Suppose we have a data set including market relative prices and real incomes of households, as well as quantities purchased of a certain good, and use regression analysis to test the model. If the regression coefficient of the relative price variable is positive (which makes the good Giffen), then the regression coefficient of the real income must be negative. If it is the case, then the model is accepted. If it is not, then the model is rejected. This is the only test that can submit the model to the falsification process. Hence, if a Giffen good cannot be found, then the model becomes unfalsifiable. Indeed, this testing is absent in the literature.

In sum, the standard consumer model is unable to generate refutable empirical propositions; so it is not a good model. This is a static model. Other models of the theory (dynamic) using utility functions will face similar problems.

Lexicographic Preferences and Hierarchy of Human Needs

The other consumer model is based not on utility functions but on lexicographic preferences. The model assumes that the individual has needs, which are hierarchically ordered. Lexicographic preferences mean that the individual seeks to satisfy his or her needs in certain order: primary needs first; only if the primary needs have been satisfied will he or she seek to satisfy the secondary needs, and so on. Then, the model assumes that each order of needs can be satisfied and that there exists the next need. The assumption of the hierarchy of needs implies no substitution between primary and secondary needs, but only within goods that satisfy primary needs, and within goods that satisfy secondary needs, and so on.

Lexicographic preferences are represented as a vector of utility functions, one for each order of needs, the order of which shows the hierarchy of needs. Lexicographic preferences are also exogenously determined. By comparison, we can say that the utility function reduces the structure of human needs, represented as a hierarchical vector of utility functions, to a singly utility function. Human needs are reduced to utility.

The model of lexicographic preferences assumes that the individual seeks to maximize the satisfaction of needs starting from the primary needs, then the secondary, and so on, up to the highest order possible, subject to his or her budget constraints. The assumption of the hierarchy of human needs comes from the work of a theoretical economist (Georgescu-Roegen 1966 [1954]) and from the pyramid of human needs developed by psychologist Abraham Maslow (1970). According to Maslow's theory, the pyramid of needs include the following order: physiological, security, social, esteem and self-actualization, where the latter implies the realization of human potentials.

Economic choice under lexicographic preferences is assumed to work as follows. For a given society, in which there will exist just one pyramid of needs, goods will enter in certain order into the consumption basket of households and leave the basket in certain order as well. Therefore, rich and poor households will differ in their consumption baskets, not only in quantitative terms, but also qualitatively, as most of the goods consumed by the poor will not appear in the consumption basket of the rich, and vice versa.

If a good satisfies several needs, its consumption will be subject to diminishing marginal valuations, which reflect the hierarchy of needs. The first units will be devoted to the most important need (physiological), and the next units available to the less important need (social companionship), and so on. Take the case of water. The first units will be allocated to satisfy primary needs, such as thirst (drinking); the next units to satisfy secondary needs, such as hunger (cooking); and then to less important social needs, such as bathing, washing, and gardening.

If different goods satisfy different needs, individuals will purchase them according to their real incomes. Consider the case of food products. At low real income, individuals will purchase a basket of food products destined to satisfy only hunger. Once this need has been satisfied, the next basket bought will satisfy hunger and social needs, such as companionship. Thus, at higher incomes, people will change the quality of the food basket purchased, where the second basket is of superior quality. Similarly, at low real incomes, people will buy a type of shoes that just satisfy the need to protect their feet, at higher real income people will buy another type of shoes, which satisfies the social need of prestige *as well*. The second type of shoes is of superior quality. Take note that in these examples, biological and social needs are distinguished, and the former has priority, which is consistent with Maslow's theory.

Considering quality, suppose good B is of lower quality compared to good C. Thus, on the criterion of quality, the model of lexicographic preferences defines a priori what goods are of lower quality and what goods are of higher quality and thus predicts their income effects. This prediction seems to be testable. However, the criterion of quality applied to goods is basically subjective and thus leads to tautological propositions: If good B is consumed by the poor and not by the rich, it must be of low quality.

Therefore, the model has only one refutable prediction: In a given society, goods enter and leave the basket of consumption goods in certain order, according to the real income of households. The fact that the poor do not consume some goods would be easy to explain for those goods that are expensive and indivisible. For example, the poor do not buy cars because the expenditure in a car would be much higher than the individual's total budget. Therefore, we may say that the poor cannot afford to buy a car. The real test is that the poor do not buy some goods even though they are affordable, for they have other priorities. Therefore, the model will be refuted if no ordering of those goods *that are affordable* is found in the basket of consumption between the poor and the rich. This testing is not available in the literature.

However, there is a very simple and direct way to submit the theory to falsification. The lexicographic theory assumes that the hierarchy of needs is ordered as follows: physiological or biological needs first and social needs second. People firstly care about their biological survival; hence, only after this need has been satisfied will they become interested in seeking social needs satisfaction.

Once the lexicographic theory is stated in this form, empirical predictions are easy to derive. Take the case of child undernourishment. Rich households should not have undernourished children, for they are already spending on goods satisfying social needs, which implies that their primary needs (hunger, nutrition) have already been satisfied. On the other hand, households having undernourished children should not be spending on social needs, because their real income is so low that they cannot even satisfy biological needs. Therefore, if we observe that households with undernourished children are spending on goods that satisfy social needs, the model is refuted.

It is a fact that undernourished children are concentrated in poor households, in rural settings and shantytowns. From casual observation, it is also a fact that households in these areas have expenditures on goods that satisfy social needs (fiestas, parties, weddings, funerals, and other social celebrations), whereas at the same time have undernourished children, which put together refute the theory. Indeed, the few available fieldwork studies over a sample of Third World countries tend to refute the theory. Poor households living with one dollar/day or two dollars/day per person do not allocate every penny to buy calories, but expenses on food count for 50% to 60% of total income and a significant part of the nonfood expenses go to festivities, weddings, and funerals (Banerjee and Duflo 2007, pp. 145–146; Collins et al. 2010, pp. 105–106). These empirical observations lead us to question the validity of the lexicographic model.

The failure of the lexicographic model seems to originate in the assumption that individuals act, firstly, as biological creatures and only then as social creatures. Poor people are interested in satisfying their primary needs only, which are physiological needs (thirst, hunger, and shelter). In order to act as social beings, they must already have satisfied their primary needs, and until then the individual does not care for social life. Therefore, the model predicts that the poor have no social life; the poor should typically be a pariah. What the observation in the real world seems to indicate, as shown above, is that the poor also live a social life and then consume goods that satisfy social needs as well. This observation refutes the lexicographic model of consumption theory.

The lexicographic model presents another problem. It does not explain savings behavior. Macroeconomic models present consumption-saving behavior, but savings are just residual and have no purpose. A consumption-savings theory is then needed. A proposal of such theory is presented now.

A NEW CONSUMPTION-SAVING THEORY

Humans are both individual and social animals, as shown in Chap. 3. As social animals, people would pursue individual and social life enjoyment. The new theory will then assume that individuals seek to live in society, as members of society, not in isolation. Human society is not just the sum of independent individuals. It will also assume a context of economic growth, which implies continuous modernization of social life.

The new consumption-saving theory will have the following set of assumptions:

(a) Humans are both biological and social creatures. Therefore, human needs include both biological and social ones. People seek to satisfy both, not in lexicographic ordering, but at the *same time*. Human needs so defined are still hierarchical, for it involves different levels of satisfaction: primary, secondary, and so on. However, the primary level includes not only biological needs (drink, food, shelter, body preservation) but social needs as well (companionship, friendship, group membership, prestige), so does secondary levels, and so on. Therefore, at the primary level, both biological and social needs will be satisfied only at a low level; at the secondary level, there will be higher level of satisfaction of both needs, and so on. We could define these levels as *standards of living*.

(b) Biological and social needs are few, as indicated in the Maslow pyramid. However, they are satisfied with the consumption of goods, which are numerous and changing in the process of economic growth, which implies a continuous modernization of social life. Biological needs are satiable, but social needs are not. People seek to catch up with this modernization, to improve their *relative* living standard (RLS).

(c) In every period, there exists a consumption frontier in society. The objective of catching up with modernization implies that people seek to adopt and adapt continuously the basket of the consumption frontier by imitating the consumption patterns of others who are closer to the consumption frontier; therefore, people seek to maximize relative consumption or relative livings standard. This assumption implies that people's preferences are not exogenous, but change endogenously over time.

(d) Savings are part of the consumer's constraints, not of his or her preferences. Human life is subject to risk, measurable and unmeasurable. Human needs also include security needs. People seek biological survival as well as social survival. People seek protection against the risk of losing the level of living standard attained by accumulating assets, which implies savings.

The new consumer-saving theory can thus be stated as the following proposition:

Alpha proposition: *People seek to maximize their relative living standard levels in society and to protect the level attained, subject to their resource endowments.*

Given his or her resource endowments and the consequent budget constraint, the individual buys a certain basket of goods, with which seeks to satisfy both his or her biological needs and his or her social needs. The set of consumption goods expands in society due to modernization, which implies that the same human needs can be satisfied with new goods; thus, individual wants and desires for new goods are socially created. People are subject to competition in the labor markets as workers and in the consumption good markets as consumers.

The workings of the theory can be illustrated as follows. Consider the frontier consumption basket as given. If the individual's real income is so low that optimal biophysical health is not affordable even allocating total income to that purpose, then the income will be allocated in part to buy goods that satisfy biological needs (and have only suboptimal physical health situation) and in part to buy goods satisfying social needs. As real income rises, both types of goods will be increased. At a sufficiently high real income, the individual will buy less goods satisfying biological needs (as optimal physical health can be attained) and will allocate the *additional* income to buy mostly goods that satisfy social needs. The ordering of goods entering and leaving the consumption basket of individuals at different income levels is thus socially determined.

The theory assumes that the individual will seek to imitate the consumption basket of others who are closer to the frontier. People adopt and adapt the consumption basket frontier by the mechanism of imitation. It is called "demonstration effect" in the literature. Thorstein Veblen, James Duesenberry, and others developed this idea. This imitation behavior is usually summarized in the saying "keeping up with the Joneses." In the context of economic growth, if real incomes rise continuously, then people adjust their initial consumption basket toward the given consumption frontier, which implies a consumption plan or trajectory.

The consumption frontier is exogenously determined. Its change originates in the innovations that lead to new consumer goods and modern ways of life. Exogenous changes in the consumption frontier will then modify the consumption trajectory of individuals. Therefore, the adoption of and adaptation to the new consumer frontier implies an endogenous change in the consumption trajectory, as people take steps toward closing the new gap. The mechanism of dissemination of the new goods is the market system. Therefore, the theory assumes that consumer behavior is changeable and that it is changed through the market system. This assumption is consistent with the biological theory of human behavior evolution (Chap. 3).

To be sure, the theory still assumes selfish behavior. Individuals still act guided by self-interest. However, their preferences are such that they do not pursue consumption in isolation, independent of what the rest do, but as members of society. People seek social companionship as part of their social needs not because they follow altruistic behavior, but because consumption is part of the social context of selfish and competitive behavior. Seeking companionship, fellowship, or even friendship is not for altruistic reasons (to be concerned about the well-being of others); it is rather partly a way of enjoying life egotistically, part of the show-off. The individual success in the competitive world needs to be shown to others and to show off through the consumption basket. Bowling alone, drinking alone, and dancing alone are not situations that people seek. The real pleasure of a person going for tourism was in the old times to send postcards back home. Today, it is to use the Internet to show photos and videos.

In contrast, the utility model assumes that people act guided by self-interest and are able to order their preferences about consumption goods. This ordering is represented by the individual utility function; that is, the *utility function is individually and exogenously determined*. Accordingly, the individual seeks to maximize his or her utility function, which is constructed independently, with total autonomy, as if he or she lived in isolation.

In short, the new theory assumes that people seek to maximize RLSs. We could use the utility function to represent the individual preferences for goods, but it would have to take a different content, in the sense that individuals would still have their personal utility functions, but it would not be individually or exogenously determined. According to the new theory, *individual preferences are socially determined, and thus they are endogenously determined*. This theory assumes that the individual acts as a member of society, not as if he or she were an isolated Robinson Crusoe. Therefore, it is better to leave aside the utility function.

The new theory assumes that consumption goods are hierarchically ordered in society, which is socially determined. *The theory predicts that goods appear in the consumption baskets of rich and poor households in a certain order*. Thus, inferior and normal goods are socially determined, and are empirically identifiable. Therefore, the theory is falsifiable upon income effects. The theory would be rejected if consumption goods showed no hierarchical ordering across income levels of households, if inferior and normal goods were not empirically identifiable. Price effects do not pose any problem on the falsifiability of the theory. The theory still predicts negative substitution effects and that a Giffen good must be an inferior good. However, there is no need to find, firstly, those strange Giffen goods to test the theory—as in the case of utility theory.

People live in a world of risks (measurable and non-measurable). Thus, people take actions to protect their attained living standards. As biological creatures, people seek physical survival. People seek to avoid death and to live a long and healthy life. As social creatures, people also seek social survival, maintaining its social position, or moving upward in the social scale, but avoiding the fall.

People face two types of risks, the bearable and the unbearable. Unbearable risk refers to losses that would imply a *disaster* for the individual, namely, falling below physical or social survival. People are risk adverse in the sense that risk is a bad (not a good). Therefore, people will be willing to play games in which the risk involved is bearable and in which the risk of losses is compensated by the higher expected gains; however, people will avoid playing games in which the risk involved is unbearable, which would lead to disaster, no matter how high the expected gains. Thus, the disaster situation operates as a constraint in people's behavior.

Therefore, people will take measures to avoid disaster situations by accumulating assets, which implies savings. People save for precautionary motives (short-run protection) and for retirement-age motives (long-run protection, which includes bequest motives). The new theory will assume that savings are part of the individual's constraints, not of his or her preferences.

A Dynamic Model of the RLS Theory

Consider, first, a short-run model of the RLS theory, in which consumption and saving behavior under capitalism are integrated into a single model. The individual is a worker and is endowed with human capital (H^*) and money stocks (M^*). For the sake of simplicity, the model will assume that the relative prices of consumption goods remain fixed. Thus, we can use the composite good theorem and consider all these goods as a single good (C); moreover, the model will assume that the price level is equal to one, so that the nominal values of any variable will also be equal to its real value.

Then the individual j seeks to

$$\text{Maximize} \quad RLS_j = f\left(C_j / C^*, G\right); f_j > 0 \tag{4.1}$$

$$\text{Subject to} \quad Y_j = g\left(H_j, L_j\right); g_j > 0 \tag{4.2}$$

$$M_j = M\left(Y_j\right); M' > 0 \tag{4.3}$$

$$N_j = nC_j \tag{4.4}$$

$$Y_j\left(1-t\right) = C_j + \left(M_j - M_j^*\right) + \left(N_j - N_j^*\right) \tag{4.5}$$

Equation (4.1) indicates the individual's preference function. RLS depends upon the basket of private consumption goods (C), relative to that of the given society's consumption frontier (basket C^*), and given the stock of public goods (G). The individual seeks to approach the consumption frontier. It follows that, given his or her resource constraints, exogenous changes in basket C^* will have the effect of changing the individual's basket C; that is, his or her preference changes endogenously.

Equation (4.2) is the production function of the real income (Y), which depends upon the endowments of the stock of human capital (H), and labor (L), where the working time is given. The income of the individual worker comes either from market wage rates or from income as self-employed, where physical capital is small and can then be ignored. Equation (4.3) is the individual's demand for money for transaction motives, which depends upon his or her income level, where the stock M represents the cash balances required for each income level. Equation (4.4) says that the amount of N in assets is needed to protect the consumption level C from shocks, where coefficient n depends on the probability of its occurrence.

Equation (4.5) is the budget constraint. Total individual income (Y) is subject to government tax rate (t), which in the aggregate finances the supply of public good G. Then, total income net of tax will be allocated to buy the consumption goods, to adjust the real cash balances required for transactions (M) in relation to his or her money endowments (M^*), and to adjust the asset N required to protect consumption from shocks in relation to his or her asset endowment (N^*). These adjustments imply increasing or decreasing consumption or saving temporarily. Suppose these adjustment are made in one period; thus, the short-run equilibrium in the remaining periods will be:

$$Y_j(1-t) = C_j^o \qquad (4.6)$$

Total income net of taxes is allocated to consumption and this basket of equilibrium (C^o) will be repeated period after period as long as the exogenous variables remain unchanged. The exogenous variables include the consumption frontier; hence, changes in C^* will lead to another equilibrium in the individual's consumption basket.

For the long-run analysis, assume that the real income is subject to risk, then so is consumption. The individual holds a stock of assets (N)—physical or financial—for protecting his or her living standard from those shocks. Shocks can hit income flows (bad weather, health problems) or the stock of physical capital (earthquake) or human capital (disability). In the short run, the individual seeks to save and accumulate assets for precautionary motives. This is already taken care of above, by assuming an adjustment of savings *in one period*.

The individual also needs assets to maintain his or her current consumption level for the retirement period, when no income flow will be coming. Thus, the individual seeks to hold assets to maintain his or her standard of living in the short run and the long run. This implies saving a fraction (s) of his or her total income *in each period*. (Business motives of savings are ignored, as the model deals with workers' behavior alone.)

What are the determinants of the saving rate? The stock of required assets depends upon the expected risk losses and upon the permanent consumption level planned, which depends upon the current real income. Let T_1 be the expected number of years of work life and T_2 of retirement life. Then, the problem of the individual is to determine the saving rate that allows him or her to accumulate assets with which to maintain the current consumption level in the retirement period as well. Thus,

$$N^* + T_1 S = N = T_2 C + N^{*'} \tag{4.7}$$

$$T_1 s Y = T_2 (1 - s) Y \tag{4.8}$$

$$\text{Then,} \, s = T_2 / (T_1 + T_2) \tag{4.9}$$

Equation (4.7) shows, on the left-hand side, the endowment of assets (N^*) and the accumulated savings in the working period, which must be equal to the demand for the stock of assets (N). This is the amount required to hold the current consumption C during the retirement period and to leave asset as bequest ($N^{*'}$), shown in the right-hand side. Just for simplicity, assume the individual plans to leave as bequest the same amount he or she received as endowment. Equation (4.8) now presents the equilibrium condition, from which the saving rate needed can be determined.

Equation (4.9) indicates that the individual will need to save a proportion of his or her current income that is equal to the number of years that he or she will be retired as proportion of total years of adulthood. If the individual plans to live 20 years on retirement after 40 years of work, then he needs to save 1/3 of his or her current income to be able to maintain the current consumption level in the retirement period. Thus, the ratio s is exogenously determined, say, by institutional norms about retirement age. The required saving rate does not depend on the income level.

For the long-run analysis, under fix income over time, we may just ignore the short-term adjustments in the cash balances and in the savings for precautionary motives as we saw above. Then, the budget constraint for every period will be the following:

$$Y_j(1-t) = C_j + S_j = C_j + sY_j \tag{4.10}$$

The saving rate comes from Eq. (4.9). Rearranging, we get

$$Y_j(1-t-s_j) = C_j^o \tag{4.11}$$

where C^o is the long-run equilibrium consumption basket. This consumption basket will be repeated period after period— for savings will accumulate financial assets over time to make this consumption level permanent—as long as the exogenous variables remain unchanged. To be sure, the same amount of savings will be repeated period after period, which will be added to the stock of assets being accumulated; hence, this stock will accumulate over time until the amount of T_2C is reached, which is the required stock to sustain permanently the standard of living associated to the current real income level.

As indicated in Eq. (4.1), if C^* remains fixed, this basket has already been internalized in the individual's preferences. At the current real income level, the gap between the frontier and the individual's consumption basket is determined, and then the individual chooses a mix of old goods and modern goods and thus seeks to approach the consumption frontier at a certain pace, as his or her real income increases. Thus, the income–consumption path is determined.

We now need to determine the effect of changes in the consumption frontier on the individual's consumption basket C^0. An increase in C^*, maintaining his or her real income fixed, widens the gap; he or she is left behind. Then, to "keep up with the Joneses" he or she will have to increase C^0. This effect results from the assumption that consumption is socially determined. Individuals imitate the consumption dictated by the wealthier members of society. The theory assumes that individuals are not isolated and autonomous people, but that they live as members of society; thus, their behavior reflects all the interactions in society.

As the consumption frontier of society expands, the individual will seek to imitate (adopt and adapt) that expansion and will seek to substitute the old goods for modern consumption goods. In principle, the individual could maintain the same consumption level for each income level, changing only the consumption structure: more quantities of modern goods and less of the old ones.

However, the substitutability between old and modern goods will be very limited because of the novelty of modern goods. Modern goods are just new satisfiers of given human needs. Furthermore, firms present and promote these goods as new "human needs." The use of advertisement succeeds in promoting this notion, as firms are able to "create new human needs" and at the same time supply the goods that satisfy them. In addition, the social pressure, the competition in the field of consumption, induced through the modernization process in consumption goods, and the shifting outward the frontier consumption, will have the net effect of increasing total consumption for each income level.

Given that real income remains fixed, the increase in consumption level will imply reducing savings, which in turn implies reducing the stock of financial assets that is *required* for protecting the real income, both in the short run and in the long run. The dilemma now facing the individual is between maintaining the old consumption basket duly protected and moving to a new, modern consumption basket that is more vulnerable. Given the assumptions of the model, the individual will be induced to choose modernization with more vulnerability.

Therefore, as the consumption frontier (basket C^*) expands, the gap with the individual's consumption basket becomes wider. The individual will then seek to close the gap with the new frontier, not at the current pace with which he or she intended to reach the old frontier, but at a higher one. Therefore, the consumption level will become higher, but more vulnerable. The new equilibrium implies that the individual's preferences have been changed endogenously, for he or she is choosing, at the same real income, a different consumption level and is willing to tolerate higher risk, including the risk that may imply disaster.

Consider now changes in the individual's real income. Assume the individual's income level increases over time, for the economy is experimenting a growth process. When the real income increases, maintaining C^* constant, the individual will increase consumption, changing his or her basket along the income–consumption path, which goes in the direction of approaching basket C^*. The income–consumption path is thus determined and it incorporates the imitation effect. In this case, the consumption path is protected through increased savings. The individual's consumption program will be realized in the long run.

Now suppose that the consumption frontier C^* also changes in the growth process, due to exogenous innovations in consumption goods. If the individual maintains his income–consumption path unchanged, he or she will be left behind. In order to catch up with the new consumption frontier, he or she will readjust the income–consumption path and will increase the consumption expenditure for each income level. This readjustment implies reducing the saving rate. As a result, total savings will not increase at the required pace; thus, the stock of assets that is required to protect the new income level will not be met. The individual has now become more vulnerable to shocks and his or her long-run consumption program (during the retirement period) will not be viable. He or she is now willing to reduce the current saving rate (s), which was the device to protect the consumption program. The consumption program over the long run has become vulnerable and he or she is now willing to tolerate this situation (which he or she did not before) in the process of adopting consumption modernization.

This is a case of endogenous change in human behavior. Consumption preferences are endogenously changed, as they are socially influenced. The individual behavior is still rational, for there is consistency between the individual's means and ends, according to his new preference. However, the objective of "keeping up with the Joneses" leads to consumerism and to a higher degree of vulnerability of his consumption program both in the short and in the long run. The actual savings rate (s) is endogenous, as it depends negatively upon the level of the consumption frontier (basket C^*), and takes smaller values than the rate that is required to protect the real income. The individual is now willing to tolerate higher degrees of risk in order to have a modern way of life. This is the result of a social imposition.

Consider now that the consumers in this model refer to the workers. Then, the aggregate behavior of workers will just be the addition of the individual behavior shown here. The model does not assume further social interactions. Therefore, in the economic growth process, in which both per capita income increases and the consumption frontier expands over time, people will be induced to increase their consumption levels due to two effects that reinforce each other: the income effect and the demonstration effect. Due to the latter effect, consumption as proportion of total income will increase and, thus the aggregate saving rate of consumers will decline. Therefore, consumerism leads workers to reduce the accumulation of assets that is needed to protect the increasing consumption levels; hence, they have been induced to tolerate higher degree of vulnerability on their consumption program. Their preferences have been changed by society.

Predictions of the Dynamic Model

We have already shown that, according to biology, human behavior is changeable and society can change it; that is, human behavior is the result of the interactions between nature and nurture factors (Chap. 3). The social environment under which consumers operate is that of economic growth and modernization of life style. Two mechanisms are at play to change consumption behavior. One is the propensity of people to imitate the consumption patterns of the wealthy, "to keep up with the Joneses." The other is the action of oligopolies to induce people to consume the goods they produce. To this second mechanism, we turn now.

The new consumer goods are the result of research and innovations, of large investments, which can be carried out by large firms only. These firms operate mostly in oligopolistic markets. Oligopolies compete not only with prices but also with sales promotion strategies, the objective of which is to have a direct impact on the behavior of the firms' customers. Human behavior can thus be controlled and changed through sophisticated market strategies.

In neoclassical economics, advertisement is the device firms use to supply information to the market about a new product, which consumers will appreciate. Information is valuable and consumers get it free through advertisement. Consumers have autonomy to evaluate the new information and make decisions about changing their behavior because their preferences are exogenously given. Advertisement changes the behavior of consumers, not by changing their preferences, but by increasing information (cf. Stigler and Becker 1977). Because of advertisement, the market demand for the product will increase to a higher level; profits will thus be higher. As in any market exchange, both consumers and producers will be better off with more information.

In contrast, the assumption established above implies that advertisement is only in part information; more importantly, it is a device to change people's preferences and increase their loyalty to the product. The idea is not only to shift the market demand curve upward, but also to make it as price-inelastic as possible. The consumers have no autonomy to have "free to choose" behavior, as they are manipulated using behavioral engineering techniques. To be sure, oligopolistic firms cannot write in the mind of consumers all they want, as if it were a blank sheet, for genes shape the working of people's mind. This is the meaning of nature and nurture interacting in human behavior (Chap. 3). The behavioral engineering techniques take into account the role of nature and nurture and yet are able to change human behavior. This is why it is sometimes called "techniques of deception."

Since firms are profit maximizers, the incentive is that in an oligopolistic market competition firms seek to maximize profits by using the advertisement device, together with prices and technology. Thus, investment in advertisement is just like any other investment, with a rate of return. In sum, oligopolistic firms have the power to change preferences in favor of satisfiers they produce through advertisement.

In this case, market power means the power to influence consumers in such a way that they can take decisions to buy a specified good almost unconsciously. From biology we know that freedom of will exists—despite the influence of nature upon human behavior—in a very limited sense: The decision to do something is made by our brain before we are aware of it, that is, free will is unconscious (Ridley 2003, p. 273). On second thoughts, individuals may revise consciously on their decisions. Advertising is the device to introduce the product in the sphere of the unconscious decisions of people. This mechanism would apply not only to new products, but also to old ones. "Capitalism leads to the crippling of the social consciousness of individuals" says Albert Einstein's conjecture (Chap. 3). This is the case in the oligopolistic market. The market power under oligopoly goes beyond price making.

The dynamic model of RLS theory can be represented in the form of an abstract process (Fig. 1.1, Chap. 1). According to this dynamic model, consumption and saving of workers are the endogenous variables of the process, whereas incomes growing at a given rate and initial endowments are the exogenous variables. Exogenous variables also include the frontier basket, the tax rate, the quantity of public goods, and the behavior of oligopolies, particularly investment in advertisement. The mechanisms include the propensity of people to imitate consumption patterns of the wealthy and behavioral engineering techniques.

The model predicts that advertisement changes consumers' preferences and that firms seek to maximize profits by investing in advertising. Facts tend to be consistent with the prediction of the model. Oligopolistic firms indeed use behavioral engineering techniques to influence the behavior of consumers. The techniques refer to sales promotions, which include not only advertisement, but also price discounts, coupons, rebates, and so on. The techniques are based on the assumption that rewarded behavior tends to persist; therefore, sales promotions should operate as rewards that persist. Empirical studies have indeed shown that sales promotions have the expected effect (Scott 2003). Because sales promotions affect behavior of consumers persistently, they change not only quantities purchased, but also preferences. Therefore, once the sales promotions are removed, consumers will continue to act as if they were not.

A recent econometric study by Chen and Waters (2016) presents an estimation of the effect of advertisement upon changing consumers' preferences. The study is based on a sample of 600 firms from the US oligopolistic industries and the period of observation is 1993–2012. Controlling for the effect of relevant observable variables in market behavior, such as relative prices and real incomes, the study seeks to estimate that part of changes in consumption behavior that is due to changes in preferences (the residual component). The result is that investment in advertisement by oligopolistic firms has a statistically significant effect upon profits, which is mostly accounted for by the changes in the preferences of consumers that advertisement generates.

The dynamic model also predicts that the basket of consumers in a given society is hierarchically ordered. Thus, we should observe a hierarchy of goods in the basket of consumption goods across income levels for a given society. Due to the differences in budget constraints, the basket of consumption of the poor will be different from that of the rich, quantitatively and qualitatively. Goods enter and leave the consumption basket in a certain order across income levels. There will be inferior goods and normal goods, which are socially determined. Inferior goods satisfy both biological and human needs at a low budget constraint, so they tend to be cheap and divisible goods; at higher real incomes, they are replaced by other goods, those that are included in the basket of richer households—the normal goods. There is no hierarchy of human needs; however, consumption goods have a hierarchy in society's consumption baskets.

According to the model, the mix of new and old goods depends upon the income levels of households. The new goods dominate in the basket of the wealthy, but some are also included in the poor's basket. The imitation propensities and oligopolistic market behavior reinforce each other to induce consumers to buy increasingly more modern goods (income elasticity is higher than 1), and thus to consumerism. This prediction is testable and constitutes a pending research field. However, the fact that poor households show undernourished children and suboptimal health conditions but are at the same time equipped with some modern goods is consistent with this prediction. Therefore, we may accept the dynamic model of the RLS theory.

BACK TO UNIFIED THEORY: A NEW EVOLUTIONARY MODEL (III)

Now consider an evolutionary model of unified theory, in which the dynamic model of the RLS theory is introduced. The dynamic model will refer to the working class as consumers. For this purpose, some structural relations are now assumed.

According to RLS theory, human needs are few, whereas satisfiers are numerous. Moreover, new goods appear in the market continuously. Consumers adopt and adapt the modern goods; therefore, their behaviors are socially influenced. The wealthy are the early adopters of the new goods as they have the economic capacity to do it. The way of life of the wealthy becomes the social norm. Workers will go through continuous adaptations over time seeking to approach the consumption frontier, a moving and elusive target.

Given that consumption imitation is a social imposition, workers will have to make adjustments of different kinds on their lives in order to compete in the consumerism game and not be left behind. What are those adjustments and ways to cope with the social imposition of consumerism?

An adjustment is to reduce saving rates, as shown above. Savings are not part of workers' preferences, but of their constraints. It is a requirement to cope with the needed assets for short-run and long-run protection of their living standards. The induced fall in saving rates implies accepting higher vulnerability of living standards.

Another adjustment is to find new ways to raise real income. Consumerism leads workers to higher demand for consumer goods, which implies higher demand for real incomes. Some wage earners may expect that through real wages alone, even if rising, they will not be able to make it. Thus, ways to make additional incomes will be pursued, which implies less leisure or less time for the family. Female labor participation in the labor force will tend to increase; multiple jobs, longer hours of work, work abroad are some of the possible adjustments. Family life and childcare will be sacrificed as result of these adjustments.

Workers who make income from self-employment as second best alternative—the underemployed—may also feel pushed to search for ways to make additional incomes. The consequences on leisure time and family time will be similar to those mentioned above for wage earners.

The pressure for higher incomes may also lead workers (and businesspersons as well) to enter into illegal activities to make more money. This is also an endogenous change in preferences, as people would be willing to engage in illegal activities now, which were unacceptable before. Illegal incomes include a variety of sources. Corruption income comes from the relations between the public and private sectors. Redistribution income comes from robberies and extortions committed by individuals upon the wealthy or upon others.

Organized crime generates income from taking advantages of the opportunities created by the prohibitions of law, such as trafficking of drugs, arms, and other commodities, and human trafficking. These activities can be seen as industries in which the norms are those of the mafia, in which failures to comply with established agreements or to refuse to accept and agreement are penalized with death ("make him an offer he cannot refuse"). Hence, society has a dual justice system: the legal and that of the mafia.

The higher demand for income that is induced by consumerism leads to the increase of illegal incomes. Thus, consumerism induces the overall increasing of illegal behavior. Illegal income alternatives can help people to close the gap, but at the cost of accepting to tolerate a higher risk now, including unbearable risk that might end up in disaster. The consequences upon the health status will be negative, as these adjustments increase the stress with which people live.

To be sure, if the consumption frontier were fixed, as in a static economic process, such social pressure for higher incomes would hardly exist. The classic study of Alexander Chayanov (Thorner, Kerblay, & Smith 1966) showed this case. In the Russian peasantry of the early twentieth century, the number of consumption goods was very limited, and peasants worked just to meet their basic needs with those goods; hence, peasants getting higher yields from their richer lands allocated less time to work in the fields and thus consumed more leisure compared to those farming in less rich soil. In this static society, the demand for real income was stable. In contrast, in modern capitalism, the demand for real income is pushed continuously by the system and people are continuously anxious about failing to have more money.

Actually, the limited social tolerance for inequality hypothesis is rooted in the consumption modernization process. People do not tolerate the gap between their income and that of other social groups because the consequent consumption gap is too large and is increasing over time. This large consumption gap is what people consider unfair and unacceptable.

Consider a new evolutionary model (III) of unified theory in which the partial theory of consumption will be introduced. As we already know, the evolutionary process contains a temporary dynamic process; moreover, we have assumed that the dynamic trajectory is a sequence of static general equilibrium situations. The static general equilibrium in the initial period is presented now.

In terms of the abstract process method, the exogenous variables include the initial inequality in the individual distribution of economic and political assets. There are two social classes, workers and capitalists. Political entitlements are equally distributed. This is then an epsilon society. Another exogenous variable refers to the state policies, such as law prohibitions and penalties, including here taxes. Finally, the economic growth process starts with a given stock of physical and human capital.

Consider that the market equilibrium is initially with excess labor supply and excessive income inequality. Therefore, the excess labor supply will seek self-employment income or seek for jobs with an expected income.

Under consumerism, the social pressure for higher incomes leads people to adjust their incomes from legal activities. Excessive inequality is conducive to seek illegal incomes, as means to redistribute income by force. Now those that constitute the excess labor supply would look for illegal income alternatives as well. Even wage earners would do that. Moreover, even capitalists would go into corruption behavior in their relations with public sector officials. Further, some people would seek to set organized crime to take advantage of the opportunities given by law prohibitions, such as drug, arms, commodities, and human trafficking.

In the economic process, there will be legal and illegal incomes. The model assumes that people act guided by the motivation of self-interest. Therefore, people choose to obey or not to obey the law, depending on economic cost–benefit considerations alone. There will be interactions between these types of incomes. The reason is that in general equilibrium, someone's income is someone else's expenditure, and vice versa: someone's expenditure is someone else's income.

Given the government policy parameters, the market system will initially solve for the prices and quantities of equilibrium, which lead to excess labor supply and excess income inequality. However, this will not the final solution, for people will adjust seeking illegal incomes, which in turn will affect market incomes, and so on, until general equilibrium is attained. Thus, the general equilibrium solution implies the existence of legal and illegal incomes. The outcome of the economic process is average income and income inequality for the initial period.

The next period will start with new stocks of physical and human capital and more new consumption goods and thus more pressure of higher incomes. The general equilibrium solution will imply a new level of average income and another degree of income inequality; it also implies the existence of legal and illegal incomes. And so on. Average income or per capita income will increase continuously over time along its transition dynamics trajectory. This income level rise over time will be accompanied by qualitative changes: increasing income inequality and increasing pollution of the atmosphere.

In the case of sigma society, the general equilibrium solution starts with a higher initial inequality in the individual distribution of endowments, due to inequality in political assets, but will have the same characteristics as those of epsilon society. The trajectory of average income and income inequality will show quantitative differences only. This is the unified model of economic growth.

Evolutionary model III predicts the following consumption patterns:

Beta proposition 1: *Goods included in the consumption basket show a hierarchical ordering across income levels of households in society.*

This prediction has already been derived above. In the economic growth process, new consumption goods will appear continuously. The hierarchy of goods will prevail, now taking into account all consumption goods, including the new set of goods. Therefore, the evolutionary model predicts that, in the economic growth process, consumption patterns change quantitatively and qualitatively. This prediction is falsifiable. Empirical research is badly needed to test the model. Household surveys do not collect data with this scientific question in mind. At a glance, however, facts seem to be consistent with this prediction, as shown above.

Globalization of the world economy is clearly homogenizing consumption patterns over time. We could say that the consumption frontier of goods is the so-called *American way of life*. This basket constitutes the consumption target for people of all classes and places. This frontier shapes the hierarchy of goods in the basket of individual people. We observe the modernization of consumption baskets not only in rich and middle-class households, but also among the poor in the world capitalism.

The second prediction is about saving rates:

Beta proposition 2: *In the economic growth process, saving rates of workers tend to decline.*

The empirical evidence about this prediction must come from household behavior, for the RLS theory refers to workers. However, most studies on consumption function refer to macro data, which includes the behavior of the capitalist class, who save for business motives, different from the precautionary and retirement motives of savings in the workers' behavior model. A study on saving rates based on household data for the USA has indeed found a constant saving rate for the period 1951–1985 and a decline for the following five-year period (Bosworth et al. 1991). This is consistent with the prediction of the model.

The third prediction of evolutionary model III is about quality of life:

Beta proposition 3: *Economic growth is accompanied by a qualitative change in human health: higher degrees of stress.*

The side effect of consumerism is stressful human life. Consumerism makes people more vulnerable to the impact of shocks. People reduce the stock of assets that serves them as a protection device against risk. People are also pushed to take illegal activities to make more income in an effort to close the gap between their consumption basket and the consumption frontier of society. People reduce the time allocated to children and family life. We could also include another adjustment: People tend to become overindebted in the effort to reconcile overspending over time. These alternatives to go beyond means are at the cost of accepting to tolerate higher risk, even unbearable risk. The result is higher degree of stress in human life. Ill health problems will appear eventually.

Facts tend to be consistent with the prediction that economic growth is accompanied by a more stressful human life. People are living longer but are sicker (shown in Table 1.3, Chap. 1). This fact would give some support to this prediction. More specifically, stressful human life measured by the category *mental and drug use disorder* leads to the same result. Deaths caused by this category of disorder in the world are available in the IHME (2016) database for the period 1990–2013. Calculated as a ratio per thousand people, this source says that *death rates* increased by 25% between 1990 and 2013.

Is Consumerism Irrational Behavior?

Rational behavior means consistency between means and ends. In this model, *given* their ends, namely, seeking to maximize RLS, rational consumers will follow the best course of action to attain those ends. Rational behavior does not refer to the ends alone or to the means alone, but to the consistency between ends and means, as discussed above. As to ends, consumers seek to catch up with modernization, to "keep up with the Joneses." Firms, through advertisement, do not change these ends. They do change the means through the supply of modern consumption goods, new satisfiers, with which consumers are induced to attain their ends, which were also created. Hence, the consumption frontier becomes a moving and elusive target.

In the model, the behavior of firms is also rational. Firms seek their ends—profit maximization—and follow the best course of action to attain them, including behavioral engineering techniques to change consumers' behavior. Hence, out of individual rational behavior, the outcome of the social interaction in the long run is not the well-being of individual consumers, let alone the common good!

In sum, according to evolutionary model III, in the economic growth process, a quantitative increase in per capita income takes place, which is accompanied by qualitative changes in society. In this case, people live an increasingly stressful life. The economic growth process cannot continue forever, for there are limits to the process now given by human-limited tolerance to stressful life. The fact that people live lives of desperation in the economic growth process can also be considered a paradox (Akerlof and Shiller 2015). On this ground alone, we can say that the economic growth process is an evolutionary process.

Figure 1.2 (Chap. 1) can be utilized to incorporate this new evolutionary model III. Along the curve R, showing the increase of per capita income over time, there will be qualitative changes in society. Along that curve, as we already know, both income inequality and degradation of the biophysical environment will increase; a third factor also increases qualitatively: selfish behavior of people becomes increasingly predominant. In this chapter, we have discovered a fourth factor: consumerism, which leads to an increasing stressful human life. Therefore, along curve R, points A, B, and C indicate qualitative changes in society, all leading to social maladies. We have economic growth with social maladies.

CONSUMER SOVEREIGNTY DOCTRINE: AN EPISTEMOLOGICAL CRITIQUE

In neoclassical economics, the market solution is considered a good social solution. The argument is that no one knows what a consumer wants better than the consumer himself or herself. Moreover, the market system is the most efficient system to acquire information about what people want. People preferences are revealed in the market demand. Market exchange is voluntary. Therefore, production under the market system is oriented to give people what they want. This is called the *consumer sovereignty* doctrine. This doctrine assumes that people's preferences are exogenously determined. What they choose in the marketplace is what they want genuinely, with autonomy.

In light of the RLS theory presented here, people's preferences for goods are endogenously determined; they are the result of social influences, including the influence of producers. Consumer's free choice is thus an illusion. Consumers are induced by firms to choose in certain ways; the consumers' decisions are not theirs alone, but include what firms want them to choose. The mechanism is the application of behavioral engineering techniques. Out of individual rational behavior, the outcome of the social interaction in the long run is not conducive to individual consumers well-being, as discussed above.

Ignoring all the other cases of market failure, such as negative externalities, the point revealed by this theory is that no mechanism exists by which the basket of consumption chosen by individuals in the marketplace serves the genuine needs of individuals themselves. Human needs are finite, but their satisfiers—real or created—can be extended at infinitum by profit-seeking oligopolies. Individuals are subject to distortions about how to satisfy their human needs. The theory predicts consumerism, which does not necessarily lead individuals to their personal well-being, let alone to social well-being. Facts tend to be consistent with this prediction. Therefore, on epistemological grounds, the consumer sovereignty doctrine does not follow from a scientific theory.

Biology has shown that the fact that humans are the product of evolution does not mean that humans are perfect creatures (Mayr 1997). This is why people living in a capitalist society, in which people seek to utilize market exchange to take advantage of opportunities in their own benefit, can change their behavior under the influence of others, who are seeking their own interests and use for that technique of deception. In such a world, individual autonomy is a mirage.

In market exchange, those able to induce the consumption of goods are selfish social actors, interested in their own profits, not necessarily in the well-being of consumers. They are no experts or scientists who know what is good and bad for the individual and society. Therefore, market exchange can cause harm either directly, as in the case of the processed food industry that is unhealthy, leading to diseases, or indirectly, by producing unnecessary goods, the production of which is energy-intensive and leads to pollution, which eventually is bad for health. It is a problem of incentives. Market exchange is based on selfish behavior.

Modern goods may be harmful (process food leading to obesity) compared to old goods (natural cereals). The reason is that goods have social marks; thus, the individual's basket of consumption goods is socially driven. The criteria to include goods in the consumption basket are primarily social, which include novelty, imitation, mode, modernization, prestige, companionship, social pressure, and so on. Social life implies the consumption of these social goods. If not, the individual could become ostracized. The individual's basket of goods is thus the result of a social imposition. Individual freedom to choose goods with autonomy is thus an illusion. Only an isolated individual (Robinson Crusoe in the deserted island) would have autonomy to choose freely.

The fundamental capitalist institutions—private property, markets, and electoral democracy—do not generate the correct incentive system to self-regulate the market of consumption goods from producing foods that harm. To be sure, this conclusion assumes a concentrated power structure, the power of which is exercised through the market and electoral democracy mechanisms.

Consider the following simple criterion of social welfare: *People live a longer and healthy life*. Consider this as a measure of social progress. A study on large samples of countries and for the last two decades has shown that indeed people are living longer, but are sicker, as was shown in Table 1.3 (Chap. 1). This fact is consistent with the predictions of the new evolutionary model (III) presented here.

In sum, the outcome of the consumption basket from the economic process in the capitalist system is socially determined—a social imposition—and thus cannot be taken as something good and thus sacred and untouchable, as the doctrine of consumer sovereignty wants us to believe. On the contrary, it is one of the areas where institutional innovations are most needed to secure social progress or better quality of society.

CONCLUSIONS

The RLS theory presented in this chapter assumes that people seek to imitate the consumption basket of the wealthy. Thus, the theory assumes the existence of a consumption frontier in society, which people seek to adopt. People do not seek to enjoy consumption in isolation, but as member of society. Therefore, the individual's consumption basket is influenced by the consumption basket of others; that is, the consumer's preference system is endogenously determined. People seek to imitate the consumption patterns of others, namely, to "keep up with the Joneses."

On the production side of the consumption goods markets, oligopolies have incentives to reinforce the human propensity to imitate the consumption patterns of others. They invest in technological innovations to create new satisfiers of human needs and then invest in advertisement to change consumers' preferences to make higher profits. Thus, consumerism dominates social life in the economic growth process.

Consumerism leads to increasingly stressful human life. This is the result of the necessary adjustments made by consumers, who are trying to live beyond their means, such as reducing protective savings and seeking more income by overworking or engaging into illegal activities.

This chapter has also shown another evolutionary model (III) of unified theory by integrating into it the RLS theory. The result is that along the curve showing the increase in the per capita income over time there will be another qualitative change in society, namely, consumerism. The model predicts that consumerism is conducive to a more modern way of life, but also to a human life that is more risky, more vulnerable, and more stressful. Data are too scarce to present a formal falsification of the model; the model is new, with new empirical variables. However, the available facts tend to be consistent with the empirical predictions of the model. There is no reason to reject the new evolutionary model at this stage of our research; thus, we may accept it.

We may summarize the results of this and previous evolutionary models. Economic growth under capitalism has benefits for society, as per capita income increases over time, but it also produces side effects, which constitute social maladies. The first evolutionary model (I) showed that economic growth is accompanied by two qualitative changes: rising income inequality and increasing degradation of the biophysical environment. Two new evolutionary models (II and III) have shown two additional qualitative changes: rising egotism and consumerism. We may consider consumerism part of rising egotism. Then, the third qualitative change that accompanies economic growth is increasing egotism.

Therefore, unified theory is able to explain why the outcome of the economic growth process under democratic capitalism has been economic growth with social maladies. The exogenous variable in each model is the initial inequality in the individual distribution of economic and political assets. Through the two basic institutions of capitalism, markets and electoral democracy, this initial inequality leads society to a concentrated power structure. The economic and political elites act guided by self-interest and thus have no incentives to generate a self-regulated economic system, in which social maladies could be eliminated and the common good attained. Furthermore, the elites are able to induce workers to increasing egotistic behavior, which leads to an increasing neglect for the common good—free-riding behavior in the production of public goods and unchecked negative externalities in private goods consumption and production. The outcome of economic growth with social maladies is just the reflection of the existence of the power structure. This is the ultimate causal factor. Facts tend to support this prediction of the unified theory.

In order to transform democratic capitalism into a society that is self-regulated regarding social maladies, some structural changes in the current way democratic capitalism functions will be necessary. Doing "business as usual" will not help. Unified theory has shown that, under democratic capitalism, individuals acting guided by self-interest lead in the aggregation to economic growth with social maladies, not to the common good—not even to their own well-being, as shown in this chapter. New public policies are needed to introduce innovations into democratic capitalism to tackle social maladies, which can be derived from unified theory.

The liberal discourse against public policies is that they are intrusions on individual freedom; moreover, the only intrusions are public policies. Political power is the only power under attack, as the existence of market power is neglected. According to unified theory, both political power and economic power constitute the power structure of the current democratic capitalism. Therefore, and before we go into the public policy implications of the evolutionary model III, the pending question is to what extent do the public policies that seek the common good constitute an intrusion into individual freedom in current democratic capitalism. This is the topic of the next chapter.

REFERENCES

Akerlof, G., & Shiller, R. (2015). *Phishing for Phools: The economics of manipulation and deception.* Princeton, NJ: Princeton University Press.

Banerjee, A. V., & Duflo, E. (2007). The economic lives of the poor. *Journal of Economic Perspectives, 21*(1, winter), 141–167.

Bosworth, B., Burtless, G., & Sabelhaus, J. (1991). The decline in savings. Evidence from household survey. *Brookings Papers on Economic Activity, 1*, 182–256.

Chen, J., & Waters, G. (2016). Firm efficiency, advertising and profitability: Theory and evidence. *The Quarterly Review of Economics and Finance, 63*, 240–248. doi:10.1016/j.qref.2016.04.004.

Collins, D., Morduch, J., Rutherford, S., & Ruthven, O. (2010). *Portfolios of the poor: How the World's poor live on $2 a day.* Princeton, NJ: Princeton University Press.

Georgescu-Roegen, N. (1966). *Analytical economics.* Cambridge, MA: Harvard University Press. Chapter 3 on lexicographic preferences was originally published in 1954.

IHME. (2016). Institute for Health Metrics and Evaluation: Global burden of disease study 2013 data downloads. Retrieved from http://ghdx.healthdata.org/global-burden-disease-study-2013-gbd-2013-data-downloads

Maslow, A. (1970). *Motivation and personality* (2nd ed.). New York: Harper & Row.

Mayr, E. (1997). *This is biology. The science of the living world.* Cambridge, MA: Harvard University Press.

Ridley, M. (2003). *The agile gene: How nature turns on nurture.* New York: Perennial.

Scott, N. (2003). Sales promotion. In B. Weitz & R. Wensley (Eds.), *Handbook of marketing.* London: SAGE.

Stigler, G., & Becker, G. (1977). De gustibus non est disputandum. *The American Economic Review, 67*(2), 76–90.

Thorner, D., Kerblay, B., & Smith, R (1966). *A.V. Chayanov on The theory of peasant economy.* Homewood, IL: The American Economic Association.

CHAPTER 5

Individual Freedom and the Common Good

Capitalism is usually presented as the realm of individual free-dom. In light of the unified theory, however, capitalism oper-ates with power relations and individual freedom is subject to intrusions through its fundamental institutions, markets, and electoral democracy. Under this particular context, what is the relation between individual freedom and the common good? This is possibly the most fundamental question in the social sciences of our time. The chapter seeks to provide a scientific answer to this question.

THE COMMON GOOD: AN ANALYTICAL DEFINITION

In neoclassical economics, the common good is contained in the Pareto optimality criterion. If someone in society can be made better off without making anybody worse off, then social well-being increases. If someone can be made better off at the cost of others being made worse off, then there are no social gains, for interpersonal utility is subjective and cannot be added across individuals to obtain a net social gain. If no one can be made better off without making someone worse off, then the situation is Pareto optimum.

© The Author(s) 2017
A. Figueroa, *Economics of the Anthropocene Age*,
DOI 10.1007/978-3-319-62584-3_5

The unified theory has developed another concept of the common good. The common good or social well-being has two components: public goods and those private goods that have positive externalities. Public goods are destined to serve the social well-being, not the individual well-being. This is the standard concept of public good. However, because unified theory includes as endogenous variables production and distribution, and assumes that not every degree of income inequality is socially tolerated, excessive income inequality has social consequences: it leads to social disorder. Social order is also a public good, in addition to the standard public goods.

On the other hand, unified theory assumes selfish behavior of social actors. Therefore, production and consumption of private goods are most likely to generate negative externalities. Therefore, private goods will be part of the common good if, and only if, they lead to positive externalities.

In contrast, the standard criterion of Pareto optimality can be attained at any degree of inequality, no matter how excessive inequality is. Moreover, income redistribution in favor of the poor does not lead to Pareto improvement. Pareto optimality is independent of income inequality. On the issue of externalities, Pareto optimality is potentially reached even in the case of negative externalities by applying compensatory measures through public policies.

Market Competition and the Common Good

The institution that is consistent with individual freedom is the market system, which implies private property rights and voluntary exchange of goods. The standard claim of the liberal doctrine that the market system is conducive to the common good is based on the following assumptions. First, the individual knows what is good for him or her better than anybody does. Second, the market is the most efficient form of disseminating information about what people want. Third, individuals will exchange goods in the marketplace guided by their self-interest; however, market competition transforms individual self-interest into the common good. If only markets were allowed to work freely, namely, without state intrusion.

These are also the assumptions of neoclassical theory, seen as a positive scientific theory. The third assumption is a critical one; it is at the core of the social sciences. The proposition that individual selfish behavior leads to the common good is the very foundation of the liberal doctrine and of individualism. If it were not true, it would be hard to give scientific foundation to the doctrine. Neoclassical theory has developed theorems showing under what conditions the proposition would be logically true. The criterion of the common good is the Pareto optimality. The conclusions are well-known. Suffice to recall here that in the presence of monopoly and oligopoly market structures, negative externalities, or if public goods are needed in society, market competition could not lead to the common good.

The problem with the Pareto optimality criterion is that it is unobservable, as discussed above. This is solved by the normative proposition that markets should be allow to work freely, without state intrusion, to attain the common good or to get closer to it. The failures of the market system can be ignored, assuming that they are of small magnitude, which will be more than compensated by market competition, which is the essential factor; thus, free markets will lead to the common good. What the state should do, if anything, is to promote free markets. In sum, the justification of the doctrine is the economic theory that assumes the very doctrine. Thus, free market is conducive to Pareto optimality, which is unobservable, but which is guaranteed if markets are free. We end up in a tautology, for this proposition cannot be proved to be empirically wrong.

Neoclassical theory shows that market structure matters for Pareto optimality. Perfect competition is a necessary condition. Many buyers and many sellers will compete to determine the prices and quantities of market equilibrium, which implies that producers supply the goods at the lowest possible cost and consumers buy the goods at the lowest possible price. However, some models of neoclassical theory claim that imperfect market structures do not matter because in the long run market competition will ultimately eliminate current monopolies and oligopolies. These are contestable markets.

The liberal doctrine sees market competition as Darwinian, in which the most talented and hardworking people survive in the market. This idea applies not only under perfect markets, in which many buyers and sellers compete, but also even under monopoly or oligopoly. The existence of a monopoly is just the result of good performance of the individual monopolist compared to the potential entrants in the industry. Moreover, the market power of the monopolist is very limited because setting too high prices to get too high profits is self-defeating, as the extraordinary profits would call for new entrants and the monopolist would be dethroned. The same would happen with oligopolies. Thus, market competition transforms individual self-interest behavior into the common good.

Contestable markets theory assumes that capital endowments are distributed equally among individuals in society, or are slightly concentrated. Only then will entrant firms exist and the mechanism work. If capital endowments are highly concentrated in a small group of people—the capitalist class—then there will be no new entrant firms to compete in all the monopolistic and oligopolistic markets of society. There will be market competition, but among the few, among those that concentrate the ownership of capital. Therefore, market structure depends upon the property structure of capital. The higher the degree of concentration of property structure, the higher the degree of oligopolistic market structures in the society. Perfect markets in society—those where the popular concepts of demand and supply apply—require a low degree of property concentration in society.

In contrast to contestable markets theory, unified theory assumes that capitalism is a class society. The degree of concentration in the property structure of capital is very high. Individual endowments are such that a small capitalist class owns most of the total capital in society. Therefore, consistent with this highly concentrated property structure, the market structure in society will be predominantly monopolistic and oligopolistic. Market competition will be imperfect, monopolistic competition, rather than perfect competition (supply and demand). To be sure, under monopolistic competition, firms seek profit maximization through strategies that involve prices, technology, and advertisement. With these elements, firms are also able to change the behavior of consumers in their own benefits (Chap. 4). Therefore, profits of these firms are uncontestable and can be repeated period after period, as long as the exogenous variables remain unchanged.

Could capital endowments be the outcome of market competition? Could market competition change the initial inequality in endowments?

As to the first question, market competition presupposes that participants are already endowed with economic assets. These endowments are subject to property rights. If such endowments did not exist, market exchange could not either. To make the asset endowments an outcome of market competition, it would require previous asset endowments, and to make these an outcome of market competition, it would require previous-previous asset endowments, and so on. Thus, we reach the logical problem of continuous regress. Therefore, to create asset endowments by the mechanism of market competition is a logical impossibility. This problem is solved theoretically by assuming that the individual asset endowments are exogenously determined. Analytically, this is the initial condition.

The second question then arises. Given the initial property structure, could it be changed by market competition? The competition among the few, the initial property structure, constitutes in itself a protection belt of the capitalist class. In the short run, given the aggregate capital stock, the prices and quantities of equilibrium determined by the market mechanism will not change the property structure. Changes in prices and quantities of market equilibrium, due to changes in exogenous variables, will redistribute profits among firms, but will not redistribute the property of capital. Even firms that experience losses, instead of profits, need not imply the owners' bankruptcy because they may be part of a portfolio of firms. A firm may indeed go bankrupt, but the individual capitalist need not.

In the long run, the capitalist class could confront competition by the process of capital accumulation. However, the capitalist class also has a protection belt in this case. The big owners will have big profits and can accumulate capital further in amounts that are higher than the other owners will. Workers could invest in capital, but that will be in even smaller amounts. Credit markets play a limited role in reducing the initial inequality, for their incentives lead them to do business with those having high collateral, that is, the wealthy. The same behavior also applies to insurance markets. Thus, market competition can hardly change the initial inequality in capital endowments even in the long run. In the process of capital accumulation, there exists *path dependence*; that is, the initial conditions, history matters.

Is the physical capital concentrated in the hands of the best possible economic elite, of the most talented people for those tasks that make a good society? Are the current economic elite the result of a Darwinian market competition?

Social scientist Vilfredo Pareto discussed this problem long ago and showed great concern with the process of elite formation. Pareto advocated a society in which social mobility was very high so that the circulation of elites was also very high, which would guarantee that there is competition among the elites from which the best elite would emerge. As John Higley (2010) summarized, "Pareto postulated that in a society with truly unrestricted social mobility, elites would consist of the most talented and deserving individuals" (p. 161).

According to unified theory, the formation of the elite comes from the initial distribution of endowments, which is exogenously determined. It does not come from the mechanism of market competition; it is prior to market competition, as shown above. Once the elite have been determined, then, and only then, the process of market competition will proceed. How can we explain elite formation? Inheritance, social network, luck, crime are some of the possible factors.

The assumption that the initial distribution of capital is exogenous to the market process and the result that market competition cannot change the initial economic elite—because capital accumulation is subject to path dependency, as argued above—imply that the circulation of elites is not endogenous. It does not change endogenously with the outcome of prices and quantities of equilibrium in the market system. Elites are protected against economic and social disasters—as losing their privileged position in society—by the size of their wealth and the path dependence it generates. They are too big to fail. It follows that the result of market competition will just reproduce the initial elite over time. Economic elites can change, but only exogenously.

Therefore, there is no mechanism of market competition to select the best economic elite in society. In order to have the best talents of society in charge of the economic process, a high degree of circulation of elites is needed. This requires a high degree of social mobility in society—as Pareto theory of elites stated—which in turn requires a low degree of inequality in the initial distribution of economic and political assets, as the unified theory states. The initial conditions of a capitalist society are far from these requirements.

The much-discussed problem of market efficiency in neoclassical economics is therefore about the *second order efficiency*, the efficiency in the working of the market system. This is a misplaced problem, for market efficiency depends upon *first order efficiency*, the efficiency of society in the selection of the economic elite. Whether the concentration of wealth in the hands of the current economic elite constitutes the most efficient allocation of physical and financial capital among individuals in society is therefore the relevant and prior question. The fact that the same elite is reproduced in the market system does not imply that it is the best elite; under this criterion of market survival, *any* elite would always be the best. According to unified theory, market survival comes from the scale effect of the large wealth endowment; that is, the scale advantage hides the inefficiency of first order, the absence of meta-competition.

What is striking is that Vilfredo Pareto is mostly known in neoclassical economics for his efficiency concept, called *Pareto optimality*. However, this concept refers to second order competition, that is, competition in the marketplace, given the wealth distribution and the composition of the elite. Pareto's concern with the circulation of elites—the first order competition, prior to market competition—is ignored in neoclassical economics.

In sum, we have two theories about market competition. The neoclassical theory assumes that economic elites can be ignored in the functioning of capitalism because in the long run they are endogenously eliminated, as a result of market competition. The force of market competition is so strong that in the long run the market system tends to operate with perfect competition, which transforms individual self-interest into the common good (Pareto optimality). In contrast, unified theory assumes that economic elites are exogenously determined, that they concentrate market power, and that elites do not circulate; thus, it predicts that the force of market competition is so weak (a second order competition) that it cannot transform the individual self-interest into the common good. The first theory predicts higher social progress in countries where freer markets prevail and the second where the initial inequality is lower.

On the predictions of the unified theory, it has already been shown that the initial inequality (variable δ) in the First World is lower than in the Third World (Figueroa 2015). Inequality refers to economic assets, including physical and human capital, agricultural land. The qualitative differences in political entitlement just reinforce the inequality in economic assets.

The long-term study of Thomas Piketty (2014) about the ownership of capital in some First World countries shows increasing concentration. In 2010, the top 1% of the population concentrated 25% of the total capital in France, 28% in the UK, and 34% in the USA; moreover, these participations increased in the period 1970–2010.

On the elite circulation, a study of the degree of elite circulation in the world economy, for the period 2002–2014, estimated a very low coefficient of circulation, of around 0.13, the perfect circulation coefficient being 1.00 (Figueroa and Rentería 2016, pp. 15–16). This result tends to support unified theory. Thus, the process of economic elite formation (exogenously determined) comes before market competition. The concentrated power structure in society tends to reproduce itself period after period. There is path dependency in market power because the initial endowments, the initial conditions count; that is, history matters.

The new literature on economic elites is concerned with the formation of the transnational capitalist class amid globalization. It has found that the role of social networks in this formation is very significant (Carroll 2010). Globalization has not led to more competing elites but to the rise of a strong transnational elite, the core of which is constituted by corporate elites from the core countries (the USA and the UK), and which form a powerful opponent for any competing faction in the global corporate elites (Heemskerk and Takes 2016).

On the prediction of neoclassical theory that capitalist countries with freer markets—freer from state intrusion—lead to higher social progress, facts tend to refute it. Social progress is higher in the First World than in the Third World; however, state intervention is higher in the former than in the latter. The First World is the richest region in the capitalist system, with the lowest degree of income inequality, in which the state has interfered individual freedom with taxes, which is, on average for the period 1990–2012, around 43% of total output, compared to only 26% in the Third World (calculation made by the author using the database of IMF 2016).

Tax rates in the First World jumped from around 10% of national income at the beginning of the twentieth century to rates of 30% (USA), 40% (UK), and between 45% and 55% in Western Europe at the beginning of the twenty-first century (Piketty 2014). Tax rates are certainly endogenous. Therefore, in the process of economic growth, First World countries have increased the production of both private and public goods, and the latter in higher proportion. This is how economic growth has been sustained. This fundamental transformation in the role of the state enabled these countries to supply public goods beyond basic law and order, such as public education, public health, and social infrastructure.

The Pareto optimality criterion will then be discarded. This is so for three reasons. First, the criterion ignores the effect of income distribution on social well-being. Pareto optimality could be reached even with a Gini coefficient of 0.80(!), as a measure of income inequality in society. Second, it is unobservable. Therefore, we could never say when social well-being has increased or not. The usual argument is to assume that free markets of higher degree—free of state intervention—imply perfect competition markets or markets closer to it, which in turn leads to Pareto optimality or are closer to it. However, this proposition is tautological, for this argument just assumes what needs to be proved. Third, Pareto optimality is derived logically from neoclassical theory; thus, its validity depends upon whether neoclassical theory is a good theory, able to explain the functioning of capitalism. However, facts refute the prediction of the neoclassical theory that income inequality does not affect the functioning of society; hence, Pareto optimality is meaningless as a social welfare criterion. The public policy proposition that free markets should be promoted is not science-based policy.

Therefore, in what follows the concept of common good will correspond to that derived from unified theory. To be sure, this theory has survived—so far—the falsification process against the basic facts of capitalism. In particular, this theory predicts that in the economic growth process increasing per capita income is accompanied by qualitative changes is society, such as rising income inequality, biophysical environment degradation, and egotism. This prediction tends to be consistent with facts.

According to unified theory, market competition cannot lead to the common good. The market system cannot operate naturally under perfect competition, which is a necessary condition to transform individual self-interest into the common good. The reason is that perfect competition markets are inconsistent with capital ownership concentration. Moreover, markets constitute the mechanism to solve the equilibrium values of prices and quantities in market exchange. The market operates as a big computer to solve the structural equations in market relations, such that the equations internalize capital ownership. A lower degree of concentration will imply different structural equations and different solutions of prices and quantities. Thus, "market failure" is a misnomer and expectation about some nice properties of the market system, such as perfect competition, is idle. The market system is just a mechanism for the exchange of goods. It is not an exogenous variable.

No Man Is an Island

The common good involves private and public goods. Private goods are part of the common good when individual selfish behavior about consuming or producing them generates positive externalities upon the rest. Negative externalities is the name for social damages that individual selfish behavior produces upon others as side effects. As members of society, where social interactions are intense, individuals acting guided by self-interest are very likely to produce negative externalities. No man is an island. Therefore, the individual freedom ends where a negative externality appears. The standard solution is to say that individual freedom may proceed if the individual can compensate those suffering the damage. In public policy, this is known as Pigouvian tax. Thus, individual freedom is socially viable as long as the state is able to apply the Pigouvian tax or other compensatory measures.

There is a logical problem with this solution. If those suffering the damage accept the compensation, say via Pigouvian tax, then we have just reached a solution via market exchange, a voluntary exchange. Then the Pigouvian tax is not needed. If the Pigouvian tax is a state imposition—reflecting the power of the political and economic elites—then the individual freedom of exercising selfish behavior is at the cost of transgression upon the freedom of the others that suffer the consequences, and who did not wish to carry out the voluntary market exchange. The Pigouvian tax is then useless. If a mining company is willing to compensate neighboring farmers for the damage caused on the land and water resources, but the farmers refuse to agree on *any* compensation, then there is no solution to the negative externality.

Public goods are genuinely part of the common good. The need for public goods makes a group of people a human society, with common problems and common fate. No man is an island. The supply of public goods needs collective solution, either in the form of collective action or in the form of democracy. Individual freedom cannot produce public goods. On the contrary, individual freedom has perverse incentives to produce public goods, for selfish behavior implies free-riding behavior.

Consider the case of human health. Selfish behavior leads people to be concerned with non-contagious diseases only, that is, with those diseases that people seek cure for on individual bases, by individual doctors. Technological progress in medicine that cures these diseases is widely celebrated. In contrast, public health is viewed as a secondary problem. Any technological progress in public health is hardly celebrated.

The difference is a matter of incentives: profits are in the market of private health services. The incentives are then perverse: the sicker the population, the higher the business opportunities to cure them privately. Thus, the profit motive has led to the misuse of antibiotics in human health with the result that antibiotics are becoming useless, as bacteria are developing resistance to them. Alexander Fleming, the discoverer of penicillin, had already warned us about this misuse in the 1940s. In public health services, incentives also tend to be perverse. The higher the public health problem, the greater the opportunity to buy votes.

Clean sky is a public good. Therefore, individual freedom cannot include the freedom to contaminate the sky and hurt the rest. There cannot be freedom to generate negative externalities. However, selfish behavior leads to pollution of the skies and to human health problems. This is a negative externality via public goods, called the problem of the commons. Furthermore, the pollution dumped into the atmosphere will remain there forever. Thus, it damages the health of not only the current generation, but the future generations as well. Therefore, the individual freedom of today harms future generations. The Pigouvian tax solution is conceptually meaningless in this case. Therefore, the biophysical environmental problem gives rise to social limits in the individual freedom to exercise selfish behavior.

Living in society implies interactions among individuals. Consider just the existence of negative externalities. Therefore, the doctrine of individual freedom faces the *fallacy of composition problem*: what is true for the individual is not true for the aggregate. Given the existence of negative externalities, not everyone can have freedom of choice. Therefore, the principle of individual freedom of choice assumes that negative externalities do not exist in the social interactions and that public goods are not required in society. That could only happen in the individual world of Robinson Crusoe. Consequently, the principle of individual freedom assumes a society in which its members are just a collection of independent people, in which social interactions can be ignored in the functioning of human society. Real-world capitalism does not correspond to this abstract world.

According to unified theory, under democratic capitalism, people act guided by self-interest. People exercise their individual freedom of choice. This selfish behavior harms the well-being of others. In brief, individual freedom of choice, selfish behavior, cannot lead to the common good. Facts are consistent with this prediction. The outcome of the economic growth process is higher incomes but accompanied by social maladies. This is no accident. Unified theory explains why this is an inevitable outcome; that is, the outcome reflects the power of economic and political elites in the functioning of democratic capitalism.

Freedom from What?

The usual proposition included in the current discourse is that, under capitalism, people are "free to choose." This is not only a fallacy, as shown above, but it is obviously incomplete. It should say *Free to Choose under constraints.* Both the rich and the poor are certainly free to choose in the marketplace; so are both the small family businesses and the corporations. However, there is a big difference in the feasible set of their choices. Given the high degree of inequality in the distribution of asset endowments, capitalism could hardly be called a society of free choice. Capitalism is not Nirvana. Freedom of choice under capitalism is *bound freedom*.

The normative proposition that capitalism is a good system because people have the individual freedom to choose has the assumption that the differences observed in individual endowments do not matter. The wealthy and the poor share this freedom. As a normative theory, the proposition needs to proof that inequality is irrelevant in the society's well-being: A capitalist society is good independent of its degree of inequality, as long as individuals are free to choose. This empirical implication is included—although implicitly only—in the discourse. According to the unified theory, this proposition is refuted by facts: inequality leads to social maladies (Chap. 1).

A normative theory deals with the question of how the world *ought* to be, whereas a scientific theory deals with the question of how the world *is*. All the same, a normative theory has to be a logical system, just like a scientific theory. Moreover, a normative theory must be derived from a valid scientific theory, which has survived the falsification process. The propositions about *ought to be* cannot contradict the propositions about *is*. Only then can the normative theory have any practical value for public policies, that is, for science-based public policies. The proposition stated above lacks this logical requirement.

What the discourse seems to defend is individual freedom from state intervention. Any state intervention constitutes an intrusion to individual freedom. This is the heart of liberalism. However, this normative proposition is refuted by facts. As shown above, capitalist societies with a higher degree of state intervention in the market system are the most developed.

Furthermore, economic power intervention through mechanisms of oligopolistic competition and advertisement also constitutes an intrusion to individual freedom in market exchange; however, it is ignored in the liberal discourse. As shown earlier (Chap. 4), the unified theory predicts that market power goes as far as to change consumers' preferences; hence, individual freedom in the marketplace is manipulated freedom. Even further, unified theory predicts that political power intervention through mechanisms of buying votes also constitutes an intrusion into individual freedom in the democratic process; hence, individual freedom as citizen is manipulated freedom. Facts are also consistent with this prediction, as shown in Chap. 2.

In sum, according to unified theory, individual freedom under electoral democracy capitalism is thus bound freedom. Individual freedom is limited not only by individual resource constraints, but also by the power of the economic and political elites. Moreover, given the existence of negative externalities, not all individuals can have freedom of choice (the fallacy of composition problem). The liberal doctrine has no scientific justification, neither theoretically nor empirically.

Freedom for What?

Individual freedom is a human right. It is valuable in itself. Freedom is preferable to non-freedom. Nevertheless, the question here is of scientific nature: what do people do with their freedom, more precisely, with their bound freedom?

According to the unified theory, self-interest, egotism is what people seek with their freedom, and increasingly so. This behavior is consistent with the institutions of capitalism: private property rights, market exchange, and electoral democracy. It is rational to be selfish, egotist, greedy, and voracious in the capitalist system. Free choice may even go beyond the constraints determined by law, when the individual finds profitable to do so. This is a positive proposition. It says the world functions in this way. This proposition is testable. The facts indeed tend to be consistent with this theory, as shown in previous chapters. The fact that, regarding the common good—production of public goods, including here social order, and reducing the biophysical degradation rate—free riding is a common behavior in the real world is indeed consistent with the theory.

For example, individuals are free to choose their number of children, whereas population control policies take this freedom away. However, reproductive freedom leads to negative externalities. Sociologist Kinsley Davis (1975) put it bluntly,

> If having too many children were considered as great a crime against humanity as murder, rape, and thievery, we would not have qualms about "taking freedom away": a person having four or more children would be regarded as violating the freedom of those other citizens who must help pay for rearing, educating, and feeding the excess children. (p. 28)

The crime would include the damage that more population inflicts upon the biophysical environment.

Under social relations that imply negative externalities, individual freedom faces the fallacy of composition problem: what is true for the individual is not true for the aggregate. Individual freedom violates the freedom of others. Not everyone can have individual freedom to behave egotistically in society, for it is a logical impossibility, as mentioned above.

An analytical distinction needs to be made now. If the theory that people behave seeking their own interest is empirically consistent with facts, it does not imply that this behavior is good for society. Unified theory has indeed shown that individual selfish behavior is conducive to social maladies. Therefore, a set of assumptions is needed to transform the positive proposition into a normative one, which should by necessity be a logical system, a normative theory. Therefore, there is no logical justification to jump to the conclusion that the observed individual freedom *ought to be* respected, much less when it is manipulated and bound freedom, and even less when this freedom is for acting egotistically. It depends upon what the criterion of social well-being is chosen and what the normative theory is to show that it is ethically justified.

Science is able to establish causality relations between endogenous and exogenous variables. However, science alone cannot decide on the values of the endogenous variables (the ends) that are socially desirable. This is an ethical or normative question. What science can say is about the consistency between ends (the endogenous variables) and means (exogenous variables), which cannot be independent of the causality relations that science has established.

According to unified theory, the individual drive of egotism dominates in the workings of democratic capitalism. The outcome of the economic growth process has been economic growth with social maladies, as predicted by the theory. Thus, it is not empirically true that individuals acting guided by self-interest lead society to the common good, defined as absence of social maladies. It is just the contrary.

The liberal discourse says that people's freedom is reflected in their voluntary behavior to choose what they want. However, what do people want? Well, people want what they do. This statement is not helpful, as we have just come full circle in the tautology. Suppose people are born with a set of likes and dislikes, which are fixed for life. People's preferences are thus exogenously determined (exogenous to the economic process, to be sure). Then we could say that people seek freedom to do what they need and want as biological creatures.

Consider now the biological theory that people behavior is the outcome of nature and nurture interactions, as shown in Chap. 3. This theory implies that the set of individual likes and dislikes is the result of both biological and social influences. People's preferences not only for goods but also for motivations are thus endogenous, not exogenous. People are products of society. The freedom they want to enjoy is to do what society tells them to do. The force of society to impose its norms now sets limits to individual freedom. Human behavior is changeable and controllable; indeed, it is changed and controlled by society. What is then the justification to accept individual freedom of choice as a normative principle? The answer needs a normative theory.

Finally, in current democratic capitalism, it is not the case that society in general influences people's behavior; it is the economic and political elites that do so. The elites can and do change and control human behavior. They have the incentives to do it. In addition, they have the instruments to do it: behavioral engineering techniques. This is what the unified theory says and its empirical consistency was presented above (Chaps. 2–4). Now we can say that people want what these elites are able to induce. Not that people will accept passively any manipulation from the market or from electoral democracy. Nature also counts. People are not blank sheets in which the elites can write anything. However, given the power of elites, entrepreneurs are masters and consumers the amateurs in the world of business, whereas politicians are masters and voters the amateurs in the world of electoral democracy.

In sum, in a capitalist society, people seek individual freedom to do mostly what they are told to do. The likes and dislikes are placed at the unconscious region of human brains, which can be the definition of domination or power. The mechanisms are subtle, but the proposition is empirically consistent with facts. Therefore, this is the likes and dislikes so constructed that guide people's behavior. People do not have total *autonomy* to decide what to do with their freedom.

On the liberal doctrine, the Milton Friedman (1962) statement quoted very often says, "Underlying most arguments against free market is the lack of belief in freedom itself" (p. 15).

This normative proposition is derived from neoclassical theory. It assumes autonomy of people as to what to do with their individual freedom, namely, preferences are exogenously determined. In addition, the term "free market" refers to markets free from state interventions only; therefore, the assumption is that oligopolistic and monopolistic market structures that are so common in the real world are operating under free markets. The assumption is that there is no such thing as market power.

According to unified theory, in contrast, democratic capitalism operates with power relations, including market power. Monopolies and oligopolies use prices, technology, and advertisement to manipulate consumer behavior. Therefore, the coexistence of free markets, with market power, and with individual freedom to choose is a logical impossibility.

From the scientific point of view, therefore, observed human behavior does not reflect human autonomy, even if it implies freedom of choice, voluntary actions. Due to the lack of autonomy, there is nothing sacred about individual freedom to choose under the current democratic capitalism. It is manipulated freedom. Consider the fictitious case in which the economic and political elites who use behavioral engineering to induce people behaving in their own benefit could change their objectives (as by a miracle) and induce people toward behaving in benefit of the common good. The principles of behavioral engineering would now be in the right hands, not in the wrong hands, as is the case today.

Now consider the case of workers' democracy instead of electoral democracy, as shown in Chap. 2. Now the good government (not the one originating from the power of money as in electoral democracy) will have the incentives to seek the common good and could then use the same principles of behavioral engineering to attain the common good. The principle of individual freedom as is practiced in today's capitalism would remain unchanged. The distortions created by government actions on human behavior would be qualitatively similar to the distortions caused by the economic and political elites today, but the objective would be to attain the common good.

To be sure, the question is not about whether human behavior should be changed and controlled. This is beside the point, for human behavior is the result of nature and nurture, of genes and social influences. Economic and political elites are already manipulating human behavior in their own interests. Rather, the question is whether a social innovation could produce social actors who have the incentives to change and control human behavior with the objective of attaining the common good.

INSTITUTIONS AS MECHANISMS OF POWER RELATIONS

In the economic growth process, per capita income rises over time along a given trajectory. This curve shows the transition dynamics moving toward its dynamic equilibrium. What is observable is the transition dynamics. According to unified theory, along the transition dynamics some qualitative changes take place in society, which transform the dynamic process into an evolutionary process.

The models of unified theory assume that the transition dynamics is a sequence of static equilibrium situations. Therefore, there is static general equilibrium in each period of the trajectory. In particular, according to model III (Chap. 4), the growth of per capita income is accompanied by qualitative changes, such as rising income inequality, degradation of the biophysical environment, and rising egotism. Over time, these outcomes by periods imply a trajectory of economic growth with social maladies.

Markets and electoral democracy constitute the fundamental institutions of current capitalism. What is the role they play in the outcome of the economic growth process?

Consider the market system first. According to unified theory, the role of the market system is to solve for prices and quantities of equilibrium in market exchange so that general equilibrium in the economy is attained in each period. The theory assumes that such general equilibrium exists and that the market system operates as if it were a machine, a big computer, which is able to solve a system of equations. The market system is thus a mechanism in the functioning of the economic process under capitalism, as discussed earlier.

According to the models of unified theory, the system of equations to be solved by the market system refers to the structural equations, which includes the social interactions within the economic process. The social interactions operate through market relations and democratic relations. In the long-run analysis, the initial inequality in the distribution of individual endowments in economic and political assets—leading to a particular power structure—is the essential exogenous variable (labeled δ). Therefore, the market solution of prices and quantities for each period—the reduced form equations showing endogenous variables as a function of exogenous variables—will imply general equilibrium with social maladies. Therefore, a different distribution of individual endowments (say δ')—and a different power structure—will determine a different set of equations, and the solution of prices and quantities found by the big computer will be different. General equilibrium *without* social maladies could be the result.

It should then be clear that the outcome of social maladies is not due to market failure, for the computer has done its task: It has solved the equations. The big computer was fed with a particular set of structural equations to be solved. The market system is blind regarding social outcomes; it just solves for prices and quantities of market exchange, which in turn implies the solution values of income inequality and environment degradation. Market failure would occur when the computer fails, and is unable to solve the system of equations, as in the hyperinflation situations. The ultimate factor explaining the outcome of economic growth with social maladies is the initial inequality in the individual distribution of economic and political assets (δ), which leads to a concentrated power structure. The market system is just the mechanism, the servant, not the master. The power structure of society is the master, according to unified theory.

If this is so, there is no logic in glorifying the market solution and taking it as sacred, and much less to consider free markets as a social objective. Unless, of course, the market solution is in one's favor. This is the case of the economic elites, who are the main beneficiaries of the market outcome, and thus preach the defense of free markets. Obviously, the discourse cannot say that what are being defended is the elites' interests. Defense of the market, and of *free* market, is a good subtlety.

Workers are usually against the outcome of the market system and repudiate the market, the computer. Even a society of workers or a society with workers' democracy would need the market system, the big computer, as the mechanism to solve for prices and quantities in social interactions. In the economic process, to be sure, the market system is a mechanism, not the causal factor.

Economic growth with social maladies is the outcome of democratic capitalism. The form of democracy, which enters into the set of structural equations of the general equilibrium, is electoral democracy. Thus, given electoral democracy, general equilibrium with social maladies is the outcome of the economic process. The political elites have no incentives to change this solution or, even worse, their incentives are perverse, as shown in Chap. 2. If the form of democracy changed from electoral democracy to, say, workers' democracy, the structural equations to be solved would be different and the solution would certainly be different. The outcome could be general equilibrium *without* social maladies.

Again, in light of this result, there is no reason to glorify the electoral democracy. Unless, of course, this system works in one's favor. The discourse of the political and economic elites is to defend the electoral democracy because indeed they are the most significant beneficiaries of this form of democracy. The fact that electoral democracy remains unchanged, in spite of much criticism of the people, just reflects the power of the elites.

The political philosophy literature presents two criteria to define freedom: freedom as non-domination and freedom as non-interference (Pettit 2016). The first criterion implies that people can exercise their basic liberties without having to depend upon the actions of others, whereas the second implies that people can exercise their basic liberties voluntarily, without coercion. According to the first criterion, state intervention is needed to reduce private domination, whereas democracy is the mechanism to avoid state domination. According to the second criterion, state intervention is bad for freedom, regardless of how democratically controlled it is. In this discussion, however, "freedom to choose as you will" assumes that *the will* is exogenously determined.

According to the unified theory of capitalism, under the current democratic capitalism, people exercise their "freedom to choose as you will" under bound freedom, where the constraints include the initial inequality in the individual distribution of economic and political assets, which leads to the power of the economic and political elites to manipulate preferences and the behavior of workers. Individual will is not exogenous, but endogenously determined. Examples of manipulation and deception mechanism in market and democratic processes can be found in Akerlof and Shiller (2015).

Moreover, individual freedom is exercised in different degrees, depending upon his or her endowments of economic and political assets. Therefore, the problem of bound freedom is the same problem of inequality.

Therefore, freedom as non-domination or as no interference could hardly exist under the current democratic capitalism. The capitalist class uses the market mechanism to exercise both domination and interference upon workers (as laborers and as consumers), whereas the political class uses the electoral democracy mechanism to exercise both domination and interference upon workers (as citizens). The fact that economic growth with social maladies is one of the basic traits of capitalism just reflects the power of the economic and political elites over workers.

Conclusions

According to unified theory, the economic growth process under capitalism operates as an evolutionary process. The three evolutionary models presented so far have shown that quantitative changes in the growth of per capita income are accompanied by qualitative changes in society, which eventually will set limits to the economic growth process. The main qualitative changes include increasing income inequality, increasing degradation of the biophysical environment, and increasing egotist drive in human behavior. The consequences upon the quality of society are higher degree of crime, violence, social disorder, and stressful human life. Economic growth with social maladies is the outcome of the economic process. The current democratic capitalism is not a self-regulated system.

Human behavior is changeable and is indeed changed by society, but in the opposite direction of what is needed for the self-regulation of social maladies. The economic and political elites are able to change human behavior in favor of their interests. People's motivations and preferences are thus endogenous. Individual freedom to choose does not mean individual autonomy of people's wants, but mostly reflects the influence of society, in particular the influence of the power structure. Individual freedom under the current democratic capitalism is bound not only by resource constraints, but also by power relations.

Not only do markets constitute the mechanism for doing business. Electoral democracy is also a mechanism for doing business, as shown in Chap. 2. These institutions of capitalism and the concentrated power structure have induced people to increasing egotistic behavior, as shown in Chaps. 3 and 4. In general, human life under current democratic capitalism tends to be dominated by the motivation of doing business, for it is not hard to extend this characteristic of economic human behavior to other spheres of life: war is business, education is business, ideological behavior is business, and even religion is business. "The business of America is business" is a popular saying, which can now be extended to "The business of the current democratic capitalist society is business, and increasingly so."

This chapter has shown that individual freedom does not lead to the common good. It has also shown that there is nothing sacred about the *observed* individual freedom to choose, market competition, democratic governments, as the current discourse says. Individual freedom is mostly an illusion. Markets and electoral democracy are mechanisms to exercise power relations. Therefore, to apply new public policies that seek the common good could not constitute an intrusion into individual freedom in the current democratic capitalism.

We can now understand, as the unified theory explains, why the observed outcome of the economic process under current democratic capitalism includes economic growth with social maladies. The persistence of social maladies reflects the existence of power relations under democratic capitalism. The power relations include the power to induce people toward egotistic human behavior. Again, there is nothing sacred in the individual freedom to choose under democratic capitalism, for this behavior is the result of social influences and power relations. Thus, the behavioral engineering that is utilized by the economic and political elites to attain their own interests could also be utilized in new public policies to attain, this time, the common good.

The assumptions of unified theory lead us to these predictions about the workings of the real capitalist world. These predictions tend to be consistent with facts, as shown in the previous chapters. Therefore, we may accept the unified theory as a valid theory of capitalism at this stage of our research. The main public policies that are derived from the unified theory—science-based public policies—will be presented in the next chapter.

References

Akerlof, G., & Shiller, R. (2015). *Phishing for Phools: The economics of manipulation and deception.* Princeton, NJ: Princeton University Press.

Carroll, W. (2010). *The making of a transnational capitalist class: Corporate power in the 21st century.* London: Zed Books.

Davis, K. (1975). Zero population growth: The goal and the means. In M. Olson & H. Landsberg (Eds.), *The no-growth society* (pp. 15–30). London: Frank Cass.

Figueroa, A. (2015). *Growth, employment, inequality, and the environment: Unity of knowledge in economics* (Vol. I & II). New York: Palgrave Macmillan.

Figueroa, A., & Rentería, J. M. (2016). On the world economic elite. *Economía, 39*(77), 9–32.

Friedman, M. (1962). *Capitalism and freedom.* Chicago, IL: University of Chicago Press, Anniversary edition.

Heemskerk, E., & Takes, F. (2016). The corporate elite community structure of global capitalism. *New Political Economy, 21*(1), 90–118.

Higley, J. (2010). Elite theory and elites. In K. T. Licht & J. C. Jenkins (Eds.), *Handbook of politics: State and society in global perspective.* New York: Springer.

IMF. (2016). World economic and financial surveys: World economic outlook database (WEO). Retrieved from https://www.imf.org/external/pubs/ft/weo/2016/01/weodata/index.aspx

Pettit, P. (2016). A brief history of liberty—And its lessons. *Journal of Human Development and Capabilities, 17*(1), 5–21.

Piketty, T. (2014). *Capital in the twenty first century.* Cambridge, MA: Harvard University Press.

CHAPTER 6

Anthropocene Age Economics

In the observed economic growth process under democratic capitalism, quantitative and qualitative changes take place. Per capita income increases over time, which is accompanied by biophysical environment degradation, rising income inequality, and a rise in the relative strength of selfish behavior over altruistic behavior. These are empirical regularities.

The evolutionary models of the unified theory have been able to explain these empirical regularities. They have generated falsifiable empirical predictions, which is an epistemological requirement for a scientific theory to be valid. These predictions have been consistent with empirical regularities. Therefore, the unified theory explains the economic growth process, including why and how economic growth has led us to the Anthropocene age.

So far, these are the findings of the book. In this chapter, the book presents the public policy implications of the unified theory. What choices does human society have in the Anthropocene age? In order to answer this question, this chapter constructs a final and policy-oriented evolutionary

© The Author(s) 2017
A. Figueroa, *Economics of the Anthropocene Age*,
DOI 10.1007/978-3-319-62584-3_6

model (IV). It is also testable. Public policies will be derived from this empirically validated model; hence, they will be science-based policies.

THE FUNDAMENTAL PROBLEM OF OUR TIME

To be sure, the social problem at hand is the scientific finding that the economic growth process under democratic capitalism is an evolutionary process. Qualitative changes that accompany economic growth set limits to it. Economic growth cannot go on forever: it is unsustainable. Therefore, economic growth with social maladies—however lamentable it is—cannot continue forever. The evolutionary models have shown that the social problem is not only the eventual collapse of the current economic growth process and its replacement by another process—the regime switching problem—but the eventual collapse of human society as we know it.

Three evolutionary models of the unified theory have been developed so far. Model I (Chap. 1) is the initial one, in which the qualitative changes that accompany economic growth include rising income inequality and degradation of the biophysical environment, which imply social maladies. Model II (Chap. 3) introduces the effect of endogenous changes in human behavior as another qualitative change that accompanies economic growth, in which egotism, as opposed to altruism, tends to become the dominant human drive. Model III (Chap. 4) in turn introduces consumerism as another qualitative change that also accompanies economic growth. Since consumerism is ultimately the result of increasing egotism, the predictions of model III can be included in those of model II. Increasing egotism does not move capitalist society in the direction of solving social maladies and becoming a self-regulated system; in addition, increasing egotism leads to another social problem, the vulnerability of life standards.

Therefore, the predictions of the three evolutionary models can be represented in Fig. 1.2 (Chap. 1). Curve R shows the quantitative changes in the growth process, namely, the constant increase in output per worker, called the economic growth curve. Qualitative changes take place along the curve R: rising income inequality, continuous and irrevocable degradation of the biophysical environment, and increasing selfish behavior, reflecting the relative rise of the human egotistic drive. These changes have social consequences, such as more intense social conflicts, leading to rising social disorder and health risk. Facts indeed show economic growth with social maladies. This type of economic growth is bound to collapse, as the human society has thresholds of tolerance to those qualitative changes. Reaching one of these thresholds, whichever comes first, implies the breakdown of the growth process.

Which Factor Will Come First?

The most famous evolutionary model of capitalism is the one developed by Karl Marx. Economic growth is accompanied by absolute pauperization of workers, due to higher unemployment and falling real wage rates. Marx's model can also be represented in Fig. 1.2. Thus, along the economic growth curve R, qualitative changes take place in society, as workers' absolute pauperization increases continuously. This situation cannot go on forever. Workers will react, social conflict will intensify, and the capitalist system will collapse (at per capita income y^*), and will be replaced by another less inhuman system. However, the basic prediction of the Marxian theory has been refuted by facts.

Unlike the Marxian model, the evolutionary models of the unified theory predict that environmental degradation (not social conflict) will set the limit to economic growth. Income inequality and selfish behavior are conducive to more intense social conflicts. However, the limit to economic growth will not come from social conflict. The current democratic capitalism operates with power relations. This power structure is so strong that it is able, by using different devices at its disposal, to circumvent workers' discontent and uprising efforts. The reproduction of economic growth with social maladies is just the reflection of the power of the economic and political elites.

Among the environmental factors, pollution (no depletion) will set the growth limit. Economic and political elites have the incentives to avoid the depletion problem of mineral resources. Scarcity of minerals will be reflected in their relative high prices, which will lead both producing and user firms to induce technological changes in the production and utilization of minerals. Minerals are private commodities. The case of pollution is different. It is the problem of the commons. Individuals have no incentives to deal with a public good and seek to follow a free-ride behavior. Governments have no incentives to deal with it because it is a long-run problem, beyond the next election, and no votes can be bought with this issue, at least compared to other more pressing current issues. Therefore, the unified theory predicts that the limitative factor will be pollution.

Figure 1.2 can be used to illustrate this prediction. Per capita income grows along curve R. This is accompanied by rising social conflict and social disorder and by degradation of the biophysical environment, as indicated by points A, B, and C. The growth process ends at point Z in period T^* because environment degradation has reached the threshold value of human health tolerance for pollution. The limit that is given by depletion of mineral resources will lie somewhere in the segment ZR. This prediction is consistent with the calculations of McGlade and Ekins (2015) showing redundancy of minerals (Chap. 1). In addition, the limits determined by social conflict also lies somewhere in the segment ZR. Therefore, the limit to growth comes from environment degradation, more precisely, from pollution. This limit is biological, not social.

The environment degradation problem has led Earth scientists to argue that the current Holocene epoch has ended and that we have now entered into a new geological epoch, in which humans have become the dominant force for change on Earth's behavior. It has been called *Anthropocene* epoch: "In 2000 Paul Crutzen and Eugene Stoermer proposed that human modification of the global environment had become significant enough to warrant termination of the current Holocene geological epoch and the formal recognition of a new 'Anthropocene' epoch" (Smith and Zeder 2013, p. 8). Biologist Edward Wilson (1998) had already envisioned this change: "We are the first species to become a geo-physical force, altering Earth's climate, a role previously reserved for tectonics, sun flares, and glacial cycles" (p. 277). Anthropocene manages to pull together all elements of environmental change, where climate change is just one of the changes happening to the Earth (Waters et al. 2016).

The Anthropocene epoch or the Anthropocene age, as we have called it from the social sciences perspective, is a new context of the biophysical environment under which the economic process has to operate. This calls for new economics. The unified theory of capitalism intends to provide such new economics, for it explains the evolutionary economic growth process with a model in which the entropic nature of the economic process is an essential factor. Unified theory is able to explain how and why we have reached the new context. Hence, science-based public policies directed to deal with the new context can be derived from this theory.

In contrast, neoclassical economics assumes, although implicitly only, the Holocene age. According to this old economics, capitalism can continue to operate as before. "Business as usual" could continue, namely, pro-growth policies could continue; however, the consequence would be economic growth with increasing social maladies and a more rapid collapse of the human species. This policy, based on the old economics, is discarded here. The question is to discuss the alternative policy: how capitalism could adjust to operate under environmental stress, under the Anthropocene age. This is the fundamental problem of our time.

QUALITY OF SOCIETY: A FINAL EVOLUTIONARY MODEL (IV) OF THE UNIFIED THEORY

The endogenous variables of the previous evolutionary models can be reduced to one: quality of society (QoS). The combination of increasing per capita income over time with rising trends in both income inequality and selfish behavior, and degradation in the biophysical environment imply a fall in the QoS in which we live. Therefore, a new (and final) evolutionary model will be constructed, which has as endogenous variable the path of QoS. QoS will also be the social welfare criterion, the common good. For the sake of simplicity, the model will assume the total human society as a single capitalist society, which produces one single good.

The final evolutionary model IV begins with the assumptions made in Table 1.2 (Chap. 1). The entropic economic process assumes that production of the single good (Y) requires stocks of capital (K) and labor (L) and a flow of mineral resources as matter and energy (N). The assumption is that the production function is *limitational*, in the sense that mineral resources cannot be substituted by either capital or labor, and is thus represented as a system of two equations. In the first equation, the production factors are capital and effective labor, which is a combination of quantities of labor with the level of technology (A). The second equation assumes a fixed quantity of mineral resources (as material inputs and energy source) per unit of output (μ). Then,

$$Y = \min\left[F(K, AL), N/\mu \right] \tag{6.1}$$

The use of mineral resources in the production process leads to degradation of the environment in the form of depletion of resources and pollution of the biophysical environment (air, water, and soil). Assume that pollution (not depletion) is the relevant constraint in setting limits to output growth. Also, assume pollution rate per unit of mineral resources is fixed (β), which translates into a fixed coefficient $(\beta\mu)$ per unit of output. Pollution rate (π), pollution concentration (Π), and total output (Y) per unit of time are then related as follows:

$$\Pi(T) = \beta NT = \beta\mu YT \tag{6.2}$$

Where $\beta\mu = (\pi/n)(n/Y) = \pi/Y$, and n is quantity of mineral resources such that $\Pi(T) < \Pi^*$.

Here the symbol T stands for *historical time*, that is, time with present and future—called the *arrow of time* in physics. The entropic economic process implies an evolutionary process and then T corresponds to evolutionary processes, with time running in one direction only. (In contrast, static and dynamic processes are mechanical and then use the corresponding concept of time as *mechanical time*, represented by t, as in the pendulum movement.)

The entropic economic process contains several properties. First, production of goods implies production of waste, pollution in this case. Second, pollution increases and accumulates over time even if the flow of total output remains fixed. Third, an increase in the level of total output Y leads to an upward shift in the trajectory of pollution. Fourth, continuous increase in Y cannot go on forever. As pollution accumulates in the atmosphere, the effect on human health will be increasingly severe. Assume that humans' tolerance for pollution is limited and equal to Π^*, beyond which human life, as we know it, cannot continue, as low availability of oxygen in the atmosphere could imply an adaptation to a more anaerobic human life. The atmosphere, the only niche of human species, would become inhabitable. Then, there is a limit to total output growth and to human survival.

In the entropic economic process, therefore, *quality of society* becomes an important concept when dealing with the objectives of public policies. This concept must come from a normative theory, rather than a positive (scientific) theory, as it deals with the question of how the world ought to be rather that how it is. Normative and positive theories are related in some particular way. Normative propositions need to be based on a scientific theory, on how the world is; otherwise, it would be quite arbitrary and useless. The question about the policy implications of a scientific theory is therefore very significant in the social sciences.

For example, the criterion of social well-being is Pareto optimum in neoclassical theory. According to this theory, in the capitalist system individuals act guided by self-interest; more precisely, individuals seek to maximize their own utility functions. Furthermore, individuals seeking their self-interest and exchanging goods in free markets generate, in the aggregate, equilibrium values of total output and its distribution.

The normative proposition about social well-being that is derived logically from this theory is based on *individual well-being*. If no individual can be made better off without making someone else worse off, then the production and distribution solution of markets is the Pareto optimum. In addition to the problem that it is unobservable, Pareto optimality is independent of the degree of income inequality in society.

In contrast, according to unified theory, the capitalist system operates with power relations. The outcome of the economic growth process includes rising per capita income accompanied by excessive income inequality and degradation of the biophysical environment. The first is cardinal measurable, whereas the latter two are ordinal measurable. (The outcome of increasing egotism is ignored for the time being, just for the sake of simplicity.) The exogenous variable is the initial inequality in the individual endowments of assets, which implies a degree of power structure concentration. Therefore, the general equilibrium is economic growth with social maladies, which reflects the power of the economic and political elites. This power structure also distorts the autonomy of individual freedom.

The concept of social well-being that is logically consistent with the unified theory is *quality of society*, for the three outcomes of the economic process imply a QoS in which people live. Social well-being therefore implies the search for higher QoS, which means a concern with the common good. This concept is not about individual well-being; it is about collective well-being, about improving the common good.

Public goods constitute the genuine part of the common good. The most important public goods, according to unified theory, include the biophysical environment and the social environment. Clean skies and social order are both public goods. They both constitute the common good. Rising inequality leads to more intense social conflict and then to social disorder. Biophysical environment degradation leads to human health problems due to pollution, to more hazardous human life due to the consequent climate change, and to additional social disorder due to the social conflicts in the exploitation of natural resources. In sum, QoS, the quality of the biophysical and social environments in which people exercise their individual freedom (without distortions inflicted by power relations), is the common good, and is the criterion of social well-being.

Economic growth (rising per capita income) has a positive effect on QoS, as more goods produced will improve people's quality of life, where goods include public goods and private goods. Income inequality has a negative effect on QoS, as it leads to higher degree of social conflict and thus social disorder. Biophysical environment degradation also has a negative effect, as it affects human health negatively and also leads to social conflict in the use of natural resources and thus to social disorder. Therefore, the positive effect of economic growth on QoS tends to be offset by the negative effects of inequality and the environment.

What is the net effect over time? At the beginning of the economic growth process, the evolutionary model IV predicts that the positive effect of income growth will dominate. As the growth process continues, the negative effect of qualitative changes will tend to become more significant, and thus the QoS will tend to level off. Ultimately, the negative effects will dominate, and the quality of life will decline over time. Therefore, the evolutionary model predicts that the QoS path will take the form of an inverted-U curve.

Figure 6.1 illustrates model IV. In panel (a), per capita income or output per worker—supposing labor force is a fixed proportion of the total population makes both concepts inter-

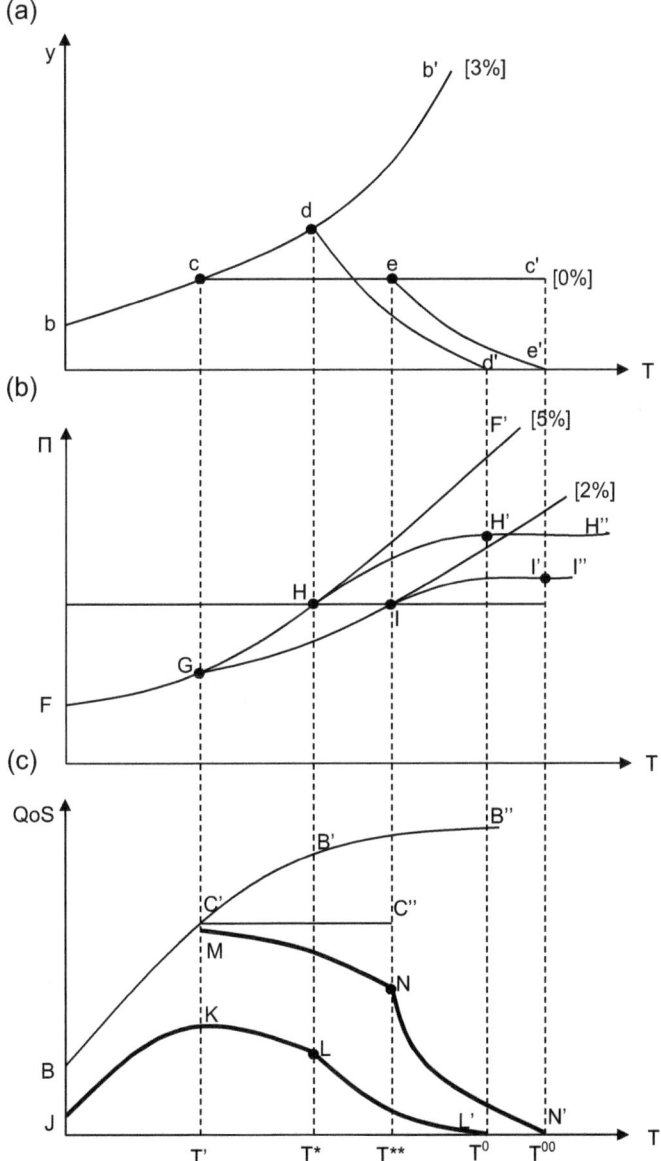

Fig. 6.1   QoS under entropic economic process

changeable—is measured along the vertical axis and time along the horizontal. It grows at a given rate (say 4% per year) along curve bb'. Assume that total income or total output grows at 6% per year and population at 2%. At each period, income inequality increases along this curve; hence, income inequality is higher at point d than at point c.

In panel (b), the concentration of pollution in the atmosphere is measured along the vertical axis. As economic growth travels along curve bb', pollution concentration grows along curve FF'. Moreover, pollution grows at the same rate of total output (6%). Therefore, pollution increases along the curve bb'; namely, it is higher at point d than at point c. Given the threshold value of pollution that humans can tolerate (Π^*), economic growth cannot go on forever. This value is reached at point H, which occurs at time T^*. From this period on, output can only fall. As total output declines, pollution rate will also decline, but total pollution concentration will still increase, although at a lower rate. When total output reaches the value of zero, pollution concentration will stop growing (point H') and will become constant. In panel (a), therefore, output per person will change: the trajectory bd turns to dd', which becomes equal to zero in period T°.

In panel (c), the vertical axis measures QoS by an index. The curve BB'' shows the transformation of output per person into QoS. The curve is increasing, indicating that the income growth effect is positive, although the effect is subject to diminishing marginal gains. The growth effect implies holding constant the other factors that change in the growth process, income inequality, and pollution. However, economic growth is accompanied by a rise in income inequality, which implies a fall in the quality of the social environment, which in turn implies a downward shift of the BB' curve. The increase in degradation of the biophysical environment that also accompanies economic growth implies a fall in the quality of biophysical environment, which in turn also implies a fall in the social environment, leading to another downward shift of the curve. Then, these two negative effects tend to bend down the curve BB″. Initially the economic growth effect will dominate, but over time the negative effects will increase over time, while the positive effect will grow at diminishing rates; therefore, the negative effects will ultimately become dominant.

At period T^*,the QoS curve has reached point L, which corresponds to point d in panel (a), whereas the segment LL′ corresponds to segment dd′, in which output per person is falling in absolute terms. Over time, the QoS will take the form of curve JKLL′, an inverted-U curve. Along the segment JK, economic growth and QoS are complementary; but along segment KL, they show a trade-off. Beyond point L, the collapse of human society will occur.

CHANGING THE TRAJECTORY WITH PUBLIC POLICIES

There is nothing deterministic about curve JKLL′ in Fig. 6.1. Economics is not physics. The evolutionary model shows that this curve is socially constructed. It reflects the pro-growth policies promoted by the current power structure, the current economic and political elites, who have the incentives to follow this policy, as they are the main beneficiaries, including the benefit of remaining as members of the elite. Therefore, the curve can be changed through social innovations. The social objective is clearly seen in the graph: How to shift the JKLL′ curve upward over time? This shift would imply a higher QoS over time and a longer period of human species survival. Consider now public policies to attain that objective.

Consider a public policy that reduces economic growth rate equal to zero at period T. In panel (a), the output per person curve changes to the horizontal line cc'. The contribution of this fixed output per person over QoS will become the horizontal segment C'C". However, the values of income inequality and pollution that accompany the growth curve will take new values along cc'. Income inequality will be equal to that at point c and therefore smaller than that at point d. This implies an upward shift of the segment KL in panel (c). Pollution will still increase, because total output is still increasing (at the rate of population growth), but at a lower rate. The new path of pollution concentration will be given by the segment GII'. At period T^* pollution concentration will be lower. This in turn implies another upward shift of the initial segment KL. Therefore, the segment KL shifts upward to become MN.

The threshold of pollution tolerance is now reached much later, at period T^{**}. Output per person now declines along segment ee' in panel (a).

Constant average income tends to maintain the QoS fixed. However, the other factors that determine the QoS, income inequality and pollution concentration, change induced by the zero-growth situation; that is, income inequality and pollution concentration decline and have the effect of improving QoS. The net effect is therefore an increase in QoS. The segment KLL' will shift upward to become MNN'.

Therefore, the no-growth policy has the net effect of improving the QoS over time. The same quantity of consumption per person will imply a higher QoS because both the social and the biophysical environments in which individuals live will be improved, which means higher QoS. On the QoS criterion, no-growth policy is superior to the alternative of pro-growth policy. Even if *total output* were set at zero growth rate, implying an absolute decrease in the quantity of consumption per person, the net effect could be an even higher QoS, because the public goods (social and biophysical environment) would improve even more and could more than compensate the loss in personal real incomes. Thus, even de-growth policies could be superior to pro-growth policies.

Now consider another public policy that is able to decrease income inequality at period T by redistributing incomes. The redistribution effect will have two parts. One is the reduction in social disorder and improvement in the social environment, which increases QoS. The other works through the diminishing marginal contribution of real income over QoS, given the concavity of curve BB". What the rich lose is more than compensated by what the poor gain. *The redistribution effect upon quality of society exists and is positive.* If the curve BB" were linear, there would not be such redistribution effect. Therefore, income redistribution increases the QoS, that is, it shifts the QoS curve upward.

Finally consider the public policy that is able to generate technological innovations that reduce the pollution rate. The effect of technological change will also have two parts. Firstly, it seeks to reduce the amount of pollution per unit of mineral resources used up in the production process, coefficient β. This implies new technologies of waste management. Secondly, it seeks to reduce the amount of mineral resources used up in the production process, coefficient μ.

Not all goods are technologically uniform in their requirements of mineral resources. Hence, in a world of many goods, changing the production structure toward those goods that are less intensive in the use of mineral resource would reduce pollution. Collectively consumed goods will economize the use of mineral resources than privately consumed goods. Consuming services instead of material goods (exosomatic gadgets) will also reduce pollution. Technological change that reduces the requirements of mineral resources per unit of output will also reduce pollution. In all these cases, the degradation of the biophysical environment will continue, but at a lower rate; thus, the QoS will be improved.

In sum, public policies of zero-growth society, accompanied by policies of income redistribution, and by policies of technological innovations that are mineral resource saving will improve the QoS over time. In panel (c), with these policies, the segment KLL' of the initial QoS curve will be shifted upward and become the segment MNN'. People will live in a society that is of higher quality and human society will survive for a longer time, although still finite time. Therefore, these policies are largely superior policies than the alternative pro-growth policy, which is conducive to the original curve JKLL'. The mathematical proof of these changes is presented in the Appendix to this chapter.

Take note that the environmental problem leads to another social conflict: the intergenerational distribution of consumption goods. More output in the current generation implies less non-renewable resources and less output for the future generations, with the bequest of a more polluted atmosphere. The concept of QoS *includes* the well-being of future generations; that is, zero-growth policies in the current generation imply improving the QoS for next generations as well.

EMPIRICAL CONSISTENCY

The endogenous variable of the evolutionary model IV is QoS. QoS will also be the social welfare criterion of the common good. Hence, it needs a precise definition. In particular, it must be observable, so that gains and losses in the common good can be known, not assumed. Thus, we can avoid the problem found in neoclassical theory, which uses as the welfare criterion a non-observable category, the Pareto optimality. The three qualitative changes in the growth process—increasing income inequality, degradation of the biophysical environment, and rising selfish behavior relative to altruistic—have consequences upon the quality of life of people, which we have called social maladies. Social maladies refer to hazardous human life and to the collapse of the human species.

Regarding hazardous human life, rising income inequality in society leads to a rise in social disorder because people have limited tolerance for inequality; it also leads to the rise in unhealthy life. If inequality had no consequences for the health of individuals, then inequality could hardly be considered a social problem. Higher environment degradation leads to social disorder due to the social conflicts about the exploitation of natural resources; through its effect on climate change, it also increases the risk of economic losses; and, finally, it leads to unhealthy human life due to pollution effects. The relative increase in selfish behavior leads to social disorder due to the negative externalities that grow unchecked and the free-riding behavior on public goods; it also leads to vulnerable life standards under modernization and the consequent stressful human life, which in turn implies an unhealthy human life.

The social consequences of the growth process outcomes can be reduced to health because they directly or indirectly, positively or negatively, affect human health. If higher social disorder and high risk of economic losses did not affect human health, directly or indirectly, they could hardly be considered social maladies. Hence, in this final model, the outcome of the economic growth process will be *healthy life expectancy*. This is, to recall, years of life expectancy corrected by the years of life with illnesses.

Because the economic growth trajectory cannot go on forever, the dynamic trajectory is only temporal. The qualitative changes that accompany the growth process make the dynamic process a mirage, for it is part of an evolutionary process. Because the period of collapse is unobservable, the degree of pollution can be used as the social welfare criterion. Given that pollution affects human health, the criterion of healthy life expectancy can summarize the concept of social maladies.

Therefore, in this final evolutionary model, the endogenous variable is QoS, measured by healthy life expectancy. Economic growth with social maladies has been reduced to this variable. Figure 6.1c now measures healthy life expectancy along the vertical axis. The effect of economic growth upon healthy life expectancy is positive, but the effect of social maladies is negative. The net effect will take the form of an inverse-U curve. Initially the net effect is positive, and thus healthy life expectancy increases over time; then the curve levels off; ultimately, the curve falls over time, as shown in the figure. This prediction of the evolutionary model is falsifiable.

Healthy life expectancy has been included in empirical work very recently. Thus, for the period 1990–2013, Table 1.3 (Chap. 1) shows that in the First World healthy life expectancy increased, but at a *decreasing rate*, namely, 2.6 years between 1990 and 2005 and only 1.1 years between 2005 and 2013. This is the relevant measure for the test because the First World data indicates the changes taking place in the frontier of quality of life in the capitalist society. This trajectory is indeed consistent with the prediction of the final evolutionary model.

Because power structure is the exogenous variables, as long as the power structure remains unchanged, the outcome of the economic process under capitalism will move along its given trajectory (curve JKLL' in Fig. 6.1c). This trajectory is conducive to the collapse of the system, for the current dynamic economic process is entropic and thus evolutionary.

According to unified theory, to be sure, the power structure can change, but only exogenously. The economic growth process does not change it, that is, power structure cannot change endogenously, because it is an equilibrium situation. The reason is that no social actor has the power and the incentive to do it. The government cannot choose another less concentrated power structure because it does not have the power to do it; it does not have the incentive either, as the politicians who control the state (or expect to) are part of the power structure. The same can be said about the capitalist class. Workers have the incentives, but do not have the power. Therefore, no social actor can change the current concentrated power structure. This power structure can only change exogenously.

As an exogenous variable, power structure is very specific. In the literature, the data set on power structure changes over time under democratic capitalism are unavailable. It is not like other macro variables. Take the case of terms of international trade, which is exogenous in the short run when analyzing the behavior of a single country or a group of countries. This variable moves up and down over time and the predictions of the macro model upon its effect on the country's output can easily be tested. Up and down variations of power structure over time are unavailable to test the predictions of the evolutionary model.

What the few empirical studies show is a very high level of concentration in the distribution of capital ownership in the First World. For a sample of 16 countries from the First World in the year 2000, the average Gini coefficient was around 0.67 (Davies et al. 2010, p. 246). In the US economy, the estimated value of the Gini index for the period 1987–2010 varies in the range of 0.834 to 0.866 (Wolf 2014, p. 40). These estimates are comparatively very high compared to the value for the Gini index observed for income inequality, around 0.33. The long-term study by Piketty (2014) for France, the UK, and the USA estimated that the concentration of capital ownership increased in these countries in the last decades (Chap. 5). Therefore, we may conclude that, in general, the concentration of the power structure has remained unchanged or increased in the First World countries in the last decades. There are no indications that capital concentration declines with economic growth. Studies are very scarce for Third World countries.

We cannot determine the effects of changing the current power structure to another less concentrated power structure by an experimental method either. Economics is not an experimental science. It is more like astronomy; its evidence comes not from controlled experiments, but from natural experiments. To repeat, we do not have those natural experiments referring to changes in power structure.

One of the main predictions of the evolutionary model—the trajectories of the endogenous variables change when power structure changes—has not been submitted to empirical refutation. Data set and empirical studies on *changes* over time in the power structure are limited, as mentioned above. We have accepted the unified theory because its other predictions are consistent with facts; namely, the prediction that, for *given* or *increasing* capital concentration, the trajectories of per capita income, income inequality, and pollution move in the same direction over time is consistent with facts. Moreover, the unified theory assumes that changes in power structure imply changes in the initial inequality, which in turn implies institutional innovations, such as massive redistribution of physical capital ownership to workers or new forms of democracy. Since this type of institutional changes have not occurred in the capitalist world, we may accept the proposition that the current power structure has remain unchanged or has increased in the last decades, but not declined.

In order to change the trajectory of the current democratic capitalism of economic growth with social maladies, and function in the new Anthropocene age, the exogenous variable power structure must decline. This requires institutional innovations, such as replacing the electoral democracy for another form of workers' democracy.

INSTITUTIONAL INNOVATIONS

In this final evolutionary model of the unified theory, QoS is endogenous and the degree of the power structure concentration is the only exogenous variable. The current power structure is highly concentrated. The concentration of capital ownership leads to economic power of the economic elites. The electoral democracy is a device to transfer the political power of the people to the government and to the political elites. Economic and political elites promote pro-growth policies, as they have the incentives to do that. Therefore, QoS over time will follow a given trajectory (curve JKLL′ in Fig. 6.1c) as long as the current power structure remains unchanged. "Business as usual" will take society along this path, until its collapse.

However, the current path is not destiny; it can be changed. Economics is not physics, as discussed earlier. Through appropriate public policies, curve JKLL′ can be shifted toward curve MNN′ in Fig. 6.1c, as shown above. These policies are not viable under the current power structure. The current economic and political elites have revealed all this time that they do not have the incentives to do it, and workers do not have the power. Therefore, capitalism needs institutional changes that can generate incentives to carry out the public policies needed to shift the current trajectory of QoS upward.

As shown earlier (Chap. 2), electoral democracy is not conducive to these policies. The current economic and political elites have the incentives to push government for pro-growth policies. The policy of zero-growth society or de-growth society would require another type of government, elected under different rules of democracy.

The current economic and political elites have no incentives to redistribute income either. Their incentives are for pro-poor policies, which are consistent with pro-growth policies. The discourse of the elites says that everyone gains with pro-growth policies, whereas income redistribution policy is a zero-sum game. This discourse makes people believe that in the context of growth the problem of income inequality is gone. This is a fallacy, as the unified theory has proven. Income inequality is determined by the initial inequality in the individual distribution of asset endowments in the long run, as predicted by unified theory. In fact, this is what has happened under democratic capitalism in the last decades: income inequality has remained at high levels or increased, but has not declined endogenously.

Finally, the current economic and political elites have no incentives to invest in new technologies that reduce pollution. According to the evolutionary model, technological change does not come from outside the economic process. It is rather an outcome of the economic process, a result of decisions taken by social actors, based on incentives. It is endogenous. In particular, capitalists invest in the generation of new technologies expecting the highest economic returns for such investment. Thus, it is more profitable for them to invest in new technologies that save labor rather than capital. It is less profitable to invest in new technologies that save energy from fossil (reduce coefficient μ), for the prices of energy are not increasing significantly to induce that investment. It is not profitable to invest in new technologies that reduce the impact of production upon the environment (reduce coefficient β), for environmental degradation is a public good problem and this effect is not translated into private costs.

Current governments have priorities that are similar to those of firms in promoting technological change. Electoral democracy is a system in which the government is subordinated to the power of capital (Chap. 2). Thus, governments support the capitalist class in following their priorities, for example, with patent laws. On the pollution problem, governments do not have incentives to reduce coefficients β and μ as priority, for it is a long-run problem, not a big issue for the next elections. Politicians could hardly buy votes with this policy offer.

In view of the perverse incentive problems that are associated to the current power structure, the new public policies require institutional changes. Thus, another form of democracy that leads to governments with the correct incentives for the common good must replace electoral democracy. The political class would then have to disappear. To regain people's political power under capitalism implies another form of democracy, namely, any form of workers' democracy. Workers' democracy would reduce the initial inequality, as it will eliminate the current inequality in the distribution of political entitlements, the coexistence of first-class and second-class citizens. Then, worker's democracy would be stronger democracy than the current one. The government could not be subordinated to the power of the capitalist class. Capitalists will have economic power, but workers will have political power.

There will be a balance of powers in society. As predicted by unified theory, the institutional change in democratic rules will lead to changes in the initial inequality, which in turn will lead to a decline in the current power structure.

The new power structure with workers in control of the state will generate the correct incentives to apply the public policies derived from unified theory. In particular, the new type of government could now use economic and social incentives, instead of relying upon economic incentives only. The new type of government will have incentives to be accountable to the workers—the people—and to the workers alone. Unified theory predicts this behavior of governments under any form of workers' democracy. The common good—the QoS—will be improved over time, even in an economic process that works under environmental stress, that is, in the Anthropocene age.

To be sure, workers' democracy is another form of democracy in lieu of electoral democracy. Therefore, workers' democracy constitutes an institutional innovation. It has nothing to do with the observed cases of access to government by the so-called labor or workers political parties, for these parties just play the very game of electoral democracy.

The effect of this institutional innovation upon power structure and public policies can be summarized in the following set of relations:

$$\text{Given } \delta \text{ and } ED \Rightarrow \delta'(>\delta) \Rightarrow PP'$$

$$\text{Given } \delta \text{ and } WD \Rightarrow \delta''(<\delta<\delta') \Rightarrow PP''$$

The first line refers to the current situation. Given the initial inequality in the individual distribution of economic and political assets (δ), electoral democracy (ED) implies a higher degree of inequality and the corresponding power structure

(δ'), which implies a set of feasible set of public policies (PP'). This is so because electoral democracy is a mechanism by which the workers' political power is transferred to the political class, as shown in Chap. 2. The second line says that the same initial inequality now with workers' democracy (WD) instead would generate another degree of inequality and the corresponding power structure (δ''), which is lower than the current ones, which in turn implies another set of feasible public policies (PP'').

We know from biology that human behavior is changeable and that can be changed by society (Chap. 3). Therefore, governments under workers' democracy will also be able to reinforce the viability and the effects of the public policies by applying behavioral engineering, but now for the common good. Capitalists and politicians use behavioral engineering techniques to manipulate the behavior of workers and induce them to behave in directions that are profitable to the elites, as shown earlier (Chaps. 4 and 5). Elites use behavioral engineering for their own benefits. Under this context, individual freedom to choose is a myth. The induced individual freedom choices are not conducive to the common good. The outcome of economic growth with social maladies is consistent with this prediction of the evolutionary model.

Therefore, under the current democratic capitalism, behavioral engineering techniques are in the wrong hands. With another form of democracy, with workers in control of the state, public policies will reflect the interests of the people and behavioral engineering could now be used for the common good.

It should be noted that even with the new public policies, the evolutionary process would still have a breakdown point in a finite period, which technological changes cannot eliminate, as shown in Fig. 6.1c. The physical laws of thermodynamics can hardly be defeated by technological change.

However, the breakdown point will occur much later with the public policies introduced by the new power structure and human life will enjoy a higher quality society.

The entropic economic process is, by nature, evolutionary. Therefore, economic growth is not sustainable. According to the second law of thermodynamics (the entropy law), the biophysical environment degrades over time continuously and irrevocably. The biophysical degradation implies a dynamic trajectory that has a negative slope over time. The only thing man can do is to change the value of the slope, postpone the breakdown period and thus the end period of human species. There is the expectation that man's creativity can generate technological changes that are so strong and occur at such a pace that it can continuously defeat the laws of thermodynamics. It would be like fighting and defeating continuously the law of gravity.

Sun energy is also seen as a possible way out to the finite nature of the economic process. This option faces some difficulties. First, the flow of sun energy reaching our planet is not as strong as would be needed to make solar energy technologically viable. Second, energy source is not the only problem, as production of goods also requires matter from mineral resources. To dematerialize the production of material goods is unviable under the first law of thermodynamics. Even the device to capture sun energy (collectors) needs matter from mineral resources. Recycling can only be partial. Third, the current firms supplying mineral resources will resist any change that implies loss in their market economic power.

Therefore, the fundamental scarcity facing human society rests upon the laws of thermodynamics. Biological species, such as the human species, need to exchange energy and must follow the law of physics, including the laws of thermodynamics. To escape from this principle, we would require the transformation of non-renewable natural resources into renewable. Mineral resources as an energy source and material input to produce material goods would enter into the economic process *as if* they were biological resources; in brief, all energy needed for human life would be coming from the sun alone and production of material goods would be dematerialized. A formidable task!

Technological innovations are not sufficient to postpone the collapse. It has to include zero growth. The quantity of mineral resources per unit of output may be decreased. If, however, the total output produced increases, then, the net emissions of pollution may even increase under technological innovations. This has been the case with the auto industry. The new technology was able to reduce the amount of gasoline per unit of car, but the number of cars has increased significantly, which in the net has increased the consumption of gasoline and thus the amount of pollution concentration.

The Holocene age, the economic growth age, is over. Sadly, we have ended this age with social maladies. Measured by social progress, economic growth has been a total waste of scarce resources. The current QoS is mediocre, which can only get worse. However, we have the chance to make some improvements with what is left of natural resources scarcity. In order to maximize the survival of the human species and still have a better-quality society new institutions are required. Therefore, the challenges for human creativity are to invent new social institutions to replace the existing ones.

Human societies have existed for many years, but economic growth has taken place in the last two centuries only, and more strongly in the last six decades, which has been sufficient to degrade the biophysical environment and move us into another geological age. The Anthropocene age is an endogenous outcome of the economic growth process. This is what the evolutionary model of the unified theory has shown. Because the economic growth process—and the economic process in general—is an entropic process, this change of ages is irrevocable. Let us not forget that the entropy law implies that time (labeled T in Fig. 6.1) can only go forward; it is irreversible. Therefore, there is no return to the Holocene age. We must now face the drudgeries of the Anthropocene age, which we humans have created.

COMPARATIVE PUBLIC POLICIES

Bio-economics, as constructed by Georgescu-Roegen, assumes that the economic process is entropic. It also assumes that the Earth is a closed thermodynamic system, as it exchanges energy but not matter with the exterior world. Finally, it assumes that the current production system is based on energy provided by fossil fuels, stocks that exist on the Earth's crust, and on solar energy. In physical terms, the laws of thermodynamics govern the economic process.

The policy implication that Georgescu-Roegen himself derived from his theoretical framework was that economic growth is unsustainable. He also said that steady-state situations are impossible, not only due to the nature of non-renewable natural resource of fossil energy, but even in the case of using only solar energy in the production process. The reason is that the production of material goods would still need material inputs, which also degrade. Recycling is always possible, but it is only partial, not complete. Complete recycling is a physical impossibility, which he called the fourth law of thermodynamics. Empirical studies have shown that recycling operates at diminishing marginal returns, which is consistent with this law (Bonaiuti 2011, p. 41).

The unified theory of capitalism has integrated the assumptions of bio-economics into a particular social context: democratic capitalism—and thus avoided Paul Sweezy's criticism (Sweezy 2017). Thus, the physical and social relations of the economic process have been integrated into a single logical system, a scientific economic theory. The evolutionary models of the unified theory have developed, gradually, the different traits of economic growth. The predictions of these models have not been refuted by available empirical data. Therefore, there is no reason to reject the evolutionary models and, therefore, we may accept the unified theory as a good approximation of the real capitalist world at this stage of our research, until new facts or superior theory appears. Policy implications have then derived from the unified theory in this chapter.

A comparison with public policies that are proposed by other fields dealing with biophysical degradation, such as environmental or ecological economics, is in order. The work by Mauro Bonaiuti (2011) presents a survey of these fields in terms of the principles of bio-economics, including here the policy debates. A group of followers of bio-economics, with Herman Daly as the main exponent, has proposed the policy of steady-state economy or ecologically sustainable economy. The idea of the steady-state economy is one in which the stocks of population and capital remain constant maintained by a sufficient low rate of output that is within the regenerative capacity of the ecosystem. Natural capital could thus be maintained intact. This position, which ignores the Fourth Law, has gained space in the policy discussion through the journal *Ecological Economics* (pp. 44–45). Bonaiuti distinguishes another group of followers who propose the policy of de-growth, which is, according to him, more consistent with Georgescu-Roegen's ideas (pp. 45–48).

The evolutionary models of the unified theory predict that economic growth is not physically sustainable. It also predicts that even a static economic process, with a given flow of output, is not. The given amount of output per year will produce a given amount of pollution per year, which will accumulate in the atmosphere. Now, suppose the output level decreases to a lower level; then, the amount of pollution per year will also be lower, and pollution will accumulate in the atmosphere. At a lower rate, but pollution will accumulate! Therefore, even de-growth is not physically sustainable!

According to the evolutionary models presented here, the steady-state economy and the ecologically sustainable economy are an impossibility. Even a static economy, with a given output flow, is physically unsustainable, as shown above. These models assume that the laws of entropy also apply to biology and ecology. Pollution is a threat to biodiversity and to ecosystems (Chivian and Bernstein 2008). The principle of ecology is that species of the planet Earth are all connected in a web of life, a single ecosystem; hence, changes in human species actions, such as polluting water tables, have consequences for the rest of the species of the ecosystem (Wilson 1998). Pollution affects the renewable resources. The case in point is fisheries in the increasingly polluted oceans. Natural capital cannot remain intact in the economic process. In the entropic economic process, the laws of thermodynamics operate continuously and irrevocably.

The evolutionary model IV presented here, from which public policies have been derived, is consistent with the assumptions of bio-economics listed above. The model does not need to enter into the debate about the fourth law of thermodynamics because it assumes that the limiting factor in the economic growth process is not matter or energy, but pollution. Then, the model predicts that at the collapse period, the Earth will be left with redundant matter and energy. Therefore, the relevant public policy objective is not to seek more economic growth, but better QoS, which is measured by healthy life expectancy. The major impact of the degradation of biophysical environment coming from economic growth is pollution and climate change, which primarily affects human health. Humans are aerobic species; becoming anaerobic would mean human evolution.

How do these public policies derived from the unified theory compare with those derived from other economic theories?

Economics is a social science. Its scope includes the production and distribution of goods in human societies. Because human societies differ in time and space, there can hardly exist a single economic theory that is able to explain all types of human societies. Economics is not physics. The principle of ontological universalism of physics cannot apply to economics. Furthermore, human societies change over time. Economics is more like biology.

Capitalism has been in operation for over two centuries now. At present, we observe the coexistence of several economic theories, each intending to explain capitalism. In order to evaluate the validity of these theories, we need a criterion to accept or reject scientific economic theories. This comes from epistemology—the formal science that deals with the logic of scientific knowledge in factual sciences. Science is epistemology. Considering the *composite epistemology*—a combination of the epistemologies of Nicholas Georgescu-Roegen and Karl Popper—the current epistemological status of the three most notable economic theories, that is, neoclassical, effective demand, and classical, can be presented succinctly as follows. Thus, we can apply the principle that science-based policies can be derived from theories that have survived the falsification process.

The foundations of neoclassical economics come from the economic theory proposed by Adam Smith (1937 [1776]). The theory assumes that in a capitalist society individuals act guided by the motivation of self-interest. Then the theory predicts that individual self-interest leads, as by an *invisible hand*, to the common good. The liberal doctrine is thus based on the invisible hand principle of Smith. If you believe in liberalism—the state should not intrude in the market system— notice that you are assuming that nothing of significance has changed in world capitalism in the last 240 years.

On the criterion of the composite epistemology, if facts refute the predictions of a scientific theory, then the theory is rejected. Facts indeed refute the predictions of the neoclassical theory: capitalism does not show the predominance of the common good; on the contrary, the persistence of social maladies, the social consequences of excessive income inequality, and biophysical environment degradation are the basic traits of capitalism, as indicated above. In seeking to explain the economic growth process, neoclassical theory assumes that this process is mechanical, not evolutionary. Economic growth can be repeated forever. Neoclassical growth models ignore bio-economics, as revealed in popular textbooks (cf. Jones and Vollrath 2013). This is, in part, the reason for its failure to explain economic growth with biophysical degradation.

The current pro-growth public policies, and the liberal discourse, come from neoclassical economics, the standard economics. According to this theory, economic growth can go on forever; there are no physical limits to growth, as discussed above. "Business as usual" is the derived policy, maintaining the institutions: free markets and electoral democracy, and the consequent individualism and selfish behavior. No need for collective actions. The problem of biophysical degradation can be ignored, as technological changes will take care of that.

Economic incentives will be able to defeat even the laws of thermodynamics of physics.

The foundations of effective demand economics come from the economic theory proposed by Michal Kalecki (1971 [1933]) and John Maynard Keynes (1936). The theory assumes that in the short run the levels of output and employment are determined by the expenditure behavior of social actors—the effective demand—to which producers react passively; moreover, the market solution is not necessarily with full employment. Therefore, the state has a role to play in the market system to reach full employment equilibrium. The state intervention doctrine is thus based on the principle of effective demand. Again, if you believe in this doctrine, you are assuming that nothing of significance has changed in the world capitalism in the last 80 years.

On the empirical refutation of the theory, unemployment in the capitalist world has always been with us. More significantly, the capitalist economy has never attained full employment in spite of the applications of Keynesian state policies. Unemployment is part of a more complex social problem—the excess labor supply—if one considers the capitalist system as composed of the First World and the Third World. Excess labor supply indeed takes the form of unemployment in the First World, and the forms of unemployment and mostly underemployment in the Third World. So far, we have been unable to observe full employment equilibrium in the capitalist system; on the contrary, general equilibrium under democratic capitalism is *always* with excess labor supply.

The foundations of classical economics come from the economic theory of Karl Marx (1938 [1867]). The theory assumes that capitalism is a class society, in which class struggle is part of its functioning. The theory predicts that in the long run the capitalist system is socially unviable and that its evolutionary process will imply increasing intensity in class struggle, which ultimately will lead to its collapse. The corresponding doctrine of class struggle to accelerate the breakdown of capitalism is thus based on the class theory of Marx. Again, if you are a believer of this doctrine, you are assuming that nothing of significance has changed in world capitalism in the last 150 years.

Empirically, capitalism is still a class society. Income and wealth inequality is still with us. The reserve army takes the form of unemployment in the First World and mostly underemployment in the Third World. Most notably, the capitalist system is still with us and the expected breakdown has not taken place. Furthermore, in the process of economic growth, real wage rates have increased, refuting the prediction of continuous *absolute* pauperization, although the *relative* pauperization of workers (inequality) is prominent.

Marxian economic theory assumes that the economic growth process is evolutionary, in which quantitative changes are accompanied by qualitative changes in society, such as relative pauperization of workers. However, Marxian economics has also ignored bio-economics, as Paul Sweezy acknowledged in the 1970s. Although bio-economics has recently been introduced into Marxian economics (cf. Burkett 2009), falsifiable models have not been developed. The assumption to ignore the biophysical environment in the economic process was fine to explain most of the past two centuries of capitalism. However, biophysical degradation is a new element in the economic process, which calls for new economics.

In sum, any scientific theory is an abstract representation of the real world. The use of abstraction implies the construction of scientific theories, in which each theory assumes what the essential elements that explain the real world are. The rest is ignored. Thus, the sin of a theory does not lie in making assumptions, which are necessary to construct an abstract world that seeks to resemble well the real social world; rather, it is having the wrong set of assumptions (ignoring elements that are essential), which can be discovered only by submitting the theory to the falsification process.

For some particular parts of the capitalist system, or for some particular research questions, or for some particular periods, each of these theories might have been valid. However, for the economic growth process, they are refuted by the empirical regularities of capitalism of the last five to six decades, as they are unable to explain economic growth with income inequality, biophysical degradation, and the consequent social maladies. On epistemological grounds, therefore, these three economic theories are rejected. Just to be sure, this conclusion has nothing to do with ideology. It is based on the composite epistemology, and the derived rules for scientific research in economics. Any researcher, following these rules, and accepting the empirical regularities, would necessarily reach this conclusion.

Conclusions

A fourth and final evolutionary model (IV) of the unified theory has been presented in this chapter. The model reduces all endogenous variables of the preceding models to QoS, measured by healthy life expectancy. The exogenous variable is the power structure. The current pro-growth policies will continue as long as the current power structure remains unchanged. These policies imply a particular trajectory of the QoS over time: an inverse-U curve overt time. The available data tends to corroborate the model's predictions. Thus, there is no reason to reject the model IV and, at this stage of our

research, we may accept it as a good approximation of capitalism under the new Anthropocene age.

Consequently, it was justified to derive the model's public
policy implications to discuss the science-based policy alternatives for the Anthropocene age. The chapter has extended the
policy implications to the world society as a whole. The alternative policies to the current pro-growth policies include no-
growth, income redistribution, and mineral resources saving
technological change. It is expected that with these policies
the inverse-U curve will be shifted upward, the implication of
which is to improve the QoS and retard the collapse of human
society, as we know it.

To change the current trajectory of growth with social maladies to a new trajectory of higher quality of life requires
higher order public policies to change the exogenous variable
of the model, that is, to dethrone the current power structure.
This in turn needs institutional innovations. Taking the capitalist system as given, the most important institutional innovation consists of dethroning the current electoral democracy
and replacing it with another form of democracy that gives
political power to the people, who in the case of capitalism are
the workers. Workers' democracy would imply a balance of
power. Under this new democratic rule, governments would
have the correct incentives to apply public policies for the
Anthropocene age, which will improve the current QoS trajectory. This institutional change would imply a re-foundation
of democratic capitalism.

Comparatively, the public policies derived from unified theory are strikingly different from those derived from other economic theories. Pro-growth policies are derived from
neoclassical economics, the standard theory. There are also differences with the fields of environment and ecological economics. A group seeks policies of ecologically sustainable

policies. No such sustainability exists according to the unified theory. Another group seek de-growth. Environment degradation in the form of pollution concentration in the atmosphere will continue even in this case, although at a lower rate of accumulation; hence, the QoS will not improve, unless the degree of inequality and technology are also changed.

In this book, unified theory has been submitted to further corroborations. By constructing evolutionary models, the theory is able to explain the role of markets and democracy—the fundamental institutions of capitalism—and that of power structure in the outcome of economic growth with social maladies. Unified theory can thus explain why and how we have ended up in the Anthropocene age. Furthermore, we need a new economics for the Anthropocene age. Therefore, the new economic principles that are consistent with the new age can be derived from unified theory. Unified theory is thus presented as the new economics of the Anthropocene age. Previous economic theories assumed implicitly the Holocene epoch; moreover, they assumed this age could last forever. Therefore, they have become old economics.

The public policies for the Anthropocene age lead to improved QoS at zero economic growth. How would a no-growth society operate? This question is discussed in the next chapter.

APPENDIX: THE EVOLUTIONARY MODEL IV

The set of relations established in the text can be summarized by the following set of equations. Equations (6.3), (6.4), (6.5), (6.6), and (6.7) are the structural equations of the model, Eq. (6.8) is the reduced form, Eq. (6.9) shows the dynamic trajectory of the endogenous variable, and Eqs. (6.11) and (6.12) resolve the changes in the trajectory due to change in the exogenous variables.

Symbols

QoS: quality of society; y: per capita income or output per worker; D: degree of income inequality; Π: concentration of pollution in atmosphere; r: growth rate of per capita income; λ: parameter of income inequality, increases with income redistribution policies; τ: technology parameter, increases with mineral resource saving innovations.

$$QoS = F(y, D, \Pi), \; F_1 > 0, \; F_2 < 0, \; F_3 < 0 \tag{6.3}$$

$$D = g(y, \lambda), \; g_1 > 0, \; g_2 < 0 \tag{6.4}$$

$$\Pi = h(y, \tau), \; h_1 > 0, \; h_2 < 0 \tag{6.5}$$

$$QoS = F(y, g(y, \lambda), h(y, \tau)) = G(y, \lambda, \tau) \tag{6.6}$$

$$y(T) = f(T, r, y_0), \; f_1 > 0, \; f_2 > 0, \; f_3 > 0 \tag{6.7}$$

$$QoS(T) = H(T, r, \lambda, \tau), \tag{6.8}$$

$H_1 > 0$ for $T < T$ and $H_1 < 0$ for $T > T$
$H_2 > 0$ for $T < T$ and $H_2 < 0$ for $T > T$
$H_3 > 0$
$H_4 > 0$

$$\partial QoS/\partial T = H_1 = \left[F_1 + F_2 \; g_1(y, \lambda) + F_3 \; h_1(y, \tau) \right] f_1$$
$$[(+)+(-)(+)+(-)(+)](+) \tag{6.9}$$

Thus, $H_1 > 0$ for $T < T$ and $H_1 < 0$ for $T > T$

$$\partial H_1/\partial r = \left[F_1 + F_2 \; g_1(y, \lambda) + F_3 \; h_1(y, \tau) \right] f_{12}$$
$$[(+)+(-)(+)+(-)(+)](+) \tag{6.10}$$

Thus, $\partial H_1/\partial r > 0$ for $T < T$ and $\partial H_1/\partial r < 0$ for $T > T$

$$\partial H_1 / \partial \lambda = f_1 \, F_2 \, g_{12} > 0 \qquad (6.11)$$
$$(+)(-)(-)$$

$$\partial H_1 / \partial \tau = f_1 \, F_3 \, h_{12} > 0 \qquad (6.12)$$
$$(+)(-)(-)$$

REFERENCES

Bonaiuti, M. (2011). *From bioeconomics to degrowth: Georgescu-Roegen's "new economics" in eight essays.* London, UK: Routledge.

Burkett, P. (2009). *Marxism and ecological economics.* Chicago, IL: Haymarket Books.

Chivian, E., & Bernstein, A. (Eds.). (2008). *Sustaining life: How human health depends on biodiversity.* New York: Oxford University Press.

Davies, J., Sandstrom, S., Shorrocks, A., & Wolf, E. (2010). The level and distribution of global household wealth. *Economic Journal, 121,* 223–254.

Jones, C., & Vollrath, D. (2013). *Introduction to economic growth* (3rd ed.). New York: Norton and Company.

Kalecki, M. (1971). *Selected essays in the dynamics of the capitalist economy 1933–1970.* Cambridge, UK: Cambridge University Press. Chapter 1 on effective demand was originally published in 1933 and Chapter 12 on capitalist threat in 1943.

Keynes, J. M. (1936). *The general theory of employment, interest, and money.* London: Macmillan.

Marx, K. (1938). *Capital* (Vol. 1–3). New York: International Publishers. Originally published in 1867.

McGlade, C., & Ekins, P. (2015). The geographical distribution of fossil fuels unused when limiting global warming to 2.6 °C. *Nature, 517,* 187–190. doi:10.1038/nature14016.

Piketty, T. (2014). *Capital in the twenty first century.* Cambridge, MA: Harvard University Press.

Smith, A. (1937). *An inquire into the nature and causes of the wealth of nations*. New York: Random House. Originally published in 1776.

Smith, B., & Zeder, M. (2013). The onset of the Anthropocene. *Anthropocene, 4,* 8–13.

Sweezy, P. (2017). A letter to Nicholas Georgescu-Roegen, July 31, 1974. *Monthly Review, 68*(9), 56–57.

Waters, C. N., et al. (2016). The Anthropocene is functionally and stratigraphically distinct from the Holocene. *Science, 351*(6269), aad2622.

Wilson, E. (1998). *Consilience: The unity of knowledge*. New York: Alfred Knopf.

Wolf, E. N. (2014, December). *Household wealth trends in the United States, 1962–2013*. Working Paper No. 20733. National Bureau of Economic Research, Cambridge, MA. Retrieved from http://www.nber.org/paper/w20733

CHAPTER 7

New Economic Principles for the Anthropocene Age

Since the end of World War II, the capitalist system has experienced rapid economic growth. Current generations only know a growing economy. A no-growth society is unknown. The arrival of the Anthropocene implies the end of the economic growth age. One of the new economic principles for the new age is zero-growth society. How would such a society function? The aim of this chapter is to present the new economic principles under which capitalism would function in the Anthropocene age.

GLOBAL PROBLEMS NEED GLOBAL GOVERNMENT

Globalization is usually seen as the increased integration of world markets of goods and financial assets. However, there are areas in which globalization is even stronger. Environment degradation and social disorder are not local problems, but global ones. Both constitute *the problem of the commons.*

In order to deal with global society, we would have to include non-capitalist societies in the analysis. Unified theory refers to the capitalist system only. Therefore, in what follows,

© The Author(s) 2017
A. Figueroa, *Economics of the Anthropocene Age*,
DOI 10.1007/978-3-319-62584-3_7

the assumption will be that capitalism is essential in the global society. Global society and capitalist society will be used interchangeably.

The biophysical environment is clearly the problem of the commons. This is just to indicate that greenhouse gases uniformly mix in the atmosphere independent of the location of emissions. Therefore, this is not a particular nation's problem, but a world problem, although governments are still national. Social order is also a problem of the commons. The excessive income inequality in the world leads to social disorder, which is not only national, but also global, such as international war and terrorism, illegal migration, illegal traffic of drugs, arms, and humans. As a result, we live in an increasingly inhospitable physical and social world. To tackle these fundamental problems of our time, which are global, we would need global policies. This implies a world government, a social innovation.

According to unified theory, the capitalist system as a whole, when First World and Third World countries are combined into one single society, can be seen, theoretically, as a sigma society: a society with several classes of citizens. Because local sigma societies are second-class societies compared to local epsilon societies, the political entitlement inequality is much higher in the capitalist system when taken as a whole relative to local situations. This hierarchy also originates in the legacy of the European colonial history of the world (Figueroa 2015). The implication is that power structure is more concentrated at the global level than at the local.

If a global government were established following the rules of electoral democracy, it would result in plutocratic governments with perverse incentives to seek the common good, as in the case of local governments (Chap. 2). The perverse incentives to seek the common good found in local electoral democracy could be even greater in the global electoral democracy.

Institutional innovations about other forms of democracy, at local and global levels, are then needed, with the aim of generating QOS-efficient governments. (To recall, QOS stands for quality of society.) These innovations should be able to eliminate the power of the economic and political elites over workers, the power of transnational corporations over local governments, the power of the First World over the Third World, and the power of first-class citizens over second-class citizens in the Third World. Thus, a new balance of power between capitalists and workers of the world needs to be established.

The standard concept of democracy is *the government of the people, by the people, and for the people*. As shown in Chap. 2, electoral democracy does not fit this concept and leads to perverse incentives in the behavior of governments. Moreover, electoral democracy implies the transfer of political power from the people to the politicians who are elected as government. Electoral democracy increases even more the power structure of society.

The word "people" in this concept of democracy assumes a classless society or an equal society. In a class society, such as a capitalist one, the people, the masses, are the workers. Therefore, the concept of democracy should be reformulated as follows: Democracy in a capitalist society is the government of the workers, by the workers, and for the workers. Thus, this type of democracy has been called *workers' democracy* in this book.

The democratic rule of selection for global government officials cannot be based on the rule of electoral democracy, for that would again lead to plutocracy. Some new method of selection must be invented to eliminate plutocracy and its perverse incentives in a global government. Chapter 2 discussed the method of sortition democracy as an alternative to electoral democracy. However, more research on theoretical and empirical work or historical experiences is still needed to find new democratic forms, which should imply political power elimination and an incentive system that is conducive to the common good policies. Any form of democracy with these characteristics would lead to a global society that is self-regulated, where social maladies are eliminated endogenously, which could be called a QOS-efficient democracy.

The concept of efficiency in the Anthropocene age implies moving the quality of the society trajectory upward as much as possible (Fig. 6.1). Governments under electoral democracy have no incentives to do this, but governments under workers' democracy should. The new institution of democracy is meant to reduce the current power structure at national and international levels. For one thing, this new rule implies the elimination of the political class and the returning of political power to workers. The economic elite will still concentrate capital, but workers will concentrate political power. A balance of power will exist.

A new form of democracy that replaces electoral democracy implies an institutional change, change in the political rules and in the political organizations, that is, a new state. The market system, the other institution of capitalism, will remain unchanged. It will function under the same rules and with the same organizations: firms and households. We should remember that the market system is just a mechanism, not a causal factor. Therefore, the market system will now solve a different set of structural equations—including the new policy priorities of workers' democracy—which will lead to different results of prices and quantities of equilibrium, and a different income distribution.

According to the unified theory of capitalism, in the economic growth process, the endogenous variables are the increase in per capita income over time accompanied by social maladies. The exogenous variable is the power structure. The capitalist system is not self-regulated to eliminate social maladies. The persistence of social maladies reflects the power of the economic and political elites. To transform the capitalist system into a self-regulated system requires, according to the theory, a change in the current power structure. This in turn implies institutional innovations. The challenges of the Anthropocene age economics require a global government based upon new principles of democracy.

We have lived in a growth-mania society since post-World War II. Hence, the endeavor to shift to a no-growth society will be a major human endeavor. The capitalist class will certainly resist this change. However, governments under workers' democracy will be in favor.

The evolutionary model assumes that mineral resources are the *limitative factor* of production; that is, mineral resources inputs, as materials and energy source, can hardly be substituted by capital or labor, which means that the increase in the use of mineral resource inputs is a necessary condition but not a sufficient one to increase total output. Consequently, zero mineral resources as inputs imply zero total output. The implication of this assumption is that controlling the exploitation of mineral resources at the world scale would be a means to control total world output.

Currently, exploration and exploitation of mineral resources are in private hands, while the property of the deposits is state owned. However, the stock of minerals in the crust of the Earth is treated as if it were a free good. No one pays for the social cost of the depletion of the stock. Furthermore, the waste generated by the use of mineral resources is dumped into the atmosphere with zero private cost of disposal. No one pays for the social cost of the consequent pollution of the atmosphere either. The stock of mineral resources and the clear skies are gifts of Mother Nature. Mother Nature has no cashier. Conceptually, therefore, depletion and pollution are part of the problem of the commons—the tragedy of the commons.

Therefore, the new rule would have to call for a World Authority in charge of the management of mineral resources to eliminate the problem of the commons. Now somehow Mother Nature will have its cashier. Then, depletion and pollution will not be free, but will have the market price. This price will be the instrument to control the degradation of the environment. However, pricing is not enough. At the market price, private demand might be so inelastic that quantities could hardly be diminished. Quantity restrictions will then be needed as a complementary policy instrument, so that depletion of the stock of mineral resources and the pollution of the atmosphere can really be under control. The well-being of future generations can thus be taken into account.

The exploitation of renewable natural resources also constitutes the commons problem. Fisheries and forests are mostly open access, with limited property rights. They are subject to overexploitation (beyond their rate of self-regeneration), and are becoming scarcer. The same problem applies to ecological biodiversity. No one is willing to pay for the reproduction of renewable natural resources. Mother Nature has no cashier in this case either. Therefore, a World Authority will also be needed in this case.

Currently the attempts to control the environment through government agreements have been a failure. Facts have revealed to us that this is the case. In a survey article for the 100th Anniversary of *The American Economic Review*, one reads the following conclusion: "Conventional regulatory policies have been excessively costly, ineffective, and even counterproductive. The problems behind what Harding [in his classic work of 1968] characterized as 'the tragedy of the commons' might better be described as the failure of commons regulations" (Stavins 2011, p. 182).

According to the unified theory, this failure is not surprising. Governments under electoral democracy do not have incentives to seek the common good and are subordinated to the private interests of the capitalist class. In the new context, the collective control of the environment will come from governments of new forms of democracy.

Currently, capitalist countries show increase in output per person or output per worker over time. According to the unified theory, the economic growth process takes the following form along the growth frontier curve. Consider again the limitational production function presented in Eq. (6.1), Chap. 6, as a system of two equations. Assume the first equation is homogeneous of degree one, implying constant returns to scale on two factors: capital (K) and the combined labor technology (AL). Suppose population grows at the rate of 2% per year, as does labor supply. If physical capital grows at 5% per year, and technological change at 3%, and labor employed at 2%, which combined is also 5%, then total output will grow at the rate of 5% as well.

These rates imply a growth of output per worker of 3% (the difference between growth rates of total output and population), which is equal to the growth rate of technological change (factor A). Thus, the source of economic growth is technological change. This growth process is repeated period after period, which leads to environment degradation continuously and irrevocable due to the laws of thermodynamics, via the pollution effect of output growth, as indicated in Eq. (6.2) of the limitational production process.

The no-growth capitalist society will perform differently. Output per worker will remain fixed. Therefore, the growth rate of technology (factor A) will be zero. Now the dynamic equilibrium in the long run, with a fixed technology (A), is obtained when the capital stock grows at the same rate of population growth rate (2%), which implies growth of total output also at 2%. This dynamic equilibrium along the growth frontier curve, with constant per capita income, could be repeated period after period, although for some finite time only, until the period of breakdown, given by the pollution effect, is reached. Therefore, no-growth society does not imply steady-state equilibrium, for such equilibrium is only temporary—it is a mirage—under an entropic economic process. To be sure, under entropic economic process, economic growth is unsustainable, but no growth is unsustainable too!

What is significant in the no-growth society case is that the use of mineral resources as mater and energy inputs will increase at the same rate as total output, that is, at 2% (vs. the 5% in the pro-growth society). Therefore, the depletion rate of the stock of mineral resources will decline and consequently the pollution rate will too. The current breakdown period will be postponed.

No Growth Implies Income Redistribution

Consider a no-growth situation everywhere in the capitalist society starting *now*. Hence, the current production and distribution situation in world capitalism would be congealed. Then this would be the initial condition of the new economic process under the Anthropocene age. The implication is that we would start with the current income gaps within and between countries. We would be congealing the current degree of excessive income inequality! This would

Table 7.1 World capitalism: income distribution, circa 2005

Group	Population	Per capita income	Total income
World	100.0	1.00	100.0
First World	*21.0*	*3.24*	*67.9*
Capitalists			17.0
Workers 1	21.0	2.43	50.9
Third World	*79.0*	*0.41*	*32.1*
Capitalists			8.0
Workers 1	39.5	0.41	16.1
Workers 2	39.5	0.20	8.0

Notes: (1) First World countries correspond to "High Income" and Third World to "Low and Middle Income" less "Eastern Europe and Central Asia" (ex-Soviet Union) and less China in the categories of World Bank. Population, Per capita Income, and Total Income come directly from the World Bank data. Total income is net national product (NNP), which is equal to 0.9 of GDP (standard assumption). (2) The share of capitalists in total income refers to profits/NNP, which is equal to 0.25 in both the First World and the Third World (Gollin 2002, Table 2, p. 470). Population share of capitalists are ignored, assuming that it is less than 1%. (3) In the Third World, Workers 1 refer to wage earners and Workers 2 to the self-employed in the subsistence sector; assuming equal shares in total labor force and assuming 2:1 ratio in average incomes (Figueroa 2010, Tables 5 and 6), their shares in total income were determined. The resulting wage rate ratios for Workers 1 in the First World and the Third World is nearly eight times, which is consistent with the ratio of six times for minimum wages estimated by ILO (2010, Table SA2)

Source: World Bank (World Development Indicators, Table 1). Taken from Web page: http://data.worldbank.org/indicator/NY.GDP.PCAP.PP.CD?end=2015& start=2014

maintain the high degree of social disorder and thus the low quality of society. Improvement in the quality of society would require income redistribution, as shown in Fig. 6.1c, Chap. 6.

Table 7.1 presents an estimate of the current income inequality of world capitalism. The rich First World constitutes nearly 20% of the total population but gets two-thirds of the total income, which implies that the remaining one-third goes to the 80% of the population living in the poor Third World. This is a significant degree of inequality, as it implies a gap in per capita income of eight times.

The share of profits is 25% of total income, which is received by the capitalist class. The size of the capitalist class is not easy to determine. However, most studies have found that it is very small, less than 1% of the population. Inequality among workers is another feature. Differences in average wage rates between wage earners in the two regions imply a gap of around six times. Workers who are self-employed in the sub-sistence sector in the Third World are the poorest in this region and thus in the capitalist system taken as a whole.

Figure 7.1 shows the same data of Table 7.1, but in the framework of the unified theory. Panel (a) depicts the current situation in production and distribution in the First World and panel (b), the same in the Third World. In each panel, the vertical axis measures output per worker and the horizontal axis the labor force. Suppose the rates of labor participation in total population are homogenous everywhere, then we can use output per worker as equivalent to per capita income, and labor force in lieu of total population to transform the data of Table 7.1 into the distribution of total income by labor force.

According to unified theory, the Third World operates with a capitalist sector and a subsistence sector, whereas the First World with the capitalist sector alone. Curves A' and A" show average labor productivity or output per worker in the capital-ist sectors, whereas curves M' and M" represent the corre-sponding marginal labor productivity. The assumption that firms seek to maximize profits implies that the real wage rate must be equal to the marginal labor productivity. The differ-ence between the average and the marginal productivities is the profit per worker. Therefore, the shaded areas indicate the share of total profits in each region and the remaining areas in

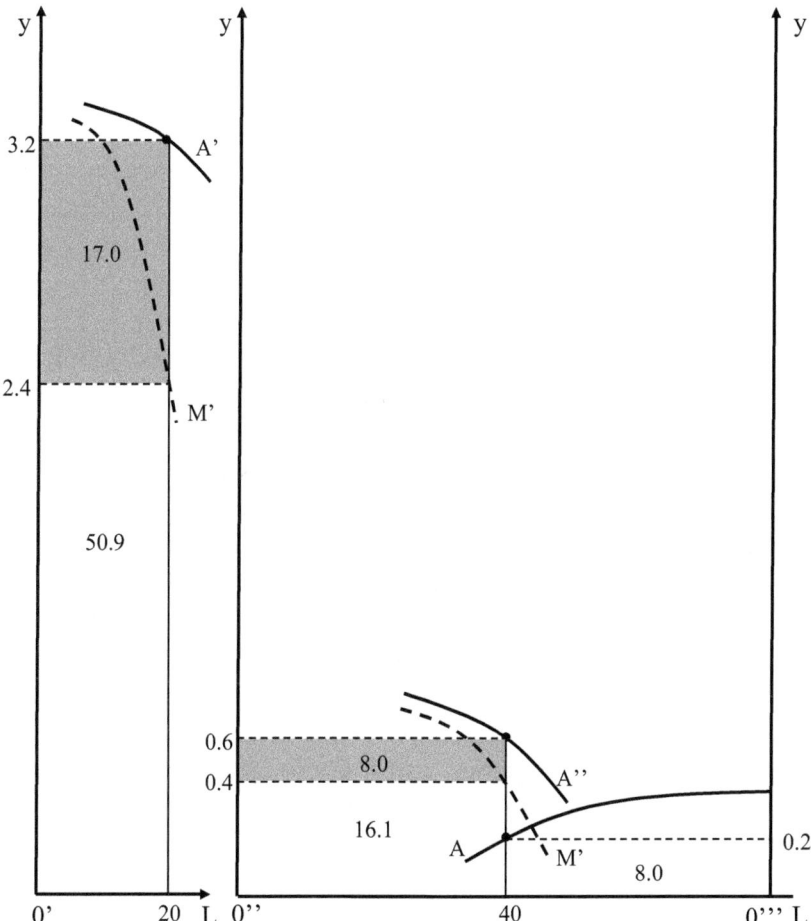

Fig. 7.1   Production and distribution in the capitalist system, circa 2005

blank are the share of wages. In the Third World, the average labor productivity in the subsistence sector is represented by the curve A, which is also subject to diminishing returns.

The excess labor supply takes the form of unemployment in the First World, whereas unemployment (relatively small) and underemployment (the dominant form, half of the labor force) does in the Third World. Because unemployment rates lie mostly in the range of 2–10% of the labor force in both regions, they are ignored in Fig. 7.1.

Note that Fig. 7.1 is constructed on scale; hence, it shows the actual figures of the production and distribution situation in the current world capitalism. The difference in labor productivity *levels*—the position of the curves—between the capitalist sectors is certainly an important feature of the production process in world capitalism. The average labor productivity of the subsistence sector in the Third World shows the lowest level. According to unified theory, differences in physical capital, human capital, and technology level with which workers are equipped explain the gaps in labor productivity levels.

Given this difference in the levels of average labor productivity, the observed differences in the wage rates should not come as surprise. The market wage rate of equilibrium cannot be independent of the average labor productivity, but a fraction of it. According to standard economics, international trade was supposed to be the mechanism to equalize real wages across countries. This has not happened and it could hardly happen, unless the average productivity levels were equalized across countries. What the graph suggests is that the Third World is able to compete in international trade with those relatively low labor productivities because their real wage rates are also relatively low.

Suppose the objective of a global redistribution policy is to *double* the income of the poorest of the capitalist system, namely, the workers at the bottom 40%, who are self-employed in the subsistence sector of the Third World, and who receive 8% of the global total income. This could be achieved, for instance, by transferring *half of the profits* received by the capitalist class in the First World, the share of which is 17%. Given the high degree of inequality, this transfer does not seem an excessive burden for the capitalist class.

The average income of the bottom 40% could then be doubled *now* with redistribution. The alternative to attain this increase is via economic growth. This can also be seen in Fig. 7.1. Economic growth in the Third World means the continuous upward shift of the average labor productivity of the capitalist sector, curve A''. The growth in the capitalist sector will imply a growth in the average income in the subsistence sector through labor absorption, given the diminishing labor returns. However, it would take many years to have the income doubled, depending on the growth rate of the capitalist sector. Following the famous "rule of 72," if the growth rate in the subsistence sector were 2% per year, it would take 36 years to double the income level of the subsistence sector. Hence, for the poor, a well-designed income redistribution is a superior alternative to economic growth. Thus, the poor would have the incentive to favor income redistribution policies instead of pro-growth policies.

The poorest of the Third World could benefit with redistribution on two accounts. Their income could be raised significantly by the between-country redistributions, as shown above, but also by within-country redistributions. Workers' democracy at global and local levels would have the incentives to carry out these policies.

This redistribution exercise shows that income redistribution is a fine policy to improve the real income of the poor population. Given the current high degree of income inequality, redistribution policy even competes favorably with the alternative pro-growth alternative. Therefore, and contrary to what the current discourse says, economic growth is not necessary to have social progress and income redistribution is not "redistribution of poverty" either. The policy of no-growth society with income redistribution in the Anthropocene age would lead to a higher quality of society, as shown in Fig. 6.1 (Chap. 6).

Income redistribution cannot be reduced to cash transfers only. This transfer would certainly imply more cash income for the poor, but they will remain poor people, that is, they will become "poor people with money." Higher money income can hardly improve the quality of life, the living standard, the degree of citizenship of the poor, as the experience with cash transfers has already shown. The theory of capabilities predicts this outcome (Sen 1992). Investment in improving human capabilities, such as health, education, social protection against risk would have to be included in the redistribution policy. The poor would then become a superior human being, a first-class citizen, a true member of society.

Redistribution policies of this type would have the effect of reducing the growth rate of population. Consider the theory that assumes that people see their children as assets. Then, the number of children of families will depend negatively upon their real income or real wealth and upon the social protection of society. This theory predicts that the poor families will have more children than the rich. This prediction is consistent with facts, in particular, when we compare the Third World with the First World. Increasing the welfare of the poor will reduce the population growth rate of society and the pressure upon depletion and pollution would be diminished.

The question is how to make redistribution policy socially viable. The transfer cited above will be unthinkable under the current power structure, especially under the current electoral democracy. Political and economic elites have no incentives to do that. People's egotist drive, which is increasingly dominant, will also oppose it. However, under the new institutions, under a new form of democracy, this policy would be socially viable. The policy of no growth with redistribution requires an institutional change in the current democratic capitalism, as discussed earlier.

Income redistribution from the First World to the Third World would be necessary for a world of peace and social order. Again, under the current institutions, this would be unviable. Not only would economic and political elites oppose it, workers of the First World would too. However, new forms of local democracy and global democracy would generate incentives in favor of redistribution.

We know that economic equilibrium under the current democratic capitalism is with inequality, with excess inequality. Thus, inequality can be seen as a social imposition. The poor are not able to choose between being poor and not being poor. Inequality makes profits viable and then capitalism viable. (Profits originate in the capitalist system because the wage rate is a fraction of average labor productivity, as illustrated in Fig. 7.1.) Therefore, an income transfer from the rich to the poor does not mean that the poor "get something for nothing," as the prevailing discourse of the elites says, while transfers to the wealthy through the public budget means "getting something for something," such as employment creation. On the contrary, not redistributing, concentrating the fruits of economic growth, has led society to live under social disorder. Redistribution is a way to reduce the social imposition upon the relatively poor.

No growth with redistribution is a policy to improve the quality of society (Chap. 6). It is not that the poor are receiving a transfer for nothing. It is a method to attain the common good. So everyone will benefit with redistribution, not only the poor, but also the wealthy. The capitalist system would still operate with property rights and the firms' drive would still be profits, but the common good would be the social objective of public policies. Workers also seek their own interests, but they would have to comply with the new rule: quality of society is a common good and has priority. Individual interests are not above the common interest as before, just the opposite.

Currently, egotism runs very strong. The profit motive leads businesses to produce modern goods, which may harm people, yet they induce people to consume these goods. This market exchange leads to higher expenditures in health services, which are financed not out of profits, but out of taxpayers' money. The profit motive also leads firms to produce goods and dump the resulting waste into the atmosphere (costless disposal), but then pollution harms people, which leads to higher expenditure in health services, not paid out of profits, but out of taxpayers' money. These are examples in which private profits are subsidized with public funds. The new form of democracy is the innovation that would be able to stop these practices applying the needed incentives, which include stopping economic growth.

Consumerism is another side effect of economic growth that the new rule of no growth can stop. For example, durable goods need not be replaced if in good condition just because the social imposition of consumerism or the mode dictates to do so. Durables can make it last longer by alterations and repairs. Recently, the Sweden government set economic incentives for repairing durable consumption goods instead of buying new ones. As this example shows, quality of life need not decrease in a no-growth society.

No-growth society does not imply lower standard of living for everyone. It does imply a context in which the scarcity of material goods generates incentives for abandoning the current "American way of life." This lifestyle is based more on exosomatic gadgets rather than on endosomatic instruments. The new economic principle is that the less physical goods are utilized to satisfy human needs and wants, society will be better off. The current individual motivation is for consuming and having or consuming more goods, which, given the scarcity of material goods, could be replaced by the motivation of seeking to become a superior human being. The new incentives are for replacing the "American way of life," which corresponds to the Holocene age, for another, simpler lifestyle that is consistent with the Anthropocene age.

According to the unified theory, rising individualism and egotism have accompanied economic growth under capitalism. The arrival of the Anthropocene age has meant the end of this evolutionary process, including the end of individualism and egotism. Therefore, the egotist human drive would tend to go in reverse in the new age, under the context of no growth and redistribution. Again, the new form of democracy would have to rely more on social incentives—instead of economic incentives only as is the case today—to reinforce the altruist human drive. This new democracy should be able to change human behavior in the direction of seeking the common good. The techniques of behavioral engineering utilized today by the economic and political elites for their own benefits could now be applied, but for the common good.

Today's capitalist society has no choice, but to become a new society, under new institutions, where the common good, not the individual interest, has the social priority. To continue under the current institutions, with individualism and egotism at its highest development, would imply both decreasing the quality of society and minimizing the period of human species survival. This is what unified theory predicts if the current economic growth continues.

No Growth Implies Breaking the Link Between Income and Employment

Economic growth under capitalism has been with persistent excess labor supply. Since the industrial revolution, technological change has implied more and more complex machines.

Mechanical energy has substituted the physical energy of workers, but the human mental capabilities have been required to operate the more intricate machines. These new technologies have been mostly labor saving. Therefore, in the economic growth process, where the average labor productive curve is shifted upward continuously, we observed increases in both wage employment and real wage rates.

In the last decades, the process of technological change has shifted from new machineries to the electronic chip revolution. Computers, smart machines, and robots are replacing workers mental functions. A smart machine can in principle replace jobs that consist in following specific instructions (an algorithm or routine). The main losers in the first industrial revolution were horses, not humans; in the current smart machine revolution, it appears that workers, and particularly unskilled workers, will be the main losers. The new technology is still labor saving, but with a stronger bias.

Therefore, *both* labor wage employment and real wage rates could hardly increase at the same rate as they did in the economic growth process of the first decades of the 1950s. This period of rapid growth with stable inequality has been called the "golden age of capitalism."

The effect of the new technology of the last decades is reflected, in part, in the increase in excess labor supply. The other effect is further increase in income inequality. Smart machine technology tends to increase the share of profits in national income, as labor costs diminish in total value added in the main industries. This technology tends to generate more jobs for the well-educated and the creative relative to the mechanical jobs. Therefore, income inequality among workers also tends to increase. This new distribution effect, rooted in new smart machine technology, is already included in the evolutionary model of unified theory, as the increase in income inequality that accompanies economic growth (Fig. 1.2, Chap. 1).

The electronic chip revolution has come at the time when capitalism is showing economic growth with social maladies, which refer to rising income inequality and degradation of the biophysical environment. The new technology leads to the production of more gadgets, which promote modernization and economic growth. It has come at the wrong time, at the Anthropocene age, at the time of shifting pro-growth capitalism to a no-growth society. This new technology can hardly facilitate the solution of social maladies. It was not designed for this either. It is the outcome of profit motives. The new technology is not part of the solution, but rather part of the problem now. We have an additional problem to solve, namely, the need of social innovations to solve social maladies created by technological innovations that go in the wrong direction.

Therefore, the problem of labor displacement by smart machines also requires institutional innovations. Economist Wassily Leontief (1983), who has studied the long-run process of technological displacement of labor, suggested two innovations: labor-sharing mechanisms (instead of having one part of the population fully employed and the other totally excluded) and income redistribution policies. The latter has already been discussed above. The technological labor displacement problem just reinforces the need for the new rule of income redistribution. Labor sharing is indeed a particular form of income redistribution among workers. Full employment policies are not helpful now, as shown above.

The old rule was that income and employment constitute the outcome of the same economic process. Labor productivity (output per worker) depends upon where the worker is employed and how he or she is equipped with physical capital, human capita, technology, and the pull of workers.

Furthermore, the market wage rate depends upon the labor productivity level. This rule is no longer viable, for the consequent excess supply of labor might be socially intolerable. The new principle in the Anthropocene age will call for weakening the connection between labor income and labor productivity.

For a meaningful discussion, we need a theory of labor markets. According to unified theory, labor markets in epsilon societies operate differently from sigma. In epsilon type societies, Walrasian wages are relevant. However, the market wage rate of equilibrium in any labor market will take a value that is above the Walrasian value. This is known as the efficiency wage rate, for it maintains the labor discipline that is needed to attain high levels of labor productivity. Unemployment is the labor discipline device. Then labor market equilibrium is necessarily with unemployment. This is the current rule.

A new rule would consist in giving the unemployed worker an income that is a fraction of the market real wage. This gap would maintain the incentives for labor market competition. This would be a kind of guaranteed minimum incomes for workers in society, as a right. The total minimum income would come through taxes from the global profits of the society. In a way, the guaranteed minimum income would be like the current unemployment insurance, except that its coverage would be wider and for longer periods. It is a new rule, for it gives workers the right to receive a share of the global profits, whenever they are excluded from contributing to those profits. Minimum wage policies would not be necessary.

In sigma type societies, Walrasian wages may be relevant for some labor markets, but not for the majority, which operate under overpopulation. This type of society is overpopulated. The excess of labor supply is so large that seeking jobs as unemployed is not good allocation of time and workers seek instead to find ways to make income as self-employed in the subsistence sector. The gap between the market wage rate and the marginal income in the subsistence sector is the labor discipline device in these cases. Unemployment is not. Labor is then allocated to the capitalist sector as wage earner and the excess labor supply is found in the subsistence sector in which the average income from self-employed is a fraction of the market wage rate. This is how efficiency wages theory works in sigma society. Hence, the majority of workers in the subsistence sector make incomes that are below the market wage rate, which is to say, they are not unemployed, but underemployed. This is the rule now.

As a new rule, consider transferring the underemployed worker an income that is a fraction of the market wage rate. This would be a kind of guaranteed minimum income for workers in society, as a right. The total minimum income would come, through taxes, from the global profits of the society. Again, it is a new rule, for it gives workers the right to receive a share of the global profits, whenever they are excluded from contributing to those profits. Minimum wage policies would not be necessary in this case either.

Compared to the current situation, these new rules would reduce inequality among workers and between workers and capitalists. They constitute mechanisms to redistribute income and maintaining, at the same time, the incentives for labor market competition.

Standard macroeconomics says that to increase wage employment, higher aggregate demand is needed, which will lead firms to produce more goods. However, more goods imply more pollution. This economic principle would not work in the Anthropocene age. Moreover, the fact is that full employment has never been attained under capitalism, and never will, as explained by the unified theory. However, the policy to improve the lot of the unemployed and underemployed would not be the full employment policy, but the new economic principles, such as income redistribution and minimum guaranteed income.

No Growth Implies Developing Meta-Innovations

Currently, both private and public sectors finance scientific research and technological innovations. These activities are thus based on the self-interest of economic and political elites. Researchers and innovators are not driven for the motivation of solving social problems or the problem of the commons, for that is unprofitable for the elites. This is why most technological solutions do not lead to social solutions.

For example, profit motive would lead to technological innovations that are labor saving, for they lead to higher profits than capital saving innovations. Scarcity or higher relative prices of material inputs will induce elites to seek innovations saving their utilization in production. In the case of the environment, energy prices have not increased steadily over time to induce new technologies that are fossil energy saving. Dumping waste into the atmosphere has been costless disposal, which has generated no incentives to seek technologies to avoid pollution, for it is a public good problem. New social technologies to deal with social maladies are also neglected under profit-driven innovations.

We are living in an age of a new technological revolution, which includes artificial intelligence, the Internet, robots, nanotechnology, and biotechnology. It occurs at the Anthropocene age, but it is not directed to solve environmental problems. It occurs at the age of highest income inequality, and yet it is not directed to deal with this social problem. To adopt those innovations as they come will not help us in solving today's fundamental problems. The fact that we have lived a long period of economic growth with social maladies reveals that these innovations have not changed the course of history. That would have happened just by accident, not by design, given the selfish motivations underlying the social actors responsible for the innovations. These types of technological innovations are endogenously determined, but they do not make democratic capitalism a self-regulated system.

In the Anthropocene age, the social demand for scientific research and innovations has clear priorities: reduce the degradation of the biophysical environment and reduce the degree of economic and social inequality in world capitalism. More generally, innovations should make the no-growth age socially viable.

Some of the priorities include technological innovations that are reducing pollution per unit of mineral resources used in production coupled with reducing the mineral resource per unit of output, also innovations in saving water resources and in saving agricultural soil. The risk that these unitary savings can be overcome by the production of a higher total output, as is the case today, is eliminated by the no-growth policy.

The fundamental problem of our time could not be solved by technological innovations alone. Social innovations and institutional innovations are also essential. Therefore, the social and institutional innovations and the technological innovations that the no-growth society needs call for interdisciplinary research. The scientific research that can lead to the needed innovations would have to include works in the natural sciences and the social sciences, taken separately and jointly, to attain unity of knowledge. The new form of democracy, local and global, is, according to unified theory, one of the fundamental   institutional   innovations   in   need   of interdisciplinary research. Thus, quality of society progress could be generated efficiently.

The Anthropocene age is the age of the common good, not of the private interests. Therefore, the much needed technological and institutional innovations can hardly be the outcome of profit motives. It must be carefully planned and the appropriate incentive system established. This implies the development of *meta-innovations*: innovations to generate innovations, which should lead to technologies to generate technologies. Making a no-growth society socially viable is quite a challenge. Innovations of higher order are needed.

THE ECONOMIC PROCESS UNDER THE NEW INSTITUTIONS

How would social actors behave under the new institutions?

The institutions of society shape the rationality of individuals. This is the basic assumption of the science of economics. Thus, under the current capitalist system, it is rational for individuals to act guided by self-interest.

Under the new institutions, capitalism remains a class society. Capitalists and workers are the basic social classes. The new form of democracy is meant to equalize the citizenship class—equalize political entitlements—in the capitalist system taken as a whole. This implies equalization in political entitlements *within* the Third World and *between* the Third World and the First World. The new democratic rule will eliminate political power and thus reduce the concentration of the current power structure. With the democratic reform, there would be a balance of power, as workers would capture the state and have political power and capitalists will retain economic power. The new government under workers' democracy would then have the correct incentive system to seek the common good. Therefore, the new institutions imply a re-foundation of the capitalist system. A new type of capitalism will operate in the new Anthropocene age.

In the new institutional context, people will find out that being egotist is not rational. People would still be free to choose what they want subject to their budget constraints, but now also subject to the new economic rules, as indicated earlier. People need not become altruists, but they will find it rational to stop behaving as they did in the old society, guided by egotism, even by voracious self-interest and greediness, and against the common good.

The liberal economic rule is free markets. Free from what? One could think free from monopolies and oligopolies. However, the doctrine of liberalism refers to free market as free from state intervention. State intervention is considered an intrusion into individual freedom. If the state happens to regulate some activities and sets fees and other penalties for infractions, liberalism defends and justifies the "revenge of the market" (such as illegal behavior) to those intrusions. Under the current rules of capitalism, selfish individuals exercise their freedom when the individual decides to obey or not to obey the law, taking into account the penalty of not obeying just as a price of a good, similar to the price to be paid to buy bread. The implication is that the individual will is above the law. State regulation is thus limited.

In the Anthropocene age, state regulation in the use of natural resources has to be effective. Individual egotism cannot be above the law. The individual should not choose to disobey the law just because the price to pay if disobeyed is affordable and, therefore, it is rational to continue doing business and polluting the environment at his or her will. Under the new institutions, money cannot buy everything.

Under the new institutions, capitalists and politicians cannot manipulate people's preferences as in the current democratic capitalist system. Capitalists will not have the power that they used to have and politicians would have been eliminated as a social group. However, the new state may need to influence people's preferences, reversing the old society's influences. We know from biology that people's behavior can change and that society does change it. Therefore, it is not a question of using or not using behavioral engineering techniques to influence people's behavior, for it is done all the time. In education, in religion, in politics, in markets. The question is how to use it for the common good, not for private interests, as is done today.

The market system would continue to play the role of the mechanism to solve for equilibrium prices and quantities in market exchange. However, the power of the capitalist class is reduced because the old power structure has been reduced. Market equilibrium with excess labor supply would still prevail, and would continue to play the role of labor discipline device. Market equilibrium with income inequality would also prevail. However, postmarket income inequality would be continuously reduced, according to the new economic rules of income redistribution. The market equilibrium with degradation of the biophysical environment would also prevail, but the degree of degradation, which is irrevocable by the law of entropy, would be lower. Therefore, the outcome from the new economic process would be characterized by no growth but higher quality of society.

Therefore, under the new institutions, people would live in a higher quality of society, where the social and biophysical environments are both of better quality, where people can live a better quality of life, develop their human potentials, and exercise their individual freedom but subject to the common good. The individual would not be able to place his or her own interests on top of the common good any longer, as is the case today.

Furthermore, because the intergenerational problem has been internalized in the new institutions, the common good includes the well-being of future generations. However, the problem of the finite survival time of the human species remains unresolved. With the new institutions, this big economic problem can be addressed in an intelligent way, which implies collectively, as it deals with a public good.

The current economic and political elites have the incentives to seek pro-growth policies over any other social objective because the elites are the main beneficiaries of the growth process. Not only have they benefited with higher relative incomes, but also the major benefit has been to maintain the privileged position they hold in society. Economic and political elites have created the discourse that economic growth is a necessary and sufficient condition for social progress. Economic growth is sold as a panacea. Facts have refuted this discourse. Economic growth has been conducive to social maladies and to the new Anthropocene age. Now we are finding ourselves discussing how to stop economic growth and how to live under a zero-growth society.

ENDOSOMATIC VERSUS EXOSOMATIC WAYS OF LIFE

Economist Nicholas Georgescu-Roegen (1971) borrowed from biologist Alfred Lotka the categories of endosomatic and exosomatic instruments to explain the nature of the economic process. Living creatures other than humans use for their survival only endosomatic instruments: those that are part of the individual organisms by birth (feet and wings). A bird flies after an insect with its own wings, which by nature are the bird's individual property. Humans also use their endosomatic instruments (feet and hands), but in addition have been able to create exosomatic instruments (machines, domesticated animals of burden, and consumption gadgets). Thus, humans were initially able to produce goods with the use of their own energy alone, later on they utilized the energy of domesticated animals, and then introduced machines, which require energy from fossils. Furthermore, the goods that humans produce today include not only food, but also processed food, and many consumption gadgets. Today humans have turned into creatures who are dependent for their livelihood on exosomatic instruments.

The scale of this stock of exosomatic instruments today must be very large. If the human species disappeared over-night, then the Earth's surface will not be like the moon's surface, but would appear covered by new and old machines, cell phones, smart phones, robots, computers, refrigerators, washing machines, cars, and many other man-made instruments. We should not forget guns and arms in this list!

Economic growth has implied technological change and the modernization of human life. Hence, economic growth has implied the production of more and more exosomatic instruments for that modernization. The production of exosomatic instruments is mineral resource intensive, for they need both matter and energy. We can then understand why in only a few decades of economic growth, the degradation of the biophysical environment has been so rapid.

Changes in lifestyle in no-growth society would imply a new lifestyle that is less dependent on material goods. Labor services are also part of social enjoyment of life. Consuming less goods and more labor services than is the case today would imply saving exosomatic instruments and having a consumption basket that is more intensive in endosomatic instruments. Music, art, science, and sports are among these services, to which we may add leisure time devoted to socializing. The consumption of these services would qualitatively make a society truly advanced and with higher quality of life than today. For one thing, producing fewer quantities of goods, which implies less depletion and pollution, people will be able to enjoy a healthier and more secure life. Furthermore, people will be socially valued not for the exosomatic instruments they have (a social imposition of today), but for whether they are better human beings. Actually, the latter is the only choice we humans have in the Anthropocene age.

Therefore, a zero-growth society need not imply human sacrifices, but it does imply another institutions, such as income redistribution and production re-structuring: more consumption of public goods and less of private consumption goods, more labor services and less material goods in consumption, more goods and services that satisfy genuine human needs and less socially driven consumption. Zero-growth society does not imply human sacrifices; it does imply living differently, living a more human life, away from the "American way of life," which is a social imposition and reflects the current power structure.

Institutional change does not imply transforming a capitalist society into a communist society. The reason is that the elites of communist societies also seek economic growth maximization. The case of China is clear. China did not ask permission from the rest of the world to contaminate the only skies we have, and has just implemented her new economic growth policy. Therefore, the debate on capitalism versus communism also belongs to the old economics.

According to modern economics, the fundamental economic problem of our time is how to construct a zero-growth society. This requires new institutions, other than those of the current capitalist and communist societies. This is against the usual view that the fall of communism has meant the end of history. According to the unified theory, we are just at the beginning of a new age of human history. The Anthropocene age is challenging us to renegotiate our path dependence with Mother Nature. This is quite a challenge because, as the saying goes, Mother Nature does not need people, but people need Mother Nature.

The question of self-regulation in human societies has been the main objective of this book. The recent Nobel Prize in Physiology has been awarded to Dr. Y. Oshumi for his research on autophagy—cellular "self-eating" process—from which we have learned about a self-regulation mechanism in human organisms. The human body is able to destroy its own cells as a mechanism to survive. It allows the body to cope with starvation and fight off bacteria and viruses. The human body is always repeating the auto-decomposition process and there is a fine balance between formation and decomposition. That is what life is about. Autophagy plays an important role in neurodegenerative diseases and its manipulation provides a key strategy for treating them.

Capitalism is not a self-regulated social system. It has no mechanisms to destroy its institutions or organizations that cause social maladies and create new ones; no fine balance exists between formation and decomposition. Thus, capitalism is unable to produce the common good endogenously. Manipulation of the system can provide that. There is nothing wrong with human behavior manipulation. The problem appears when manipulation is not for the common good, but for private interests, as is the case now.

References

Figueroa, A. (2010). Is education income equalizing? Evidence from Peru. *CEPAL Review, 102*(April), 113–133.

Figueroa, A. (2015). *Growth, employment, inequality, and the environment: Unity of knowledge in economics* (Vol. I & II). New York: Palgrave Macmillan.

Georgescu-Roegen, N. (1971). *The entropy law and the economic process.* Cambridge, MA: Harvard University Press.

Gollin, D. (2002). Getting income shares right. *Journal of Political Economy, 110*(2), 458–474.

ILO (International Labor Office). (2010). *Global wage report 2010/2011.* Wage Policies in Times of Crisis, Geneva.

Leontief, W. (1983). National perspective: The definitions of problems and opportunities. In *The long term impact of technology on employment and unemployment.* Washington, DC: National Academy Press.

Sen, A. (1992). *Inequality re-examined.* Oxford: Clarendon.

Stavins, R. (2011). The problem of the commons: Still unsettled after 100 years. *The American Economic Review, 101*(1), 141–188.

CHAPTER 8

Epilogue

Science seeks to explain the real world. Empirical regularities constitute the real world to be explained. In this book, the empirical regularities to be explained by economics refer to the economic growth process under the capitalist system in post-World War II. Facts indicate that the continuous increase in per capita income (economic growth) is accompanied by qualitative changes in society: rise in income inequality, in degradation of the biophysical environment, and in the dominance of selfish human behavior, the consequences of which are social maladies. Economic growth is thus accompanied by social maladies.

Scientific explanation of facts needs theory. This is an epistemological dictum. No theory, no scientific explanation. The book uses the unified theory of capitalism to explain those facts. The theory was developed recently and was constructed to explain the entropic economic process. It is unified in the sense that it seeks to explain the two parts of the capitalist system, the First World and the Third World taken separately,

© The Author(s) 2017
A. Figueroa, *Economics of the Anthropocene Age*,
DOI 10.1007/978-3-319-62584-3_8

and then capitalism taken as a whole. It is unified also in the sense that it seeks to explain the short run and the long run in a single logical system. The long-run analysis incorporates the thermodynamic laws of physics into the economic process. Therefore, the theory seeks to comply with the criterion of unity of knowledge, the other epistemological requirement for scientific knowledge. Unified theory was able to show consistency with available empirical regularities.

We can accept a scientific theory as valid only provisionally, until new empirical regularities or new superior theories become available. We get nearer and nearer the truth by the iterations of theories, facts, and testing.

In this book, unified theory has been submitted to more confrontations with the real world. New empirical regularities include the persistence of social maladies under democracy and the increasing dominance of selfish behavior that accompanies economic growth. Evolutionary models of the theory have been developed with the intention to explain those new empirical facts.

According to evolutionary models, the economic growth process is seen as a process in which quantitative changes over time are accompanied by qualitative changes, which then set limits to the repetition of the process. The outcomes of the evolutionary process, the endogenous variables, include increasing per capita income over time accompanied by increasing income inequality, increasing degradation of the biophysical environment, and increasing egotism in human behavior. The exogenous variable is the initial inequality in the individual distribution of economic and political assets, which leads to a concentrated power structure. The causality relation—relation between exogenous and endogenous variables—is thus established. The mechanisms by which the power structure causes those outcomes include the market system and the electoral democracy—the two fundamental institutions of capitalism—and the physical laws of thermodynamics, which make the economic growth process entropic and evolutionary.

The evolutionary models show that the economic and political elites do not have the incentives to solve social maladies. Workers do not either, as they become increasingly dominated by their egotist drive, which is *endogenously* changed by the self-interest of the elites. Therefore, it is corroborated that the current democratic capitalism is not a self-regulated system. As long as the current power structure and the basic institutions remain unchanged, economic growth with social maladies will be repeated period after period.

In an evolutionary model, however, the economic process cannot be repeated forever. There are threshold values of the qualitative endogenous variables that society can tolerate. In the particular evolutionary model IV of the unified theory, the degree of income inequality cannot increase beyond what society can tolerate; the biophysical environment cannot degrade—mineral resource depletion or pollution of the atmosphere—beyond what human life, as we know it, can tolerate. Thus, these threshold values will determine the limit to economic growth, whichever comes first. The evolutionary model predicts that environmental degradation in the form of pollution will come first.

This prediction of the model is consistent with facts. According to Earth scientists, our planet has already entered into a new age, the Anthropocene. The name of the age means that human behavior is now the main factor determining the fate of the planet. Economic growth has been conducive to the qualitative change of our planet. Economic growth is already proceeding under ecological stress—also under social stress, we should add.

Economic growth has a positive effect on human well-being, as consumption goods increase over time, but social maladies and the environment imply negative effects. The evolutionary model also predicts that the latter effect will tend to dominate over time; thus, the *net effect* of economic growth tends to become negative. The quality of society will eventually tend to fall with economic growth: its trajectory has the inverse-U shape. Finally, the evolutionary model predicts that economic growth is ecologically unsustainable; it can be repeated, but for a finite period only. Human society is thus an endangered species. The laws of Mother Nature—the laws of thermodynamics—are irrevocable and constitute the true law of scarcity.

The empirical predictions of the evolutionary model tend to be consistent with facts. We can then accept the model as a good approximation of the capitalist world, at this stage of our investigation. The implication is that the initial conclusion that the capitalist system is not self-regulated is corroborated. Current democratic capitalism could no reduce or eliminate social maladies endogenously.

Scientific knowledge provides useful knowledge, although not always good news. The scientific findings of the evolutionary model reveal to us the fundamental problem of our time: How should human society adjust to the Anthropocene age.

A scientific theoretical model that is valid leads to science-based public policies. The causality relations established by the model give scientific justification to public policies. The evolutionary model is a valid one, as shown in this book. The causality relations established indicate that, in the long-run economic process, power structure is the exogenous variable and economic growth with social maladies is the endogenous one. The mechanisms through which this causality relation operates include the market and the electoral democracy—the fundamental institutions of capitalism—and the physical laws of thermodynamics.

Under current democratic capitalism, the public policy is pro-economic growth. The economic and political elites promote pro-growth policies because they have the incentives to do it. They are the main beneficiaries of economic growth. The benefits include not only higher relative incomes, but also the maintenance of the privileged position they hold in society. Therefore, we can conclude that current public policies are endogenous.

According to the evolutionary model, the pro-growth policies have led society to the Anthropocene age. The continuation of these policies would tend to reinforce the social maladies relative to the positive economic growth effect. In addition, we already know that the higher the economic growth rate, the shorter the period that this process can be repeated and thus the shorter the period of the planet as the human niche. This relation also implies another: the higher the rate of economic growth, the higher the inequality in human well-being between the current and future generations.

We need to examine alternative public policies. However, given that public policies are endogenous, *alternative* public policies cannot be discussed maintaining the current power structure and the same institutions fixed. That discussion will be dreaming.

The book proposes an alternative public policy that seeks to improve the quality of society: shifting outward the inverse-U curve. This objective can be attained by setting the economic growth rate equal to zero as a necessary condition. This is intended to control environmental degradation in the

Anthropocene age. How would a zero-growth society function? New economic principles are needed and they are discussed in the text. The more salient point is that income redistribution would be part of the new rules. The high degree of income inequality in the capitalist world makes redistribution an instrument to raise *significantly* the standard of living of the poor. A society with a lower degree of income inequality is a high-quality society. The degree of social order and peace is higher. Therefore, with these policies, the quality of society can be improved over time and the period of human survival extended. The evolutionary model IV predicts these relations.

The predictions of the model IV are consistent with facts. Measuring quality of society by *healthy* life expectancy as an endogenous variable, the available data across countries indicate that the years of healthy life expectancy indeed depend upon income levels and income inequality. There is no reason to reject this model at this stage of our research and we may accept it as a good approximation of the real world.

The evolutionary model also predicts that the current power structure has no incentives to apply these public policies. Therefore, the power structure must be changed. Redistributing the capital ownership to generate a classless society is also dreaming. History supports the view that capital redistribution has come from catastrophes, such as epidemics, revolutions, and wars of mass (Scheidel 2017). What is left is changing the political power distribution. Electoral democracy is a mechanism by which the people—the workers, under capitalism—transfer to the government their political power. The political class competes to capture the state through this mechanism. The competition involves money and the participation of the economic elite, which transforms democracy into plutocracy.

Replacing electoral democracy by other form of democracy in which the people retain their political power would eliminate the political class. It would also eliminate the intervention of economic elites in public policies. Democracy would no longer be plutocracy. This reform in the democratic system implies a new power structure, less concentrated, with a balance of power. The economic elite exercise market power and the workers—the workers are the people under capitalism—control the state. The democratic reform implies an institutional innovation: a re-foundation of the capitalist system.

Therefore, in order to carry out the alternative public policies proposed above, the current power structure needs to be changed, which in turn requires an institutional innovation in the democratic system. The government under the new form of democracy will then have the incentives to apply those public policies that seek the common good, the quality of society. These alternative public policies are in accord with the new economics for the Anthropocene age—the unified theory. Pro-growth policies, by comparison, belong to the old economics, as the Holocene age, when natural resources were not the root of scarcity, is still assumed.

According to the unified theory, current democratic capitalism is not a self-regulated system. It needs to be transformed into a self-regulated system to deal with the new context of the Anthropocene age. How to do this? Institutional innovations, such as dethroning electoral democracy and replacing it with any form of workers' democracy, needs to be designed by the collaborative work of scientists (from both the natural and social sciences), thinkers, and social innovators. This is a challenge to human intelligence, to *Homo sapiens*. The economics of the Anthropocene age developed in this book may be useful in such endeavor. This is, hopefully, the expected contribution of the book.

REFERENCE

Scheidel, W. (2017). *The greater leveler: Violence and the history of inequality from the stone age to twenty-first century.* Princeton, NJ: Princeton University Press.

INDEX

© The Author(s) 2017
A. Figueroa, *Economics of the Anthropocene Age*,
DOI 10.1007/978-3-319-62584-3

Pareto optimality, 153, 160
pro-growth discourse, 66
no-growth society, 33, 219, 227, 230,
    235, 238, 241, 245, 246, 250
non-renewable natural resources. *See*
    mineral resources
normal goods *vs.* inferior goods, 114,
    124, 137
nsumer behavior, standard theory of
    lexicographic preferences model,
    115–20

O
Olson, M., 54
omega society. *See* omega theory
omega theory (explains Third World
    with weak colonial legacy),
    25
Orwell, G., 89
Oxfam, 28

P
Pareto optimality, 153–6, 160, 161,
    163, 190, 191, 199
Pareto, V., 160
    and circulation of elites,
        159
perverse incentive system under
    electoral democracy, xiii, 63, 84,
    86, 224, 225
Pettit, P., 177
physics and economics, xvii, 195, 203,
    211, 213, 215
Pigouvain tax, 165
Piketty, T., 68, 161, 163, 202
political class
    and democracy failure, 42
    perverse incentives to seek common
        good, 224
    power origin, representative
        democracy, xvi, 58

political elites, xiv, xv, 15, 32, 49,
    65–7, 69, 70, 77, 84–6, 101,
    111, 150, 167, 169, 172–4,
    177–80, 186, 191, 195, 203,
    204, 225, 227, 237, 239, 244,
    249, 257, 259
political entitlements, by type of
    capitalist society
    citizenship equality (epsilon and
        omega societies), 246
    first and second class citizens (sigma
        society), 13, 14, 33, 41, 44, 56,
        80, 205
pollution
    and human health, ix, 23, 24, 33,
        166, 190, 192, 213
    as problem of the commons, 223,
        224, 228
Popper, K., 5, 6, 11
popperian epistemology. *See*
    falsificationism; falsification
    process
population growth, endogenously
    determined, 94
population, initial conditions by type
    of capitalist society
    overpopulated (omega and sigma
        societies), 13, 15, 22, 25, 63,
        242
    underpopulated (epsilon society),
        13, 14, 63
power relations
    in electoral democracy, xvi, 41, 71,
        84, 177–9
    in market exchange, 175, 176,
    179
power relations under capitalist
    institutions
    electoral democratic system, 57,
        59–67, 72, 85, 86, 150, 175
    market system, 150, 175, 176
power structure and initial inequality,
    x, 57, 58, 70, 202, 206, 256